THE LITERACY COACH'S HANDBOOK

Also from Sharon Walpole and Michael C. McKenna

Assessment for Reading Instruction, Second Edition
Michael C. McKenna and Katherine A. Dougherty Stahl

The Building Blocks of Preschool Success
*Katherine A. Beauchat, Katrin L. Blamey,
and Sharon Walpole*

Differentiated Reading Instruction:
Strategies for the Primary Grades
Sharon Walpole and Michael C. McKenna

Differentiated Reading Instruction
in Grades 4 and 5: Strategies and Resources
*Sharon Walpole, Michael C. McKenna,
and Zoi A. Philippakos*

How to Plan Differentiated Reading Instruction:
Resources for Grades K–3
Sharon Walpole and Michael C. McKenna

The Literacy Coaching Challenge:
Models and Methods for Grades K–8
Michael C. McKenna and Sharon Walpole

Promoting Early Reading:
Research, Resources, and Best Practices
*Edited by Michael C. McKenna, Sharon Walpole,
and Kristin Conradi*

Reading Assessment in an RTI Framework
*Katherine A. Dougherty Stahl
and Michael C. McKenna*

Reading Research at Work:
Foundations of Effective Practice
*Edited by Katherine A. Dougherty Stahl
and Michael C. McKenna*

THE LITERACY COACH'S HANDBOOK

A Guide to Research-Based Practice

SECOND EDITION

Sharon Walpole
Michael C. McKenna

THE GUILFORD PRESS
New York   London

© 2013 The Guilford Press
A Division of Guilford Publications, Inc.
72 Spring Street, New York, NY 10012
www.guilford.com

Printed in the United States of America

This book is printed on acid-free paper.

Last digit is print number: 9 8 7 6 5 4 3 2 1

Library of Congress Cataloging-in-Publication Data

Walpole, Sharon.
  The literacy coach's handbook : a guide to research-based practice / Sharon Walpole,
Michael C. McKenna. — Second edition.
    p. cm.
  Includes bibliographical references and index.
  ISBN 978-1-4625-0770-2 (paperback) — ISBN 978-1-4625-0771-9 (hardcover)
  1. Reading (Elementary)—United States. 2. Literacy programs—United States—
Administration. 3. Group work in education—United States. I. McKenna, Michael
C. II. Title.
  LB1573.W364 2013
  379.2'40973—dc23
                         2012032836

To our children,
Patrick, Jimmy, and Katy McKenna,
and Kevin and Peter Walpole.
They are always with us as we think about
the classrooms we need for other people's children.

About the Authors

Sharon Walpole, PhD, is Professor of Reading at the University of Delaware, where she teaches undergraduate courses on language and literacy development in kindergarten and first grade, master's courses on content-area reading instruction and organization and supervision of the reading program, and doctoral seminars on literacy and educational policy. She has extensive school-based experience, including work as an elementary literacy coach. Dr. Walpole has also been involved in federally funded and other schoolwide reform projects. Her current work involves the design and effects of schoolwide reforms, particularly those involving literacy coaches. She has coauthored and coedited five other books with Michael C. McKenna, and her articles have appeared in journals including *Reading Research Quarterly*, the *Journal of Educational Psychology*, *Elementary School Journal*, *Educational Researcher*, *Reading and Writing Quarterly*, and *The Reading Teacher*. In 2007, she received the Early Career Award from the National Reading Conference for Significant Contributions to Literacy Research and Education.

Michael C. McKenna, PhD, is Thomas G. Jewell Professor of Reading at the University of Virginia. He has authored, coauthored, or edited more than 20 books and over 100 articles, chapters, and technical reports on a range of literacy topics. His research has been sponsored by the National Reading Research Center and the Center for the Improvement of Early Reading Achievement. Dr. McKenna is the cowinner of the Literacy Research Association's Edward B. Fry Book Award and the American Library Association's Award for Outstanding Academic Books. He has served on the editorial board of *Reading Research Quarterly*, and his articles have appeared in that journal as well as the *Journal of Educational Psychology*, *Educational Researcher*, *The Reading Teacher*, and others. He now works extensively with literacy coaches in Georgia and Virginia.

Preface

It is hard to believe that nearly a decade has passed since the first edition of this book was published! During this time our work in schools with coaches, teachers, and principals has continued to inform our understanding of the problems coaches face, and we are ever indebted to them for their insights. The last decade has also produced new research and new standards, which have broadened the lens through which we must now view coaching.

Consistent with this broadened view, we have widened the scope of this book in two major ways. First, we have extended our initial focus from grades K–3 to PreK–5. The K–3 orientation was primarily the result of two major federal initiatives, Reading Excellence and Reading First. In their aftermath, elementary coaches are now far more likely to work in schoolwide settings and these often include prekindergarten. Second, we have addressed writing directly. Long relegated to second-class status by federal reforms, writing has received scant attention in many books for coaches, and it is time we brought writing instruction into focus.

These changes have meant that revising the book has nearly amounted to rewriting it. We have, however, retained most of the earlier organization, which seems to have served our readers well. But within each chapter much has been added, and the remainder brought up to date.

In Chapter 1, we revisit the six key roles of a literacy coach, but we describe them in the new context of the International Reading Association standards, which were adopted after the first edition. We are pleased that the new standards embrace these roles and that they articulate them usefully by suggesting specific tasks that a coach should be able to perform.

Exactly how a coach working in a specific school setting goes about accomplishing these tasks is a combination of art and science. At the time of the first edition, very little research had been conducted in the area of coaching, and our suggestions for how a coach might go about implementing reading research were admittedly more art than science. All that has changed. So much has been learned about effective coaching that we have added Chapter 2, which has no counterpart in the first edition, in which we summarize important findings about coaching and distill them into take-away messages.

The next two chapters create a solid foundation for the remainder of the book. Chapter 3 provides the "big picture" of a coach's work. It presents overviews of schoolwide issues involving assessment, tiered instruction, grouping, materials, and scheduling. More than ever, we are convinced that it is essential that coaches be able to view the fine-grained, day-to-day problems they face through this larger lens. It is also important that they possess a working knowledge of research into effective practice. Chapter 4 summarizes this research. In the area of reading, we begin by briefly revisiting the National Reading Panel's report, and we then bring it fully up to date. In the area of writing, we have started from scratch to summarize key findings. In the preschool arena, we start with the report of the National Early Literacy Panel, and we amplify and extend its findings.

Chapter 5 addresses key issues related to assessment. The coach's role in administering, compiling, and interpreting results is closely examined. We again use the cognitive model of reading assessment as a strategy for making sense of the data coaches need. In revising this chapter, we address a pair of important new topics as well: the Common Core State Standards and the use of lexiles as a means of gauging the match between students and books.

Chapters 6 and 7 address the best uses of time. In Chapter 6, we examine approaches to scheduling, and we offer examples from a variety of grade levels and school contexts. We describe the problem of scheduling both whole-class and small-group instruction in a way that makes the best use of specialists. A coach must consider two types of schedules—those within the classroom and those across the grade level—and how the two fit together. This chapter offers suggestions for how to address both types. Chapter 7 speaks to the amount of time we should devote to the key components of literacy instruction. We use the metaphor of a diet to discuss what constitutes the best balance, depending both on assessed needs and the developmental expectations at each grade level. We extend the issue of whole-class and small-group instruction by suggesting how deliberate changes in diet can result in a healthier literacy program.

The next two chapters address commercial core programs and interventions, together with the often unhappy relationship between the two. In Chapter 8, we examine the issues surrounding the selection and use of a core program. Beginning with a brief history of how these programs have evolved, we offer suggestions about evaluating a core and how to avoid the problem, present in so many schools, of a patchwork quilt of supplementary commercial materials. In Chapter 9, we move on to intervention programs. We begin by exploring the arguments for early interventions, but unlike in the first edition we then examine two issues of current importance in effective coaching. We first consider how coaches can help to coordinate the use of these products in response to intervention. Then, in keeping with the idea that coaching must be a K–5 effort, we describe how interventions in the upper-elementary grades must be part of the response-to-intervention framework. Just as Chapter 8 includes suggestions for selecting a core program, Chapter 9 offers guidelines and resources for weighing the strengths and weaknesses of commercial interventions.

The final two chapters are devoted to questions of how a coach can move a school forward. In Chapter 10, we describe in detail a number of avenues open to coaches for providing quality professional development. In light of so many opportunities, we also discuss the need to craft a coherent professional development plan. Because we view coaching as an act of leadership, Chapter 11 closes the book with a discussion of this topic. In this chapter, we examine leadership at the staff, building, and district levels, and we advocate for coaches to play a role at all three. We then turn to the problem of struggling and resistant teachers and how to coach them, and we offer advice from the field.

As in all of our books, we are guided by a number of key beliefs that define us as educators. We believe that some instructional practices are more effective than others and that some teachers need to be coached in how to implement them. We believe that in order to be effective, coaches must embrace, not just reluctantly accept, their role as leaders. We believe that principals have a responsibility to support the work of coaches, just as we believe that coaches bear a responsibility to continually sharpen their skills. Finally, we believe that every teacher, even the best, can advance his or her practice and that coaching is the best avenue for achieving this goal.

SHARON WALPOLE
MICHAEL C. MCKENNA

Contents

CHAPTER 1.   What Is a Literacy Coach?   1

   Literacy Coach as Learner   3
   Literacy Coach as Grant Writer   4
   Literacy Coach as School-Level Planner   5
   Literacy Coach as Curriculum Expert   6
   Literacy Coach as Researcher   7
   Literacy Coach as Teacher   10
   The Literacy Coach: An Evolving Role   11

CHAPTER 2.   Research on Literacy Coaching   17

   The Bad News   18
   Take-Home Message 1: Coaching Does Not Always
       Change Instruction or Achievement   19
   Take-Home Message 2: Use a Coaching Model
       to Guide Your Time and Activities   20
   Take-Home Message 3: Coaches Cannot Be Effective
       Unless Their Work Is Integrated with the School's Climate   22
   Take-Home Message 4: Align Your Coaching Goals with the Goals
       of Other Leaders   22
   Take-Home Message 5: The Needs of Teachers Are Real
       and Must Come Before the Needs of Coaches   23
   Take-Home Message 6: Be Ready to Learn Many Things
       on the Job   24
   Take-Home Message 7: Be Ready to Differentiate
       for Preschool Teachers   25
   Take-Home Message 8: Be Ready to Build
       Your Coaching Toolbox   26

Take-Home Message 9: Be Sure to Find Out Whether Teachers
Implement New Approaches 27
Take-Home Message 10: Use Multiple Assessment Measures
to Track Student Achievement 29

CHAPTER 3. **What Is a Schoolwide Literacy Program?**   30
Schoolwide Research 31
Assessment Systems 36
Grouping Configurations 43
Materials and Strategies 47
Allocation of Time 50
Systems for Teamwork 54
Taking Stock 55

CHAPTER 4. **Finding and Applying Reading Research**   56
Scientifically Based Reading Instruction 57
Evidence-Based Reading Instruction 58
How Much Do We Know? 59
Phonemic Awareness 59
Phonics 62
Fluency 66
Vocabulary 69
Comprehension 72
Writing 79
Spelling 87
How Can We Keep Up? 89

CHAPTER 5. **Reading Assessment**   97
Types and Uses of Tests 97
An Assessment Strategy 99
Interpreting Outcome Scores 102
Multiple Assessment Hats of the Literacy Coach 105
Improving Group Achievement Scores 109
A Final Word 113

CHAPTER 6. **Instructional Schedules**   115
Representative Schedules 116
Porter Highland School 120
McMillan Academy 122
Bradenton Elementary 123
White Oak School 125
Time for Teaching 126
A Word to the Wise 131

CHAPTER 7. **Instructional Tasks and Procedures**   133
Stage Theories in Reading and Spelling 134
Instructional Emphases 136
Instruction for Preschool Readers and Writers 138

Instruction for Kindergarten Readers and Writers 139
Instruction for First-Grade Readers and Writers 143
Instruction for Second-Grade Readers and Writers 148
Instruction for Readers and Writers in Grades 3–5 152
Building a Program 157

CHAPTER 8. Selecting Materials and Programs 158

A Brief History of Core Programs 158
Present-Day Core Programs 162
Today's Core Components 163
Pros and Cons of a Core Program 166
Thoughtful Systems for Evaluating Materials 168
The Problem of Layering 169
A Final Word 175

CHAPTER 9. Schoolwide Response to Intervention 176

What Is the Argument for Aggressive Early Intervention? 177
What Are the Specifics of RTI? 181
How Is Research Informing RTI Efforts? 183
Selecting Intervention Programs and Practices 188
Planning an RTI System 189

CHAPTER 10. Providing Professional Support 192

Professional Development Research 193
A Model for Professional Support 194
Professional Support and Coaching 198
Planning and Implementing Schoolwide
 Professional Development 199
Nuts and Bolts 199
Using Data 201
Book Clubs and Study Groups 202
Lesson Planning 204
Observation and Feedback 206
Modeling 212
Pacing Professional Support 214
Establishing Coherence 215

CHAPTER 11. Leadership 216

Conceptualizing Leadership 216
Issues of Authority 219
Supporting the Struggling Teacher 222
What About the Resistant Teacher? 223
Many Voices 224

References 231

Index 247

THE LITERACY COACH'S HANDBOOK

CHAPTER 1

What Is a Literacy Coach?

> Once there was a peddler who sold caps.
> But he was not like an ordinary peddler,
> carrying his wares on his back.
> He carried them on top of his head.
> First he had on his own checked cap,
> then a bunch of gray caps,
> then a bunch of blue caps,
> and, on the very top,
> a bunch of red caps.
> —ESPHYR SLOBODKINA (1940, n.p.)

For a literacy coach, a stack of caps might be the perfect analogy. A literacy coach is not a principal, not an assistant principal, not a reading specialist, and not a teacher. On a given day, he or she probably dons each of these caps, but not for long. In fact, a literacy coach is fashioning a new cap—one that fits better than any of those, and one that reflects the needs of the teachers in a particular school building. Ten years have passed since we first wrote these words. During those 10 years, thousands of schools have hired literacy coaches. Hundreds of books and articles have documented and directed the work of those coaches. But we still see coaches filling constantly evolving roles.

Because this new edition will be read with new eyes, we want you to take a moment and answer this chapter's overarching question before you start reading. We think that many of the people who read the first edition of this book had no preconceived notions about coaching, but we doubt that that is true for you now. What is a literacy coach? How would your definition of what a coach is influence what a coach needs to know and be able to do? How would it influence a coach's use of time every day?

Our definition of a coach surely colors the answers we will offer in these pages. You need to know our bias about coaching right from the start: A coach is a teacher's teacher. A coach accepts, understands, and addresses the real needs of adult learners in specific schools with the same unfailing, relentless, positive energy that our very best classroom teachers bring to their work with children.

Literacy coaches can make a difference. In the first edition of this book, we introduced Cece Tillman, a literacy coach in a small rural elementary school serving children of struggling families. Her school had applied for a Reading Excellence grant and had 2 years of funding for new curriculum and assessments and extensive professional development opportunities for teachers. She stepped into the role of coach with no role models and plenty of work. Achievement was weak across grade levels. The reading curriculum was vague and implemented haphazardly. Teachers had no common professional development. There were few materials to support fluency work, and the existing phonics program was not used consistently. There was no plan to develop vocabulary knowledge, even though children appeared to have weak vocabularies. Few teachers understood or taught comprehension strategies. There were no formative assessments or strategies for grouping that all teachers used. Standardized test data, though bleak, were not surprising given what Cece knew about her school. A summary of these stark data appears in Figure 1.1.

A decade later, a different profile has emerged for Cece's school. The most recent accountability data indicated that it was meeting adequate yearly progress (AYP), with Title I Distinguished status. Checking in on Cece herself, we found her donning even more hats. Her work as a coach inspired her to tackle new tasks. She has earned a certificate in administration, taught as an adjunct instructor at night in a teachers' college, coached in middle school, and even taken on teaching and learning in math classrooms. Many coaches will find themselves in situations similar to Cece's—facing substantial hurdles; we hope that they will someday look back knowing that they have accomplished what she did, both for herself as a professional and for her community of teachers and learners.

We first conceptualized the role of the literacy coach to include six "caps," pictured in Figure 1.2. Our role definitions for the elementary coach were widely cited, even in the International Reading Association (IRA) standards document for

Subtest	Score
Reading	33
Language Arts	29
Mathematics	19
Science	30
Social Studies	32

FIGURE 1.1. Percentile ranks corresponding to group mean scores on Stanford Achievement Test—Ninth Edition for Mt. Pleasant third graders, 2000.

middle school and high school coaches (International Reading Association, 2006). As we reprise those roles today, we think that they remain powerful organizers. However, they are not all required in all settings. The roles of a particular literacy coach in a particular school will be influenced by that school's organizational structure and maturity; we will share more about how the school's needs must shape the coach's roles in Chapter 11.

Roles of school-level personnel change because the job of school changes. Compared to the schools we wrote about in 2004, we now have more diverse learners, higher expectations for student learning, new and different ways of assessing students, and a new vision of schooling as a birth-through-college-and-career enterprise. We also see the roles of individuals within schools in a more specialized way. If you don't believe us, access any one of the resources listed in Figure 1.3 and take the challenge we present there. We hope you will see these realities as opportunities for growth rather than as problems too daunting to tackle. Given the realities of schools, a literacy coach must be a leader in positive, proactive response to change.

LITERACY COACH AS LEARNER

Successful literacy coaches must make a substantial and permanent commitment to their own learning. That message is surely not surprising. Literacy coaches are responsible for understanding what is known about the developmental processes of reading and writing, about teaching and learning, and about the design and delivery of professional learning opportunities. We are more convinced now than ever that the effective literacy coach must have more than a strong knowledge base;

FIGURE 1.2. Roles of a literacy coach.

| **Demographic changes** |
| *http://nces.ed.gov/surveys/sdds/2010/index.aspx* |
| The National Center for Education Statistics has Census data for 2010 available. You can access data for your state or school system. You can download reports to look across years. See whether your own state or district has a more diverse student population now. |
| **Changes in expectations** |
| *www.corestandards.org* |
| In 2010, the National Governors Association Center for Best Practices and the Council of Chief State School Officers released the Common Core State Standards for English Language Arts and Math. Pick one grade level and read the standards for yourself. Compare them to your state's old standards and see whether these are more rigorous. |
| **Assessment changes** |
| *www.parcconline.org* |
| *www.smarterbalanced.org* |
| In September 2010, two consortia were awarded $330 million to develop assessment systems for the Common Core State Standards. Both groups promise "next generation" assessments, including performance tasks and aligned formative and summative assessments. See whether your state has joined and how the tests promised differ from your old test. |
| **Instructional role changes** |
| *www.reading.org/General/CurrentResearch/Standards/ProfessionalStandards2010.aspx* |
| In 2010, IRA released new standards for reading professionals. There are six standards and seven roles—including one for the reading specialist/literacy coach. Choose a role that you have already assumed or one to which you aspire and see whether you currently meet the standards. |

FIGURE 1.3. Signs that times have changed and will continue to change.

a good coach must also possess the tools and dispositions to learn continuously." Figure 1.4 provides some web-based sources that can help to keep you current. Working in a changing world means that knowing where to find information is critically important. For this reason, we refer you to our go-to websites throughout this book.

LITERACY COACH AS GRANT WRITER

Frequently, school-level reform efforts require money—money for new curriculum materials, money for additional intervention personnel, money for new technologies, money for professional development. State and federal moneys, once available through pro forma grant competitions, are increasingly scarce and competitive. They demand extensive research and careful writing. There are also other kinds of grants, including those offered by foundations and local businesses. These tend

Source	Website
International Reading Association	*www.reading.org*
Center on Instruction	*www.centeroninstruction.org*
National Center on Response to Intervention	*www.rti4success.org*
RTI Action Network	*www.rtinetwork.org*
International Dyslexia Association	*www.interdys.org*

FIGURE 1.4. Sources for the coach as learner.

to be more targeted and are frequently overlooked, but they should be on every coach's radar.

There are advantages to applying for grants. Bringing in additional funds can help convince administrators skeptical of coaching that a coach is worth having. Grant awards are also a source of positive public relations. They make an entire school look good. In addition, literacy coaches who have money to spend on new initiatives can connect with teachers who may have previously been reluctant. We realize that literacy coaches are busy and that grant writing takes time. We argue, though, that it is more reasonable to ask coaches to take the lead on grant-writing tasks than it is to ask classroom teachers to do it.

The first order of business is to make sure you are in the loop about funding opportunities. Find out about how notifications are made by your state department of education. This is most likely done through a page of the department's website, which you should bookmark and check regularly. There may also be e-mail distribution lists you can join that inform possible grantees of new competitions. Remember too that not all funding opportunities are through governmental agencies. Figure 1.5 provides some additional resources that may prove helpful. Because grants differ considerably, it is important to size up a funding opportunity from the outset. The estimated time required to write the application must be weighed against the amount of funding, the restrictions on its use, and the likelihood of success.

LITERACY COACH AS SCHOOL-LEVEL PLANNER

Literacy coaches, especially those who work in school-level initiatives funded through state and federal grants, are often site-based school reformers. They are charged with working in every classroom so that every teacher can have the support he or she needs to implement a specific, school-level program. They work with all teachers to understand and implement a *schoolwide reading program*—a

Source	Website
Donors Choose	*www.donorschoose.org*
NEA Foundation	*www.neafoundation.org/pages/educators/grant-programs*
National Council of Teachers of English	*www.ncte.org/grants*
Lowe's Toolbox for Education	*www.toolboxforeducation.com*
Public Education Network	*www.publiceducation.org/newsblast_grants.asp*

FIGURE 1.5. Sources for the coach as grant writer.

concept we unpack in Chapter 3. One of the challenges that almost all literacy coaches face is that of time. Schools need to protect time for teaching and learning *and* for professional development and collaboration. They must focus on the actual time available—inside school days and teacher contract hours that typically are not getting any longer. We talk about the nuts and bolts of scheduling in later chapters. However, we want you to know from the start that your own use of time as a coach will be influenced by the extent to which you are working in a school with a strong plan.

LITERACY COACH AS CURRICULUM EXPERT

Although curriculum is more than materials, among the barriers to effective literacy instruction are inexplicit, uncoordinated instructional materials. Schools tend to add new materials without removing the old, and teachers (who are natural hoarders!) have burgeoning shelves and closets (not to mention garages and attics) filled with an array of resources. The result is often a crazy quilt of programs and materials that are used in uncoordinated and inconsistent ways. Literacy coaches work with teachers to evaluate instructional materials currently in place against research-based standards, and help to locate and implement new materials that are better matched to the research base and to the needs of children. Literacy coaches help other school leaders navigate the complex (and expensive!) world of educational publishing.

In a tight economy, with new standards looming, schools may also put off purchase of new materials. In that case, curriculum expertise is even more important. Literacy coaches can collaborate with teachers to understand current resources as having strengths and weaknesses. They can help teams to decide how to make the best use of available resources and how to supplement them in weak areas. Once a curriculum is in place, the coach takes on what we see as the most important role: the role of researcher.

LITERACY COACH AS RESEARCHER

Literacy coaches are charged with answering questions few PhD-level researchers would be able to answer easily. These are complex questions, to be sure, with high-stakes consequences for children:

1. To what extent are teachers able to implement the school's curriculum?
2. To what extent are student needs being addressed by the school's curriculum?
3. In what ways must the curriculum be supported and/or modified to promote both teacher implementation and student achievement?

Building research skills was extremely challenging work for Cece, and a description of her journey can help you see how the multiple caps of the literacy coach are worn. Her story here may also help you to see the real promise of coaching.

The reality of school-based data collection and analysis is messy. In the summer of 2002, Cece learned about assessments for phonemic awareness, decoding, fluency, and comprehension for each grade level. She also participated in a calendar-building exercise, where she first marked specific times during the year when data could be reported to various stakeholders (children, parents, teachers, administrators, central office staff, and the state); she then planned backward for the data to be collected, entered, and analyzed, as well as for the training of personnel doing the data collection. Clearly, all of these constraints on the data collection system meant that it was the number-one priority.

Cece chose assessments for phonemic awareness, decoding, and fluency that summer. She investigated assessments that researchers had mentioned during technical assistance workshops. She used the Internet to gain access to test materials and reviews. She contracted for staff training with trainers recommended by the test designers. Initial assessment training was scheduled for teacher workdays before school opened in 2002. Training sessions included both collection and interpretation of the assessment data.

Implementation of the assessment plan was an enormous challenge. Cece decided to use a schoolwide assessment team (SWAT) approach, which we discuss further in Chapter 3. The team members started by establishing interrater reliability. The five testers first worked together: One child was tested by one team member, with the other four observing and shadowing the scoring. They shared their scores and resolved discrepancies. Then they called another child. When they had reached agreement, they began to work as partners, still using one member to test and the other to shadow and score. Finally, they were ready to work alone. This procedure established reliability in the initial data set, and it also established trust and respect among the team members.

After the data were collected, Cece struggled with some of the nuts-and-bolts issues in data management. She struggled to organize her data efficiently on the computer. Some of the big issues were managing such a large data set and providing timely classroom reports to teachers. By the middle of the year, Cece was working with technology specialists in her district's central office to design a more user-friendly system that was geared directly to her needs.

Once the data were organized, Cece summarized the results and shared them with her teachers. She quickly learned to create graphs and charts that depicted the progress made by individual children, classes, and grade levels. The first wave of data was very powerful. Teachers clearly saw that the children's performance was unacceptable, and they felt compelled to do something about it. As the year progressed, teachers realized that assessment-based instruction was very difficult. Cece commented at the time:

> "One of the biggest weaknesses I see across the board is the fact that most all of our teachers teach books and programs, not kids. There is very little informal assessment going on in classrooms. Teachers seem reluctant to evaluate kids' work to determine if their teaching is causing students to learn or not. And when they do evaluate, they seem unsure of how to plan for small groups or redesign lessons to teach students the skills they aren't getting with whole-class instruction. Breaking the barrier to show teachers how to teach small groups effectively will be a huge jump in the project. Getting them to use informal assessments will help our students gain by leaps and bounds. One teacher has discussed how difficult it is to do (and I realize this is so)—but I pointed out to her how much better it will be to know each step of the way how the students are doing, rather than teaching the book all year, coming down to the end, and suddenly realizing that several children don't know any of the material that they have covered all year."

This reluctance was gradually replaced with confidence. By the spring of year 1, teachers reported that the biggest change at the school was the use of data to drive instruction. Even though changing their instruction to meet student needs continued to be difficult, teachers were convinced that it was essential. Teachers began to ask for more data and to use these data to assign children to heterogeneous classrooms for the coming year.

Data analysis led to constant changes in the plan. For example, at the beginning of October, Cece analyzed developmental spelling data (Ganske, 2000) and realized that first graders were not able to apply specific phonics features in spelling that they had already been taught in their phonics program. She purchased additional reading materials to allow children to have more practice with these features, she established a greater emphasis on spelling in the curriculum, and she worked with the first-grade team to build these changes into their instructional schedule and into the interventions.

Adjustments were made in other segments of the curriculum as well. Data drove these adjustments, and Cece observed that teachers became partners with her, both in collecting and interpreting data:

"Once the initial fluency assessment was given, we determined that most of our kids were reading accurately, but with depressed rates. Using our core materials, as well as passages with the same phonic patterns, teachers now assess one child per day (they usually do more) and record their speed and accuracy. In addition, they do various interventions with students. They can choose between timed partner readings, repeated readings, and group timed readings. They turn in a chart to me and they have graphs to use with individual students. All teachers are sharing results and setting goals with students."

In her role as researcher, Cece had to learn to observe teachers in ways that were helpful to them. She had to negotiate her role as observer, and doing this was a roller-coaster ride. At first, she observed but was unwilling to provide any specific feedback. Later, she observed but was too critical. Gradually, she worked together with other literacy coaches and with her principal to build a metaphor for observation. In terms of observation, Cece was the "good cop." She shared with teachers that she was in their classrooms to learn. And so she began to observe in order to answer questions that would first and foremost make her a better coach: "What can I learn about the curriculum today that can help me to understand its strengths and weaknesses?" and "What can I learn about individual teachers today that can make my professional development more effective?" She had to abandon the "bad-cop" role, which included observations to answer a very different question: "Is this individual fulfilling his or her professional responsibilities?" In order for her to adopt the good-cop stance, her principal had to assume the role of bad cop. His observations of teachers became linked more closely to their instruction and to the instructional initiative at the school. Cece noted that, by December, the system was working:

"I think I had gotten bogged down, and I am now back on track. I realized that I had turned into the bad cop. I needed to step back and realize that my job is not to enforce but to model and offer professional development."

As Cece grew into her role as researcher, drawing upon her skills as planner and curriculum expert, she approached roadblocks in various places in the curriculum. She eventually realized that the data supported her work with teachers:

"If student learning becomes the focus, then I can use shared decision making to bring more teachers on board and cause 'buy-in' to what I am doing. For instance, I plan to share info about our fluency weaknesses and assessment data to get input from the team as to the direction of staff development. In addition, this can help pave the way for study groups and small-group staff development on a needs- and interests-based model. Many of the teachers are beginning to recognize areas in which they need more knowledge, which allows me to pull appropriate resources to meet these needs."

What Cece was learning was that the road to school change was long and winding, but that data she collected about teachers' instruction and children's learning provided her with a road map.

LITERACY COACH AS TEACHER

The No Child Left Behind Act of 2001 brought unprecedented funding for professional development for teachers in struggling schools. The legislation itself *required* districts to provide professional development to K–3 teachers and special educators. The goal of the legislation was to provide sufficient support to develop the knowledge and skills of classroom teachers so that they could change student achievement. In our current work in schools, we often see professional development organized through collaborative professional learning communities. We will describe models for providing site-based professional development in schools in Chapter 10.

Cece designed a professional support system for her teachers. First, she arranged for curriculum representatives to show teachers how to use new materials in their classrooms. The goal of these sessions was to support immediate changes in teacher practice. Cece was able to work with these representatives so that their presentations were targeted directly to the needs of her school, and also to the demands of the schoolwide commitment to use evidence-based instructional strategies.

Cece used study groups to provide professional development herself. These sessions were conducted initially after school every week. By January, Cece realized that she needed more time and that this time should be during the school day. She began to meet with each grade-level team weekly for 45 minutes. The goal of these sessions was to build teacher knowledge targeted specifically to the needs of each grade level.

Cece brought professional resources into the building. She purchased professional books consistent with the initiative, and she lent them to teachers. She also subscribed to *The Reading Teacher* for the school and joined the IRA Book Club.

Cece used her role as teacher to address what she was learning in her role as researcher. She was concerned that teachers were starting to recognize that students needed intervention, but that they were unable to provide it. She saw this dual realization as a clear indication that she needed to provide professional development:

"It is a management issue. I see the need for professional development in managing small groups. They have little experience (nor do I) in managing several groups. I would like some guidance here as to resources and ways to help them. They recognize the need, but it is a management nightmare for them. I can sympathize, and am trying to decide how to get the resources they need to be able to do this effectively."

Cece learned to manage her professional development sessions so that they were more interactive. She learned that teachers could work together productively, especially if they worked in groups, to reflect on the implications of research for their work in the classroom. She also learned that she had to be very specific about how new ideas could be addressed within the framework of the curriculum and materials that they were using.

As we look back at our work with coaches and look forward to new initiatives in schools, we know that some of the issues that Cece faced are timeless ones. We also know that individuals with her commitment to children's learning can make the same commitment to teachers' learning. We hope that many of you will join us in the complex work of coaching. In doing so you will be building on the work of previous coaches in federally funded school reform programs (Reading Excellence, Reading First, Early Reading First, and Race to the Top) and in district-level programs. You will also be adding to our understanding of the role of the literacy coach.

THE LITERACY COACH: AN EVOLVING ROLE

In 2000, the IRA released a position statement on the roles of the reading specialist. This statement argued for a three-part role, with leadership skills, diagnosis and assessment skills, and instructional skills all serving the overall goal of improving student learning. In 2004, IRA released a position statement on the roles and qualifications of the reading coach. The statement described the direct work that coaches do with teachers, and argued that they needed deep understanding of reading—that coaches needed in fact to be reading specialists. In 2006, IRA partnered with professional organizations in math, English, social studies, and science to craft standards for middle school and high school coaches. Those standards highlighted the leadership skills for coaches in those schools and also the discipline-specific literacy content that coaches needed to understand. In 2010, IRA released new standards for all reading professionals. The standards are high, and they show that school systems are complex organizations, relying on people with different roles to enact these standards in coordinated ways. They include education support personnel, preschool and elementary classroom teachers, middle school and high school content teachers, middle school and high school reading teachers, reading specialsts/literacy coaches, teacher educators, and administrators. We applaud this vision, but we also know that most schools do not have many individuals already meeting these high standards. Perhaps that fact is among the best reasons to consider literacy coaches as part of the team—they can meet school-based personnel where they are and help them to enact these rigorous standards.

We experienced one disappointment with IRA's standards. They define the reading specialist/literacy coach with a single strand of standards and evidence. We know that IRA wanted to highlight the fact that an individual should not coach teachers if he or she does not have the deep knowledge of reading development and instruction that a reading specialist needs to work with children who struggle. However, we hope that some day a coach will be a reading specialist who decides to focus attention on design and delivery of professional learning. That might mean that an individual first studies to be a reading specialist, then works in that role, and then goes back to school to study the nuts and bolts of adult learning, school leadership, and professional development. The decision to work with teachers instead of children comes with a responsibility to tackle an entirely new set of knowledge and skills. Figure 1.6 is our own concept sort of the IRA evidence that individuals meet its standards for reading specialists/literacy coaches. We have reshaped the evidence for IRA's six standards into our original six coaching roles. There is a very good match.

As we reflect on IRA's standards and performances, we see them as a chance to take stock. We don't know any individual coaches who can do all of these things! We can't do them all ourselves. However, the role of coach as learner is ever present. As you begin this book, use these performances as a self-assessment. Which are strengths for you already? Which provide opportunities for you to grow? When you are done reading, come back to your self-assessment and decide whether your knowledge and skills have been expanded. Whether you are an acting coach or an aspiring one, we hope that this book will provide you some support. Our caps are off to you already.

Learner

- Interpret major theories of reading and writing processes and development to understand the needs of all readers in diverse contexts.
- Demonstrate a critical stance toward the scholarship of the profession.
- Read and understand the literature and research about factors that contribute to reading success (e.g., social, cognitive, and physical).
- Interpret and summarize historically shared knowledge (e.g., instructional strategies and theories) that addresses the needs of all readers.
- Demonstrate an understanding of the research and literature that undergirds the reading and writing curriculum and instruction for all PreK–12 students.
- Use instructional approaches supported by literature and research for the following areas: concepts of print, phonemic awareness, phonics, vocabulary, comprehension, fluency, critical thinking, motivation, and writing.
- Provide appropriate in-depth instruction for all readers and writers, especially those who struggle with reading and writing.
- Demonstrate an understanding of the ways in which diversity influences the reading and writing development of all students, especially those who struggle with reading and writing.
- Provide differentiated instruction and instructional materials, including traditional print, digital, and online resources, that capitalize on diversity.
- Provide students with linguistic, academic, and cultural experiences that link their communities with the school.
- Use literature and research findings about adult learning, organizational change, professional development, and school culture in working with teachers and other professionals.
- Articulate the research base related to the connections among teacher dispositions, student learning, and the involvement of parents, guardians, and the community.
- Join and participate in professional literacy organizations, symposia, conferences, and workshops.
- Demonstrate effective use of technology for improving student learning.

Grant writer

- Explain district and state assessment frameworks, proficiency standards, and student benchmarks.
- Analyze and report assessment results to a variety of appropriate audiences for relevant implications, instructional purposes, and accountability.
- Demonstrate the ability to communicate results of assessments to various audiences.
- Demonstrate effective interpersonal, communication, and leadership skills.
- Demonstrate an understanding of local, state, and national policies that affect reading and writing instruction.
- Write or assist in writing proposals that enable schools to obtain additional funding to support literacy efforts.

(cont.)

FIGURE 1.6. Items from the IRA Standards for Reading Specialists/Literacy Coaches. Available at *www.reading.org/General/CurrentResearch/Standards/ProfessionalStandards2010.aspx.*

- Promote effective communication and collaboration among stakeholders, including parents and guardians, teachers, administrators, policymakers, and community members.
- Advocate with various groups (e.g., administrators, school boards, and local, state, and federal policymaking bodies) for needed organizational and instructional changes to promote effective literacy instruction.

Curriculum expert

- Develop and implement the curriculum to meet the specific needs of students who struggle with reading.
- Demonstrate knowledge of and a critical stance toward a wide variety of quality traditional print, digital, and online resources.
- Support classroom teachers in building and using a quality, accessible classroom library and materials collection that meets the specific needs and abilities of all learners.
- Lead collaborative school efforts to evaluate, select, and use a variety of instructional materials to meet the specific needs and abilities of all learners.
- Assist teachers in developing reading and writing instruction that is responsive to diversity.

School-level planner

- Support teachers and other personnel in the design, implementation, and evaluation of the reading and writing curriculum for all students.
- Work with teachers and other personnel in developing a literacy curriculum that has vertical and horizontal alignment across PreK–12.
- Lead schoolwide or larger-scale analyses to select assessment tools that provide a systemic framework for assessing the reading, writing, and language growth of all students.
- Collaborate with others to build strong home-to-school and school-to-home literacy connections.
- Advocate for change in societal practices and institutional structures that are inherently biased or prejudiced against certain groups.
- Demonstrate how issues of inequity and opportunities for social justice activism and resiliency can be incorporated into the literacy curriculum.
- Arrange instructional areas to provide easy access to books and other instructional materials for a variety of individual, small-group, and whole-class activities and support teachers in doing the same.
- Modify the arrangements to accommodate students' changing needs.
- Create supportive social environments for all students, especially those who struggle with reading and writing.
- Create supportive environments where English learners are encouraged and provided with many opportunities to use English.
- Understand the role of routines in creating and maintaining positive learning environments for reading and writing instruction using traditional print, digital, and online resources.
- Create effective routines for all students, especially those who struggle with reading and writing.
- Use evidence-based grouping practices to meet the needs of all students, especially those who struggle with reading and writing.

(cont.)

FIGURE 1.6. *(cont.)*

Researcher

- Analyze classroom environment quality for fostering individual motivation to read and write (e.g., access to print, choice, challenge, and interests).
- As needed, adapt instructional materials and approaches to meet the language-proficiency needs of English learners and students who struggle to learn to read and write.
- Demonstrate an understanding of the literature and research related to assessments and their uses and misuses.
- Demonstrate an understanding of established purposes for assessing the performance of all readers, including tools for screening, diagnosis, progress monitoring, and measuring outcomes.
- Recognize the basic technical adequacy of assessments (e.g., reliability, content, and construct validity).
- Administer and interpret appropriate assessmentst for students, especially those who struggle with reading and writing.
- Collaborate with and provide support to all teachers in the analysis of data, using the assessment results of all students.
- Use multiple data sources to analyze individual readers' performance and to plan instruction and intervention.
- Analyze and use assessment data to examine the effectiveness of specific intervention practices and students' responses to instruction.

Teacher

- Inform other educators about major theories of reading and writing processes, components, and development with supporting research evidence, including information about the relationship between the culture and native language of English learners as a support system in their learning to read and write in English.
- Inform educators and others about the historically shared knowledge base in reading and writing and its role in reading education.
- Model fair-mindedness, empathy, and ethical behavior when teaching students and working with other professionals.
- Communicate the importance of fair-mindedness, empathy, and ethical behavior in literacy instruction and professional behavior.
- Support classroom teachers and education support personnel to implement instructional approaches for all students.
- Lead teachers in analyzing and using classroom, individual, grade-level, or schoolwide assessment data to make instructional decisions.
- Provide support and leadership to educators, parents and guardians, students, and other members of the school community in valuing the contributions of diverse people and traditions to literacy learning.
- Plan and evaluate professional development initiatives using assessment data.
- Assist teachers in understanding the relationship between first- and second-language acquisition and literacy development.

(cont.)

FIGURE 1.6. *(cont.)*

- Support classroom teachers in providing differentiated instruction and developing students as agents of their own literacy learning.
- Support and lead other educators to recognize their own cultures in order to teach in ways that are responsive to students' diverse backgrounds.
- Engage the school community in conversations about research on diversity and how diversity impacts reading and writing development.
- Collaborate with teachers, parents and guardians, and administrators to implement policies and instructional practices that promote equity and draw connections between home and community literacy and school literacy.
- Use knowledge of students and teachers to build effective professional development programs.
- Use the research base to assist in building an effective, schoolwide professional development program.
- Promote the value of reading and writing in and out of school by modeling a positive attitude toward reading and writing with students, colleagues, administrators, and parents and guardians.
- Collaborate in, lead, and evaluate professional development activities for individuals and groups of teachers. Activities may include working individually with teachers (e.g., modeling, co-planning, co-teaching, and observing) or with groups (e.g., teacher workshops, group meetings, and online learning).
- Demonstrate the ability to hold effective conversations (e.g., for planning and reflective problem solving) with individuals and groups of teachers, work collaboratively with teachers and administrators, and facilitate group meetings.
- Support teachers in their efforts to use technology in literacy assessment and instruction.

FIGURE 1.6. *(cont.)*

CHAPTER 2

Research on Literacy Coaching

M y, what a difference a decade makes. When we wrote the first edition of *The Literacy Coach's Handbook* (Walpole & McKenna, 2004), and then followed with *The Literacy Coaching Challenge* (McKenna & Walpole, 2008), we drew more upon our personal experiences in coaching initiatives that on any concrete research base. Times have changed. As we prepared this revision, we struggled to keep up with the important new insights that researchers are providing. If you are new to coaching, you may want to read this chapter now and then read it again after you finish the rest of the book. Research findings in any area make more sense if you know more about that area. For us, each new research finding colors our general understanding. The book that you are reading today reflects both our experiences with coaching and the research we have read and used to guide and interpret our experiences.

Literacy coaching surely benefited from a perfect storm. Beginning in 1998 with the authorization of the Reading Excellence Act, and continuing in 2001 with the Reading First and Early Reading First sections of the No Child Left Behind Act, coaches had jobs. Federal dollars were allocated to thousands of schools to support the professional development of teachers. Coaches were hired because they were the logical choice; site based coaching had all of the ingredients of effective professional development. It was content focused, involved active learning, was coherent with the rest of the work of teachers, was of sufficient duration, and involved collective participation of all teachers in a school (Desimone, 2009).

In 2009, we were invited to write a review on coaching for the National Reading Conference (now the Literacy Research Association; Walpole & McKenna,

2009a). At that time, we could see themes emerging in the research. To organize our thoughts, we began to consider coaching as part of a causal chain, depicted in Figure 2.1. We are pragmatists. We think about coaching as one of many resources that schools may choose to use, and we do not want to use any resources that are ineffective. On its face, coaching efforts are designed to cause changes in teacher actions, changes that influence student achievement. That might be a simple enough concept, except for the circle surrounding those efforts—the context. In coaching, as in nearly every aspect of education, the context really matters. The same coach using the same methods to coach the same teacher in two different instructional contexts might get very different results because of the context in which coaching occurs.

Many of the initial research efforts were descriptive. They described coaching efforts, revealing the complexities of coaching. Often, they used case study methods to detail barriers to an individual coach's effectiveness. They described individual coaching contexts and individual coaching relationships. More elusive, though, were studies linking coaching to changes in teaching or to changes in student achievement. As we update the themes that we found in our 2009 review, though, the findings are richer. We first present each theme along with relevant findings generated after our review. Then we add new themes that were not present in the original review.

THE BAD NEWS

A high-profile study released in 2008 put a damper on the K–3 coaching movement and on its Reading First venue. Garet and colleagues compared professional

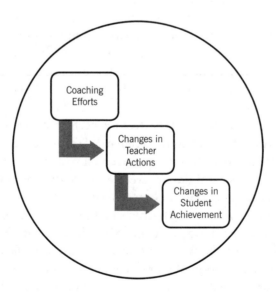

FIGURE 2.1. Causal chain inherent in coaching.

development and professional development plus coaching with second-grade teachers. Both conditions yielded increases in teacher knowledge. Unfortunately, though, neither condition was observed to influence instruction or student achievement. Does this mean that coaching does not work? To us, it means that coaching does not *always* work. The devil is in the details.

TAKE-HOME MESSAGE 1: COACHING DOES NOT ALWAYS CHANGE INSTRUCTION OR ACHIEVEMENT

One important finding of the research on coaching is that its characteristics vary incredibly. We tried to capture this variability on a scale used in geology to describe the hardness of minerals (McKenna & Walpole, 2008). At one end of the scale are the "hardest," most intrusive models, where the goals of coaching are set in advance. Our own model, reform-oriented coaching, is a hard coaching model. It is not appropriate for every school. It assumes that current teaching practices are responsible for inadequate achievement and must be replaced. It relies on research to suggest new practices. And it continually evaluates those choices for the results they provide—first for teachers and then for students. Our reform-oriented coaches, then, are important actors in school-level reform efforts. They are responsible for designing that reform and for providing the professional development that teachers need to implement it.

At the other end of the scale are "softer," less-intrusive models. New teacher mentoring programs, for example, allow coaches and teachers to work together to solve problems, as the teacher's expertise gradually and safely improves. Another example is cognitive coaching (Costa & Garmston, 1997), which supports a shared setting of goals, with the coach helping a teacher express a goal, make a plan to address it, and collect data during instruction to illustrate the teacher's level of success with the goal. Because the teacher directs the goal setting, coaching is invited by the teacher rather than imposed by administrators; coaching of this kind is consequently much less intrusive than the reform-oriented coaching Cece enacted in Chapter 1.

In our 2009 research review, the models that we found differed in the extent to which the instructional goals were negotiated in advance. In some models, the instructional target is established up front (e.g., implement a differentiated instruction program), and the coach's job is to use his or her skills to support teachers as they learn the new target. These up-front models tend to use observation and feedback fairly formally, and they often come with protocols for observation. In other models, the goal is broader (e.g., improve student comprehension), and the coach must decide and/or negotiate both what instructional practices to target and how to support teachers to learn them.

Our own thinking about coaching models has led us to conclude that only the former—up-front models—are likely to result in substantive achievement gains.

We have learned about additional up-front models since the 2009 review. Content-focused coaching (CFC) is a coaching model with a very specific aim: to increase the quality of teacher talk during comprehension lessons. The model is based on findings from the work of Isabel Beck and Margaret McKeown. CFC coaches are trained specifically to support teachers' use of vocabulary techniques (Beck, McKeown, & Kucan, 2002) and Questioning the Author (Beck & McKeown, 2006). CFC coaches work one-on-one and with grade-level teams. They develop teachers' understanding of the theory underlying these discussion approaches. They co-plan comprehension lessons. They also model, co-teach, observe, and provide formative feedback. Not surprisingly, data from fourth- and fifth-grade teacher surveys in 16 schools indicated that individual CFC coaches varied in the frequency with which they were able to accomplish these tasks (Matsumura, Sartoris, Bickel, & Garnier, 2009). While none of these coaching activities is new, what is important about CFC is that the coaching goal is clear from the outset.

Literacy Collaborative (LC) coaching is another up-front model that focuses on implementation of a set of specific practices in K–2 classrooms. LC coaches are selected the year before they begin coaching, and they are trained in the target practices while they maintain their own teaching responsibilities. Then they move to half-time teaching and half-time coaching. Teachers begin the LC implementation with seminars led by LC professional development staff members, and then the coach works one-on-one with teachers over several years. The coaching goal is two sessions per month per teacher, although that goal is not always realized (Atteberry & Bryk, 2011).

Instructional coaching, a movement gaining momentum, is much less specific in terms of its instructional targets than CFC or LC and is not necessarily limited to literacy. However, its description provides a fair appraisal of the opportunities and challenges of coaching (Knight, 2005). Instructional coaches rely on relationships and persuasion rather than formal position to leverage instructional change. They see teachers as equal partners in the coaching relationship, with choices about what they learn. They must actually recruit teachers in the school into coaching relationships, and targets are individualized around what the designers call the big four: management, content planning, instruction, and formative assessment. Instructional coaches are trained and supported through the University of Kansas Center for Research on Learning.

TAKE-HOME MESSAGE 2: USE A COACHING MODEL TO GUIDE YOUR TIME AND ACTIVITIES

The influence of schools and districts as organizational contexts for coaching really cannot be overemphasized. In 2008, we argued that even within the same district, individual schools could differ in their support for coaching. In fact, that same year, Walpole and Blamey shared results of a study of the very coaches to whom the first volume of this book was dedicated: the Reading Excellence Act (2001) coaches in the state of Georgia. All of the coaches were participating in the same professional development program, but they enacted their roles differently. Coaches tended to take on the role of director if the school's reading program needed to be designed from scratch, or mentor if the reading program was running well in general and they could focus more attention on the individual needs of teachers.

If we assume that school and district characteristics influence the extent to which coaching is enacted well, it makes sense to identify those characteristics that may help or hinder coaching efforts. A revealing new perspective on the relationship between school characteristics and coaching success involves the school's collaborative climate. A collaborative climate for teacher learning is one in which teacher teams work together to learn, setting their own goals and evaluating their success. Professional learning communities (DuFour, DuFour, & Eaker, 2008) are one example of an effort to create a collaborative climate; they assume that teachers working together as equals can solve problems of practice and student achievement. Coaching is different than this type of teacher-led professional learning because nearly all models of coaching (peer coaching excepted) rely on a difference in expertise between teacher and coach. Coaches often prompt and guide collaboration among the teachers they serve (by leading book studies, data reviews, grade-level meetings, and so forth); however, the type of collaboration fostered by coaches is bound to differ from the collaboration we would expect to see in a climate where all teachers are regarded as fellow inquirers and an equal level of expertise is assumed. We were not surprised that a recent study of CFC found that the model was not fully implemented in schools that already had a strong climate for teacher collaboration (Matsumura, Garnier, & Resnick, 2010). If teacher teams have already set their own goals, they may not be willing to abandon them for the goals of a coach. Although excellent coaches are strong collaborators, it may be that the goals of coaching and the goals of true teacher collaborations are at odds with one another.

Mangin's (2009) surveys of assistant superintendents in districts with coaches highlights this possibility. The assistant superintendents reported that the coaching climate in their districts was influenced by the broader state and national school reform climate; because schools were under pressure to increase student achievement, and coaches might help them, coaches' roles were supported. However, when that climate (and the funding associated with it) changed, support for coaching changed. Schools could no longer afford the "luxury" of a coach—even though they had previously viewed coaches as essential. The climate for coaching was also influenced by student achievement data. When data were poor, coaches' efforts were lauded. When data were good, it was difficult to justify the work of the coach. In the end, Mangin found that the most supportive district context for coaching relied on data to justify the need for the coach, addressed the coaching role directly as a service to teachers, and used teacher exposure to previous one-on-one support to set the stage for coaching.

TAKE-HOME MESSAGE 3: COACHES CANNOT BE EFFECTIVE UNLESS THEIR WORK IS INTEGRATED WITH THE SCHOOL'S CLIMATE

In 2008, there was already initial evidence that the relationships between coaches and administrators mattered, both at the district level and at the building level. Since then, coaching has surely caught the eye of researchers in the area of educational administration. Check the references in this chapter; you will see that many of the studies we are summarizing for you were published in administration journals. That fact may stem from a growing realization that coaches work as part of a fairly complex system of instructional leaders, and it may be time to think about the work of that entire leadership team instead of just the work of coaches (Gallucci, Van Lare, Yoon, & Boatright, 2010).

Administrators, especially principals, matter to the work of coaches. In a study of the relationship between principals' actions and CFC, principals who treated their coaches as valued professionals, endorsed their coaches as sources of literacy expertise to teachers, and actively participated in the CFC program had coaches who simply spent more time actually coaching. They met more often with grade-level teams and they observed teachers more frequently (Matsumura et al., 2009).

TAKE-HOME MESSAGE 4: ALIGN YOUR COACHING GOALS WITH THE GOALS OF OTHER LEADERS

In 2008 coaching initiatives already included teachers at varying levels of expertise. New teachers, teachers without formal teaching credentials, and teachers in schools with high turnover might be expected to need intensive coaching support. Researchers reported on the coaching challenges associated with these needs; in all cases there were coaches who experienced both positive and negative interactions with teachers.

Coaches may initially assume that all teachers should welcome coaching, but that simply is not the case. We are now beginning to understand why some teachers are more receptive to coaching than others. Resistance may become evident in the amount of time teachers make themselves available for coaching. Time is critical, of course, because regardless of the coaching model employed, one constraint on the effects of any coach is the amount of time actually spent with teachers. There appear to be several reasons why some teachers are available for more coaching than others. In a study of LC coaching, teachers who were newer to the profession, more willing to try new things, and viewed themselves as connected to their colleagues spent more time with their coach (Atteberry & Bryk, 2011). In contrast, teachers who make themselves available for less coaching may be motivated by fear of change, low self-efficacy, honest philosophical differences, low expectations for students, or refusal to acknowledge the coach's expertise (McKenna & Walpole, 2008).

Yet another source of resistance lies in the fact that coaches are not typically expected to teach. Mangin's work with assistant superintendents reveals another way that coaching programs interact with the needs of teachers. Schools are always dealing with limited resources. Often, literacy coaches move from roles as reading specialists (serving struggling children directly) to coaches (helping teachers serve struggling children themselves). This shift is not embraced in all schools or by all teachers, particularly when the role of the reading specialist as point person for struggling children is well institutionalized (Mangin, 2009). Coaches whose role transitions from serving struggling readers to serving their teachers should anticipate that this change will be a strain on some teachers.

There are also positive themes. While previous descriptions of coaches' work may have focused on the direct services coaches provide (e.g., modeling and formative feedback), it seems that there is more to it than that. Coaches encourage, facilitate, and demonstrate for individual teachers. Coaches help teachers read and understand educational research, and they perform a crucial service by interpreting data. In broad strokes, teachers appreciate this support. Coaches who work in ongoing collaborations tend to focus their work on groups of teachers, and these teachers appreciate the coaches' support of their collaborative work with peers (Vanderburg & Stephens, 2010). It may be that when coaching efforts are directed at a group, resistance diminishes because individual teachers feel more secure and less threatened.

Positive findings about the ways that coaches serve teachers' needs abound in the literature. Consider these findings from teachers in 20 Reading First (RF) schools after multiple years of coaching. More than 90% of teachers agreed or strongly agreed with these statements: (1) the RF coach is an important source, (2) the RF coach understands student needs, (3) the RF coach helps me solve problems, (4) the RF coach is an important resource, and (5) I feel comfortable talking to my coach (Bean, Draper, Hall, Vandermolen, & Zigmond, 2010). We see this feedback as high praise, and we have no doubt that it was well earned through hard work, both in terms of formal coaching and what these authors call COTF: coaching on the fly.

TAKE-HOME MESSAGE 5: THE NEEDS OF TEACHERS ARE REAL AND MUST COME BEFORE THE NEEDS OF COACHES

In 2008, we highlighted the importance of trust in relationships between coaches and teachers. We know more now about the personal skills necessary for coaching, and this knowledge bodes well for those of us who support professional learning for coaches. It goes without saying that coaches need literacy expertise. In addition, though, they need a unique skill set including excellent communication skills, strategies for building relationships, an understanding of change management, and an understanding of strategies for leading professional development (Gallucci et al., 2010).

Jacy Ippolito (2010) unpacked one of the challenges coaches face in their interactions with teachers: the need to balance support with pressure. The coaches he studied engaged in both directive work with teachers and in responsive work, often within the very same interaction. They employed protocols (sets of specific procedures) to help them make the shift quickly. They also made their work more effective through shared instructional leadership with their principals and teachers. This strategic flexibility is one of the personal skills that successful coaches may need if they are to be goal directed yet at the same time responsive to teacher needs. We argue, in fact, that it is really not possible to accomplish the goals of coaching without being responsive.

Developing the coaching skill set is a tall order for any one person. The good news, though, may be that coaches develop their skills in phases. Blachowicz and her colleagues invested years supporting coaches in urban schools in Chicago. As they reflected on their coaches' learning, they saw movement. Coaches approached very new ideas in "survival" mode, struggling even to understand them at a basic level. After survival, coaches moved to development of craft knowledge—they had to actually employ a new instructional strategy themselves. Finally, they moved to differentiation ability. They understood the concept so deeply that they could meet individual teachers wherever they were on this continuum (Blachowicz et al., 2010).

TAKE-HOME MESSAGE 6: BE READY TO LEARN MANY THINGS ON THE JOB

Early Reading First initiatives drew our attention to coaching in the preschool setting, and we found a large literature there that we had not examined previously. Although we might have incorporated preschool coaching research within the themes we had already examined, it makes sense to treat it separately. This is because preschool teachers tend to differ from their elementary counterparts in important ways. Generally, preschool teachers are more transient and have less formal education than other teachers. They may harbor anxiety, uncertainty, or indifference toward literacy instruction (McMullen, Elicker, & Goetze, 2006). Consequently, coaching initiatives serving preschool teachers are different from those serving other teachers.

Effective preschool initiatives tend to pair more formal, outside-the-classroom sessions with one-on-one sessions. Landry, Swank, Smith, Assel, and Gunnewig (2006) found that children in classrooms with teachers receiving mentoring had increased scores on comprehension and expressive vocabulary measures over children in classrooms with teachers not receiving mentoring. For this study, mentoring included 1-hour weekly site visits to support lesson planning, model instructional strategies, analyze assessment data, and set individual teacher goals for improvement. Hsieh, Hemmeter, McCollum, and Ostrosky (2009) examined the impact of in-class coaching on early childhood teachers' use of instructional strategies in the area of literacy. Participating teachers' use of the targeted instructional strategies increased as a result of coaching and continued after coaching was suspended.

Similarly, Neuman and Cunningham (2009) worked with early childhood educators in three groups: (1) those enrolled in a community college course in emergent literacy, (2) those enrolled in the same course but who had also been randomly assigned to work with a coach during weekly coaching sessions, and (3) those who were neither enrolled in the course nor working with a literacy coach. Results indicated greatest gains on the environmental rating scale for teachers who had attended the course and received weekly coaching. In addition, children in the classrooms of teachers who had attended the college course and received coaching made greater gains in measures of vocabulary and concepts of writing. In a follow-up study, though, Neuman and Wright (2010) dropped the combination of the college course with the coaching. They compared coaching alone to professional development alone; coaching alone improved the educational environment, whereas the college course alone did not.

Not all studies have shown positive results of coaching early childhood educators. One such study used an approach similar to that of Neuman and Cunningham (2009). Early childhood educators who had enrolled in a Heads Up! Reading course were compared to educators in the same course who also received coaching and to a group of educators who were not enrolled and who did not receive coaching (Jackson et al., 2006). On measures of environment, educators enrolled in the course made gains over the group of educators not enrolled in the course, but coaching did not add value to the course. Although many factors might explain this finding, we clearly have more to learn about how best to serve the needs of preschool teachers.

TAKE-HOME MESSAGE 7: BE READY TO DIFFERENTIATE FOR PRESCHOOL TEACHERS

The potential of technology as an effective coaching tool has emerged since our initial review. Issues of access and scale, for example, have led researchers to investigate whether coaching can be accomplished in a distance-learning environment. Findings have been mixed in that not all teachers will access web-based resources with the same frequency, and yet at the same time there are more and more resources available on the Internet.

Video-enhanced cases are also a new tool for coaches. Powell, Diamond, and Koehler (2010) designed multimedia cases for preschool teachers and tracked their use. Teachers responded well to the video component, which presented instructional examples in real classrooms. However, they did not use the full range of resources. The authors caution that the use of web-based resources as a professional development vehicle, without coaching, may not yield positive results across classrooms. The combination of coaching and such resources, though, may be ideal.

Not all tools require great technical skills. Protocols and procedures are new on the coaching landscape. Perhaps because more coaching models are available, or perhaps because of the rise of professional learning communities (PLCs) with norms and protocols, there are protocols available for nearly every aspect of coaching—from observation and feedback to data analysis to small-group problem solving meetings to book studies.

TAKE-HOME MESSAGE 8:
BE READY TO BUILD YOUR COACHING TOOLBOX

Self-report data indicate that teachers think that coaches do influence instruction. In the South Carolina Reading Initiative, teachers reported that coaches helped them try new instructional strategies in their classrooms, use different assessments, and teach based on the results of the assessments (Vanderburg & Stephens, 2010). However, the fact that teachers think that coaches help them change instruction is not the same as data that document such a change. In some cases, coaching does not alter practice. In fact, coaching can sometimes have the opposite effect. For example, one recent study found that beginning teachers being mentored, even by expert teachers, declined in their use of target practices (Roehrig, Bohn, Turner, & Pressley, 2008). The key to understanding why coaching is sometimes ineffective may lie in its relationship to other professional development.

The best-designed studies of coaching use the strategy we described in the section on preschool coaching (see Take-Home Message 6). They compare teachers who receive professional development followed by coaching with teachers who receive the same professional development without coaching. Carlisle and Berebitsky (2011) conducted such a study with a large group of first-grade teachers. They found that both groups of teachers learned about beginning reading content from the professional development, but those with a coach implemented more small-group instruction and less whole-class phonics instruction. The coaching, then, added value in terms of these practices. Interestingly, the study's design was very similar to Garet and colleagues' (2008) bad-news study, with entirely opposite results. Remember that in all coaching efforts, the details matter. Coaching plus professional development may work only when both are very directly related to the day-to-day challenges that teachers face.

Our own examination of the relationship between coaching and instruction reveals some of the complexities inherent in the job. We worked in 116 RF schools in Georgia. Our instructional goal was to increase the quality of daily read-alouds from children's literature and the quality and focus of small-group instruction. We designed a multiyear coaching support program for the state, and we were interested in the degree to which differences in coaching were associated with differences in instruction. We designed instruments to capture potential differences in coaching and their relationships to differences in instruction. Highlights of our study are provided in Figure 2.2. You will see that we found differences by grade level. The same coaching strategies yielded different relationships with instruction at different grade levels. By far the most influential characteristic of coaching, though, was its level of principal support (Walpole, McKenna, Uribe-Zarain, & Lamitina, 2010).

TAKE-HOME MESSAGE 9: BE SURE TO FIND OUT WHETHER TEACHERS IMPLEMENT NEW APPROACHES

Coaching *can* be associated with increases in student achievement. It seems, though, that the more specific the coaching program and target the greater the associated student achievement. Carlisle and Berebitsky (2011) studied coaching with a clear target: enhanced first-grade decoding. They found that first-grade teachers with coaches employed small-group instruction more frequently and had higher student growth in decoding than first-grade teachers without coaches.

Because coaches typically work across grade levels, it makes sense to look at achievement beyond just first grade. In a study of the work of 12 RF coaches, Elish-Piper and L'Allier (2011) examined the relationship between the time that coaches spent with teachers and the specific activities they engaged in together, on the one

Coaching characteristics	Teaching characteristics			
	Small-group work	Effective reading instruction	Read-alouds	Good management
Collaboration	Third grade	Third grade		Third grade
Focus on differentiation		First grade		
Support from the principal	Kindergarten, first grade, second grade			First grade, second grade

FIGURE 2.2. Positive relationships between coaching and instruction.

hand, and growth in fluency, on the other. Overall time spent with the coach was associated with greater gains in achievement in kindergarten and in grades one and two, but not in third grade. In addition, time spent conferencing, administering and discussing assessments, modeling, and observing was likewise associated with gains, but again only in K–2. These findings suggest that more coaching is better and that how coaches use their time is important. The results for third grade raise issues as well. They reinforce the emerging idea that the same coaching approaches are unlikely to work at all grades.

Research now allows us to go beyond first-grade decoding and elementary school fluency. In a multiyear coaching effort in 10 urban schools, third graders, fifth graders, and eighth graders experienced increased pass rates on their state criterion-referenced test. Description of the coaching program, designed and supported by a university team, indicates that it was a carefully thought-out reform-oriented coaching model. Coaches and teachers learned together, and student achievement improved (Blachowicz et al., 2010).

We first became colleagues over a decade ago during the Reading Excellence Act Coaching Initiative in Georgia. This initiative also produced gains on state achievement tests. Individuals in 20 of the 55 schools in the professional development project consented to additional data collection. During the years of the study, those 20 schools made AYP on the state's assessment system at a rate greater than the rest of the state's Title I schools; one year after the initiative, 100% of the study schools made AYP (Walpole & Blamey, 2008).

A study of similar size (17 schools) using the LC coaching model compared achievement before and after implementation of LC (Biancarosa, Bryk, & Dexter, 2010). Using a combination of formal and informal measures, researchers estimated the value added by coaching; there were student achievement gains each year and they increased over time, perhaps as the coaches and teachers increased their skills. In an even more stringent analysis, using control schools that also had literacy coaches, CFC produced achievement gains for English language learners (ELL) in 15 schools on a state achievement test. ELL achievement scores in the CFC schools were higher than the control schools and nearly as high as their English-speaking peers; a focus on comprehension and discussion may be a worthwhile coaching target (Matsumura, Garnier, Correnti, Junker, & Bickel, 2010).

A very large middle school study in Florida provided mixed results. With nearly 1,000 schools and 4 years of state reading data, researchers were able to track achievement over time for four cohorts of students. The researchers compared schools with coaches to schools without coaches. Coaching was associated with growth in reading achievement for middle schoolers in two of the four cohorts (Lockwood, McCombs, & Marsh, 2010). Similar to the study's authors, we choose to take a "half-full" approach to this finding, focusing on the two cohorts with positive effects rather than the two with no effects, especially because the cohort with the longest experience in coaching had the largest achievement effect. For older students, it may be that coaching takes a longer time to yield results.

TAKE-HOME MESSAGE 10: USE MULTIPLE ASSESSMENT MEASURES TO TRACK STUDENT ACHIEVEMENT

You will see us return to these take-home messages and to research throughout this book. Remember: If you are a coach, you are a professional development researcher. We hope that you will engage in design research; this means that you will continue to improve the professional development you provide to your teachers as you gather information on its effectiveness. You may change the way you use time, you may change your strategies for working with teachers, and you may change your instructional goals as you learn more about effective approaches or when data reveal new challenges. Changing your coaching strategies when they do not work for the teachers you serve is a hallmark of good coaching. In the chapters remaining in this book, we try to give you choices consistent with research on coaching, consistent with research on reading development and instruction, and consistent with what we know about real teachers and schools.

CHAPTER 3

What Is a Schoolwide Literacy Program?

We have always liked the term *coach* to refer to those site-based professional development providers who are the audience for this book. Other names for this position include reading specialist (especially one who takes on the leadership and professional development roles that IRA has long advocated), mentor, or collaborative consultant. We like coach because its use in sports is so familiar. A coach helps an entire team achieve a particular goal. A coach works with player development, but only insofar as it is consistent with team strategies and team development. A coach is different from a personal trainer. A coach is different from a physical education teacher. And a soccer coach is different from a baseball coach! A coach needs to know both the game being coached and each player's strengths quite intimately. For us, the literacy coach's game is the schoolwide literacy program.

Despite what vendors of reading materials might argue, a schoolwide literacy program is more than a set of commercial materials provided for every classroom. There is a lot of jargon to sort out. A *comprehensive literacy program* is a set of commercial materials addressing instruction and intervention for all learners at all grade levels. A *core program* is a set of commercial materials used by all learners organized by grade level. A *supplemental program* is a set of materials used in concert with a core program to offset its weaknesses. We see a schoolwide literacy program as more than materials, however. A *schoolwide literacy program* is a plan for using personnel, time, materials, and assessments designed specifically to meet the needs of the children it serves. It should be organic—constantly adapting to new information. In this chapter, we explore some of the characteristics of effective programs and then consider variables that building-level leaders must consider in defining and revising their particular program.

SCHOOLWIDE RESEARCH

The widespread use of the term *schoolwide* to refer to the characteristics of a school's plan for literacy instruction began in 1988 when the Title I law was changed to allow schools serving higher percentages of struggling families to use their federal Title I resources flexibly. These schools can opt to use Title I funds schoolwide (for all students) or to provide targeted assistance (for those who qualify based on achievement). Since that time, *schoolwide* has taken on meanings far beyond the federal Title I funding stream, but we want to stress the initial definition, that "schoolwide" Title I is more flexible and less bureaucratic. More flexible also means more complex to design and study. Research on schoolwide literacy initiatives must weigh the effects of different factors, each of which can be targeted for reform: leadership and organization for instruction, instructional materials, teacher implementation, and teacher knowledge. Researchers who consider all these things at once have much to say about the characteristics of effective reform initiatives. Others have also located especially effective schools for study. These real-life models should guide building-level leaders in the creation of their schoolwide programs. It is useful to step back and identify characteristics associated with schoolwide success as you define your own program.

Effective Schools

The search for characteristics of effective schools has engaged researchers in public policy, in educational administration, and in all content areas. Most of these efforts have combined the results of multiple cases to look for common threads. Wohlstetter and Malloy (2001) offer these characteristics of effective schools:

- They have a current vision for teaching and learning that is consistent with state and national standards.
- They have the power to make changes in teaching and learning for their building.
- They distribute power among a team of leaders.
- They develop knowledge and skills for teachers in an ongoing way.
- They collect and communicate information.
- They reward individual and group success.
- They gather resources from outside the school to advance their mission.

Interestingly, while they use literacy as a venue for describing these characteristics, these authors see each item on their list as an issue of individual school organization and governance rather than as a component of instructional leadership or program development. It may be wise to think about the intersection of governance issues and instructional planning.

Some researchers have considered specific types of schools. "Beat-the-odds" schools—schools whose performance exceeds what might be predicted based on student demographics—are a common target. Johnson (2002) summarized nine case studies of high-performing, high-poverty urban elementary schools. These schools had impressive standardized test scores, including (but not limited to) high reading achievement scores. Johnson identified several trends that were apparent across the sites:

- They targeted a visible, attainable goal that could be tracked across the school year. For example, they focused on improving attendance or increasing the number of books read.
- They focused energy on providing services to children, rather than on negotiating personal or professional relationships between adults.
- They set high, clear standards for children's behavior, so that the environment was conducive to teaching and learning.
- They created a collective (rather than personal) sense of responsibility for increasing achievement.
- They enhanced building-level instructional leadership, either through redesigning the role of the principal or by creating new curriculum support positions.
- They aligned their instruction with state and federal standards and with assessments.
- By investigating needs across the school year, they supported teachers with the materials and training that they needed to be successful.
- They allocated time for teachers to collaborate, to plan, and to learn together during the school day.
- They reached out to parents.
- They created additional time for instruction.

Johnson's characteristics of successful elementary schools encompass those listed by Wohlstetter and Malloy (2001) but include more of the nuts and bolts of planning.

Literacy achievement is always an attractive target. Researchers at the Center for the Improvement of Early Reading Achievement undertook a large-scale study of effective schools (Taylor, Pearson, Clark, & Walpole, 2000). They selected 14 schools in four different states with impressive literacy achievement—specifically, schools with both better standardized test scores and a larger proportion of children qualifying for free and reduced-price lunches than their district neighbors. In other words, these schools "beat the odds" by achieving well despite high poverty. Surveys, interviews, observations, time logs, and both researcher-collected and state-level achievement tests were analyzed for two target classrooms at each grade (kindergarten through third grade). In that group of potentially very successful schools, three schools emerged as most successful. They shared some important characteristics that separated them from the other schools in the study:

- They had strong links to parents (e.g., site councils, meetings, phone calls, surveys, letters, newsletters, and work folders).
- They had collaborative models for specialists to support classroom teachers.
- They had better building-level communication about children's achievement and about curriculum implementation, both within and between grade levels.
- They had a systematic procedure for evaluation of student progress, including a regular assessment schedule, a system for sharing and reporting data, and a system for using data in instructional decision making.
- They spent more time in small-group instruction, with those groups formed and reformed on the basis of achievement.
- They had small-group early reading interventions, including both national reform models and locally developed models across the elementary grades.
- They offered integrated, ongoing professional development programs for teachers.

These schoolwide findings can surely be used to guide reform efforts. Other researchers, working at virtually the same time in other settings, have reported almost identical characteristics of especially successful schoolwide literacy programs (e.g., Mosenthal, Lipson, Sortino, Russ, & Mekkelsen, 2002; Taylor, Pressley, & Pearson, 2002; G. G. Duffy & Hoffman, 2002).

Effective Reforms

Admiring the work of successful sites does not solve many problems for struggling schools. For them, it is the process that matters first. How does a school move toward the characteristics of effective schools identified above? Edward Kame'enui, Deborah Simmons, and their colleagues (e.g., Simmons, Kuykehdall, King, Cornachione, & Kame'enui, 2000) have provided a commonsense model of reform that they call the *schoolwide literacy improvement model*. They propose five stages for this model:

1. Describe the context thoroughly, including attention to curriculum, instruction, assessment, and interventions.
2. Form instructional groups, using achievement data.
3. Design coordinated instruction for all groups, adopting new curriculum materials if necessary.

4. Set goals that can be evaluated through data collection during the year, and adjust grouping and pacing plans accordingly.
5. Evaluate the success of the program for children at the end of the year, and adjust instruction and intervention programs accordingly.

In order to move through these stages, schools must set clear benchmarks for student achievement and select valid and reliable assessments to measure student progress. The stage of designing coordinated instruction *may* require commercial reading materials but *must* require an instructional schedule that allows time for teaching and learning and for student practice. An added bonus of a coordinated schedule is the potential for sharing and coordinating resources (including personnel) so that students have access to intervention (Coyne, Kame'enui, & Simmons, 2004).

Not all successful schoolwide reform cases incorporate new materials. In a recent elementary school case study (Fisher & Frey, 2007), researchers worked with a high-poverty, low-performing elementary school to establish a set of shared beliefs. The beliefs were broad enough to inform many aspects of instructional planning. They included a commitment to the social nature of learning, to extended conversations, to integration of reading, writing, and oral language, and to a gradual release of responsibility. These core commitments informed a rich instructional framework that included instructional strategies for modeling, guided practice, collaborative learning, independent practice, and assessment. To enact their framework, they added comprehensive professional support (formal professional development, collaborative teacher learning communities, and peer coaching). Reflecting back on the initiative after 6 years, from a place of increased achievement, participants attributed their success to the shared instructional framework, to increased instructional time, to creating positive habits in the students, and to professional support for teachers.

It may take more than just establishing a process for designing the schoolwide model, though. Teachers may need ongoing and intensive professional development resources; this fact bodes well for the hiring of coaches. In a recent middle school reform initiative, this same team of literacy researchers (Fisher, Frey, & Lapp, 2011) participated in schoolwide program design. They engaged in a collaborative process to arrive at a set of schoolwide strategies, and they provided outside-the-classroom professional development to build teacher understanding of why and how to use the strategies. When they investigated one strategy closely, though, they found that teachers needed an additional set of supports, through weekly coaching, to influence student achievement.

What case studies of schoolwide reform have in common is that they are intensive, multiyear operations. Struggling schools sometimes think that they don't have time to engage a process. The complex policy environment in which schools operate influences the success of schoolwide initiatives. Conflicting state and federal requirements as well as quickly shifting accountability tides may take schoolwide programs off track, causing them to expend all of their energy on standardized test preparation (e.g., Sunderman & Mickelsen, 2000). This is unfortunate; there is no evidence that a struggling school can be immediately transformed into a successful one.

Embracing Tiered Instruction

The concept of tiered instruction has provided a new opportunity for schoolwide thinking, and it may speed the process of reform efforts. We build on the history of literacy program effectiveness and promising reform efforts when we embrace tiered instruction. Tiered instruction, for us, is not simply a set of regulations for response-to-intervention (RTI) efforts. Rather, it is a mindset that should define all schoolwide literacy programs—and all content-area reforms, for that matter. Tiered instruction is a system for designing and providing instruction, measuring its effects, and then modifying it. We introduce tiered instruction here because we want you to focus your attention from the start on high-quality classroom instruction. In most of the schools we visit, more efforts are expended on the second and third tier than the first. Conceptually, that is a schoolwide mistake. An investment in the quality of initial instruction reduces the need for more expensive efforts (in time and money and personnel). Figure 3.1 is an overview of the most common tiered model.

While we want you to consider Tier 1 an important planning target, we also want you to anticipate that some children will need additional opportunities to learn. We, like Coyne et al. (2004), see a schoolwide, tiered model as a plan to teach all children to read by embracing our responsibility to teach each child to read. While tiered instruction might reduce the number of students requiring special education over time, that is not our primary reason for embracing it. Tiered instruction requires schoolwide collaboration and careful monitoring of students'

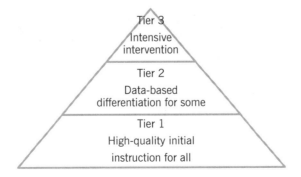

FIGURE 3.1. Conceptual model for tiered instruction.

progress (Wanzek & Vaughn, 2011), actions with the potential to benefit all learners.

As we have worked inside schools to promote the success of schoolwide efforts, we have been informed by the work of our colleagues who are studying effective schools, effective change processes, and tiered instructional designs. You will see their influence in the topics that follow. They represent our own efforts to bring this research into practice—to work with schools to become exemplary sites through building-level reform initiatives. The interrelated facets of schoolwide efforts are represented in Figure 3.2. The remainder of this chapter provides specific guidance for each of these aspects of schoolwide planning.

ASSESSMENT SYSTEMS

Whether you are emulating the work of effective schools or designing a tiered instructional program, you need clear information about student progress. Assessment data inform the design of a schoolwide program in many ways. Data can be used to identify the immediate instructional needs of children, guide their instruction, and measures the success of the program in the short and long term. This issue is so important that we deal with designing an assessment system as a separate topic in Chapter 5. Here we discuss broader issues in the management of assessments.

FIGURE 3.2. Schoolwide planning.

Scheduling Assessments

School-level assessments should not be a surprise to teachers. A well-designed literacy program has a clear schedule for conducting assessments. This schedule is created before the school year begins and provided for teachers to use to plan their work. Figure 3.3 provides such a calendar for an elementary school. Note that we have left the actual assessment names out; you can fill them in after considering ideas in Chapter 5. At this point, though, we begin to establish a common assessment vocabulary. Screening assessments are brief assessments given to all students to rule out more basic skills deficits. Informal diagnostic assessments are given only to those children identified through screenings. They are used to pinpoint skill needs. Progress monitoring assessments are used to measure the effects of instruction; they are specific to the type of instruction provided. Outcome assessments are used to measure program quality.

As you schedule assessments, be mindful of the burden they place on classroom teachers and on the instructional schedule. Keep track of *all* assessments on a central calendar to avoid assessment overload. Also, make sure that your assessments are collected and reported on a schedule that meshes with the school's overall calendar.

Collecting Assessments

At the start of a schoolwide reform effort, a literacy coach faces a particularly difficult conundrum: Assessments are best conducted by the classroom teachers who will be using the data to drive their instruction, but assessment training takes time. One thing is certain: Conducting schoolwide assessments without the training required to ensure that all testers can administer the tests reliably is a waste of teaching and learning time. Helping teachers learn to administer and interpret assessments is an important form of professional development and should be a focus of coaching whenever new assessments are adopted or new teachers are hired.

One possibility for dealing with testing is a model based on gradual release of responsibility; the literacy coach takes much of the testing responsibility at first, and then scaffolds the responsibility onto the teachers. In the first phase, the literacy coach works with a small SWAT to administer the initial screenings. This team begins by simulating and practicing the testing with adults, moves to group testing of individual children with reliability checks, and finally proceeds to testing throughout the school. Classroom teachers can watch some of the testing of their own students and start to familiarize themselves with the procedures.

In the next stage of testing, the SWAT members provide training to all of the classroom teachers (in the case of a newly adopted test), and the teachers function as members of the team in their own classrooms. In that way, the teachers can

	1	Interest and motivation inventories
First 9 weeks	2	Screenings for word recognition or fluency or comprehension
	3	Informal diagnostics (if needed)
	4	Writing samples
	5	State of the school
	6	Progress monitoring
	7	Progress monitoring
	8	Progress monitoring
	9	Reports to families
Second 9 weeks	10	State of the school
	11	Writing samples
	12	Progress monitoring
	13	Progress monitoring
	14	Progress monitoring
	15	Progress monitoring
	16	Progress monitoring
	17	Progress monitoring
	18	Reports to families
Third 9 weeks	19	Screenings for word recognition or fluency or comprehension
	20	Informal diagnostics (if needed)
	21	Writing samples
	22	State of the school
	23	Progress monitoring
	24	Outcome test practice
	25	Progress monitoring
	26	Progress monitoring
	27	Reports to families

(cont.)

FIGURE 3.3. Assessment schedule.

	28	Writing samples
	29	Progress monitoring
	30	Progress monitoring
Fourth 9 weeks	31	Progress monitoring
	32	Progress monitoring
	33	Progress monitoring
	34	Outcome testing
	35	State of the school
	36	Reports to families

FIGURE 3.3. *(cont.)*

learn to administer the tests and also collect some of the data for their own students. Other members of the team are still participating, to help the teachers get the data collected with the least possible time taken away from instruction.

Finally, responsibility can be released to the teachers to collect their own screening data. Using the assessment calendar, a whole staff of teachers can learn to collect data that can be used to fine-tune their own instruction and look at issues of overall program success. In order to do that, the literacy coach must first provide an overview of the testing dates (as in Figure 3.3), then schedule the actual testing dates, then plan backward to schedule the training that teachers will need in order to be ready to administer the tests.

Summarizing Assessment Data

We have worked with many schools that have collected extensive assessment data but not used it for instructional decision making. The barrier is summarization; no staff member is actually charged with collecting and making sense of the data. This is surely an important job for a literacy coach. Sometimes it is simply "math fear" that prevents building-level leaders from summarizing school-level data. Actually, very little mathematical knowledge is necessary; certainly statistical analysis is unnecessary. Literacy coaches would be well served by a computer spreadsheet program that allows calculation of four figures—total number (n), percentage (%), mean or average (M), and standard deviation (SD)—and by a coding system for disaggregating data to show the performance of specific groups of children (e.g., by grade level, teacher, socioeconomic status, gender, ethnicity). All four of these statistics can be calculated automatically by the computer.

Figure 3.4 provides an illustration. It is a summary sheet from a kindergarten team meeting. The data are simple: the total number of letter names and letter

Letter names, Sept.	Letter names, Jan.
At risk (n = 9; 16%)	
M = 1.5	M = 5.6
(SD = 1.8)	(SD = 5.2)
Progressing (n = 48; 84%)	
M = 17.1	M = 22.9
(SD = 7.0)	(SD = 3.7)

FIGURE 3.4. Kindergarten letter-name and letter-sound data.

sounds each kindergarten child could produce, given a sheet of random letters. The data are summarized for two separate groups. The nine at-risk children began the year with a mean score of 1.5 letter names and a standard deviation of 1.8. The small standard deviation score means that the individual data points were close to the mean score. One reason for this is the nearness of the "floor"—the lowest possible score—which in this case is zero. By January the mean had risen to 5.6, but the standard deviation was much larger. There was low achievement overall, but the individual children varied more in their scores than they had in September. The at-risk children were responding to instruction at vastly different rates. The pattern was the same for the letter sounds.

The cohort of 48 students who were on track (progressing) exhibited a different pattern. They entered school with a larger mean score for letter names (17.1) and a large standard deviation (7.0), but by January they had progressed to a mean score of almost 23 letter names with a smaller standard deviation (3.7). (The smaller standard deviation is due in part to the nearness of the "ceiling"—the highest possible score—which, of course, is 26.) Regardless of their initial status, the progressing students were responding to instruction in fairly similar ways, and they were close to mastery. The same pattern was true for these children with respect to letter sounds.

Technology for summarizing the results of data has changed drastically in the time that we have been working with coaches. Many schools now have comprehensive web-based systems for keeping track of all kinds of data; many states have web-based systems for analyzing and summarizing the results of state tests at the level of the individual item; commercial vendors provide web-based systems for screening and for monitoring progress. But buyers beware. It is easy to become distracted by attractive formats for representing results and to give specific assessments more attention than they deserve. Schoolwide leadership teams must develop their own assessment literacy such that they do not confuse attractive output with important information.

Communicating Assessments

If a literacy coach has scheduled building-level assessments, created a system for collecting the data reliably, and summarized the data, there is one step remaining: Those data must be made public to all of the school's stakeholders. There are two internal sets of stakeholders (the entire staff and the individual classroom teachers) and two external sets (the district office/school board and the parents). All of these stakeholders deserve to know about student achievement.

One set of stakeholders is the full staff—all adults who work with children in any capacity. In order to develop a shared sense of responsibility for the achievement of all children, all adults should be well informed about the strengths and weaknesses of the instructional program that are identified in the data. Summary data, as described above, can be presented to teachers in a "state of the school" address; you will see that we schedule four such addresses in Figure 3.3. The purposes of such an address are to share insights into the current achievement of children and to take leadership in using those insights to respond immediately to student needs.

Figure 3.5 is an excerpt from a handout shared with teachers during a state of the school address. The data presented are for first grade, although the format was exactly the same for all grades. For each grade level, the literacy coach reviewed the goals for that grade level in school-specific language. Next, she reviewed basic initiatives in classroom instruction. In this case, the school was using a new core program to coordinate instruction in decoding, high-frequency words, and text reading. Finally, she defined current tiered offerings. A daily small-group intervention served those children identified through the schoolwide screening, and a tutoring program served the weakest-performing children in twice-weekly sessions.

The next slide, the "New Data" section, told the whole staff that the two interventions mentioned above were insufficient for all children to meet grade-level expectations. In fact, to translate the data into time, 15% of the children were months behind and 22% were several weeks behind. For those children, then, changes in the interventions were necessary. The data prompted the literacy coach to implement changes right away.

Creation and delivery of a state of the school address legitimizes a schoolwide literacy program. In our work with schools, collection, summarization, and interpretation of data are essential to garner support for instructional changes. Initially, though, communicating problematic data is one of the most difficult tasks of the literacy coach; eventually, however, such communication is the cement that binds the teachers' collective instructional efforts to the evidence of student and program progress. It also holds building-level leaders accountable to the schoolwide plan by forcing the whole staff to consider the data and to contemplate additional efforts and programs in response to the data.

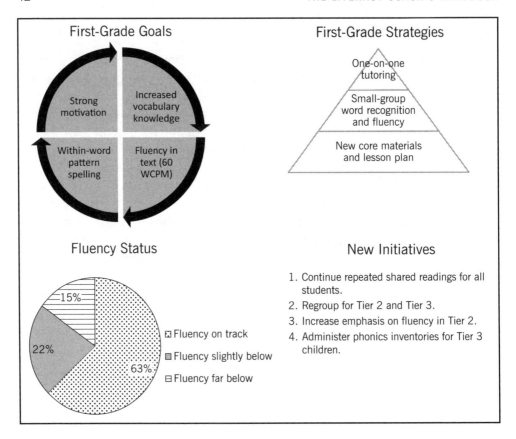

FIGURE 3.5. First-grade portion of state of the school address.

Another important set of stakeholders in the school consists of the individual classroom teachers who are delivering instruction. Summaries of assessment data across the grade levels should be communicated in public; analysis of particular classroom variables should be communicated in private. At a basic level, individual teachers should compare the data from their children to the data across their grade level to see whether their own classes are contributing positively or negatively to the overall mean, and to identify those individual children whose achievement is especially low. As we see it, one job of the literacy coach is to help teachers interpret their own data and to reflect on their own practices in relation to those data in an environment safe from evaluation. At times, classroom formation skews classroom performance (e.g., when all struggling children are clustered into specific classrooms). However, the goal of schoolwide improvement should be that all children receive the type and amount of instruction they need to achieve at grade level, regardless of where they start.

The state of the school address and the classroom teachers' individual data constitute the internal data communication variable; the same data should be reported externally to the district office. You will notice in our figures that no individuals (teachers or students) are named. Personal information is shared only with the classroom teachers. In sharing assessment data externally, this assurance of privacy is essential. The state of the school address should be communicated to district leaders to keep them informed about the progress of the schoolwide initiative. In an individual building, a literacy coach and a principal might choose to invite these external stakeholders to the schoolwide meeting or to host individual sessions for them.

These very same data should be used to communicate student achievement to parents. It is the responsibility of the literacy coach to ensure that parents are informed about their children's progress in the school's literacy program. This may mean that report cards must be reformatted. At the very least, however, parents must know what the school's goals are and where their children are performing in relation to those goals. We are concerned when children are evaluated only for their effort and attitude on their report cards, rather than for their achievement. Parents have a right to know where their children stand.

Planning Assessment

To sum up, a literacy coach must oversee the establishment of a unified, building-level assessment program. There are several essential steps:

1. Select assessments that address key components of reading development.
2. Create a calendar for assessment.
3. Train teachers to conduct the assessments.
4. Share assessment results with school stakeholders: the whole staff, the individual teachers, the district, and parents.
5. Use data to continually evaluate the success of the program and to make adjustments.

GROUPING CONFIGURATIONS

Assessing student needs is the first step toward addressing these needs. A schoolwide literacy program incorporates structures to gather assessment information and use it to form and reform instructional groups. Broadly defined, *grouping* is any system through which children are assigned to different instructional settings in order to better address their needs. A schoolwide literacy program will take a schoolwide stance on how, when, and why students are grouped for instruction. We know firsthand that that stance will likely be visited and revisited. Because grouping practices require teamwork and influence time for teaching and learning, they are vitally important to schoolwide programs.

Grouping practices have long been a source of controversy. The essence of the controversy is this: One-size-fits-all instruction will not accommodate the range of needs in a classroom, *and* always grouping children for instruction by their achievement is not necessarily the answer. Like others in the field, we advocate neither homogeneous nor heterogeneous groups, but rather a planful mixture (e.g., Caldwell & Ford, 2002; Reutzel, 1999)—with heterogeneous grade-level class-rooms engaged in whole-class instruction, and then also regrouped at specific times during the day into flexible homogeneous groups. We also recognize that controlled heterogeneity may be more reasonable for teachers than totally hetero-geneous classrooms. For example, if we rank order children by achievement and then assign them randomly to classrooms, every teacher will be faced with the full range of proficiency levels—a daunting task. The alternative of tracking—assigning children to classrooms in order to create nearly homogeneous groups—has its own set of problems, both social and pedagogical (Slavin, 1987). To avoid both problems, many leadership teams choose to cluster children in groups in each homeroom so that it will be easier for teachers to regroup them. Each classroom, then, might begin with three, or at most four, basic groups. Figure 3.6 illustrates these three basic approaches to assigning children to homerooms.

Flexibility is the key here; we define *flexible* groups as groups formed and reformed at regular intervals on the basis of new student achievement data. We also label the choices that follow as *regrouping* rather than *grouping* options, to emphasize that they are all ways to meet the individual needs of children who are first grouped into heterogeneous classroom groups and then regrouped for a spe-cific portion of time for specific reasons, and that these decisions are periodically reevaluated.

Some major approaches to regrouping for reading instruction (including costs and benefits) are the following.

	Class A	Class B	Class C
Heterogeneous assignment	3 very low 4 slightly below 8 at grade level 4 slightly above 3 advanced	3 very low 4 slightly below 8 at grade level 4 slightly above 3 advanced	3 very low 4 slightly below 8 at grade level 4 slightly above 3 advanced
Homogeneous assignment (tracking)	9 very low 12 slightly below	24 at grade level	12 slightly above 9 advanced
Controlled heterogeneous assignment (clustering)	6 very low 7 at grade level 9 advanced	3 very low 4 slightly below 8 at grade level 6 slightly above	8 slightly below 9 at grade level 6 slightly above

FIGURE 3.6. Three approaches to assigning children to homerooms.

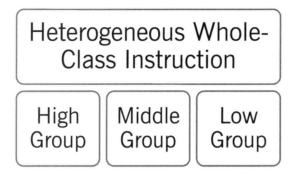

FIGURE 3.7. Flexible within-class regrouping.

Flexible Within-Class Regrouping

In this plan, children are assigned and reassigned to one of a small number of groups in their own classroom based on achievement (see Figure 3.7). They then receive instruction geared directly to their needs. The potential benefits of this grouping plan are that group membership can easily be adjusted without altering schedules, and that only one adult is responsible for the bulk of instruction for an individual child and for communicating progress to parents. The potential costs are that the number of actual groups in a classroom may be prohibitive, and that teachers must prepare to teach multiple lessons each day based on the needs of each group.

Flexible Same-Grade Regrouping

Under this plan, students are assigned to heterogeneous homeroom classes for most of the day, but are regrouped according to achievement level for a portion of their reading block (see Figure 3.8). All teachers are potential reading teachers for all students at the grade level, and additional staff members can be added. In the figure, four homerooms are regrouped into six reading groups with the addition of two adults. A potential cost of this plan is that many children will not receive reading instruction from their homeroom teacher. To contend with this problem, clear systems for communication must be established. Valuable instructional time can also be lost as children make their way from one room to another. A potential benefit of this plan is that each teacher only has to plan instruction to meet the needs of one specific group (in addition to the grade-level group) each day.

Flexible Across-Grade Regrouping

This plan dates to the late 1950s, when it was introduced in Joplin, Missouri, by Cecil Floyd (Floyd, 1954). As in same-grade regrouping, students are assigned to heterogeneous classes for most of the day, but move to homogeneous rooms

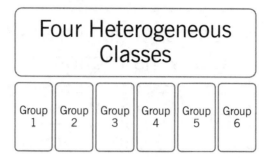

FIGURE 3.8. Flexible same-grade regrouping.

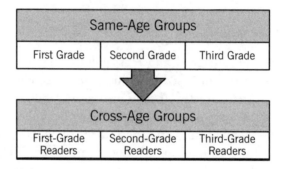

FIGURE 3.9. Flexible across-grade regrouping.

for reading (see Figure 3.9). Unlike same-grade grouping, the Joplin plan involves regrouping children of different grade levels together for reading instruction. Advanced second graders might join average-achieving third graders, for example. The potential benefits of this plan are especially apparent for the strongest- and weakest-performing readers: The instructional needs of these children in several grade levels might be very similar, and their small numbers at each grade level or in each heterogeneous classroom might prevent them from receiving the instruction they need. The potential costs of this plan are mainly in the constraints it places on the master schedule (e.g., all teachers at all grade levels must have their uninterrupted reading block at the same time) and in "selling" the plan to teachers who might question the wisdom of mixing children by age.

Heterogeneous Paired Regrouping

This plan is derived from the instructional approach called peer-assisted learning strategies, championed by Doug and Lynn Fuchs and their colleagues at Vanderbilt University (see *http://kc.vanderbilt.edu/pals* for more information). Heterogeneous pairs are formed by rank ordering students from highest to lowest on an assessment. The student list is split in half, with the strongest student paired with

(strongest student) 1	7
2	8
3	9
4	10
5	11
6	12 (weakest student)

FIGURE 3.10. Heterogeneous paired regrouping.

the strongest student in the second half (see Figure 3.10). The pairing procedure ensures that the partners have different skill levels, but that the distance between them is controlled.

A schoolwide program must address the issue of grouping in a systematic way. Unfortunately, research has not revealed any one ideal grouping plan. Each school must carefully consider a host of factors in order to reach a decision. Once a decision is made about how to group children, there are natural planning correlates, and they are cumulative. If flexible within-class grouping is chosen, then the logistics of that grouping and regrouping must be established (when, how, and by whom). If flexible same-grade regrouping is chosen, then to the logistics above must be added the need to schedule a consistent protected time for instruction within each grade level. If flexible across-grade regrouping is chosen, the scheduling demand for protected time is extended to more teachers. We believe that a grouping philosophy should be established schoolwide, and grouping procedures employed systematically. This policy ensures that all children are participating fully in the schoolwide program. In fact, we believe that a literacy coach should be intimately involved in regrouping children because those decisions are high stakes in nature, especially for children who are struggling.

MATERIALS AND STRATEGIES

A schoolwide program is informed by assessment data and addresses student needs with resources aligned with research and with the needs of children. In a broad sense, strong building-level leaders become wise consumers of the commercial materials available for reading instruction; rather than viewing these products themselves as literacy programs, effective leaders view commercial materials as tools within literacy programs that are much more. In Chapter 8 we discuss selection of commercial materials in depth. For now, we focus on the role of these resources in a schoolwide literacy program. We challenge literacy coaches to consider a systematic approach to the selection of curriculum resources. In fact, we challenge them to make choices that could be summarized in the template in Figure 3.11. You can see that we are influenced by research on literacy development. In a schoolwide program, this template can be used for planning at each grade level. It may be that particular commercial products are listed in more than one category at more than one grade level, but it is important to question whether and how these programs correspond to research in each curricular area. You can use the procedures presented in Chapter 7 to consider programs in this way.

To choose commercial resources wisely, the literacy coach must consider the potential benefits of whole-class and small-group instruction, individual practice, and intervention. For us, *whole-class instruction* is undifferentiated, grade-level instruction. The goals of whole-class instruction are to provide all children with basic access to grade-level concepts and vocabulary, and to develop literacy skills and strategies according to an explicit, systematic, grade-appropriate scope and sequence of instruction. Although this portion of the instructional day is necessary, it is also insufficient. For some children, this grade-level instruction will be so far distant from their level of performance that they will be unable to use it to address their skill and strategy needs. This will likely be true for both the highest achieving *and* the lowest-achieving readers.

	Whole-class instruction	Small-group instruction	Individual practice	Intervention
Vocabulary and oral language	All grades	ELLs	All grades	ELLs PreK
Phonemic awareness	PreK Kindergarten Grade 1	PreK Kindergarten Grade 1		Kindergarten Grade 1 Grade 2
Alphabet knowledge and decoding	PreK Kindergarten Grade 1	PreK Kindergarten Grade 1 Grade 2	PreK Kindergarten Grade 1	Grade 3 Grade 4 Grade 5
Automaticity and fluency	All grades	All grades	All grades	All grades
Comprehension	All grades	Grade 2 Grade 3 Grade 4 Grade 5	All grades	ELLs Grade 2 Grade 3 Grade 4 Grade 5

FIGURE 3.11. Curriculum resources in a schoolwide reading program.

The "small" in *small group* is a designation of the differences in needs. In forming these groups, needs are more important than numbers; members of these groups have only "small" differences in their needs. By *small-group instruction*, we mean instruction within the regular reading block provided by the classroom teacher (or the designated teacher for within-grade regrouping or across-grade regrouping), with materials selected to match the needs of particular children. You will see later that we consider small-group, classroom-based instruction Tier 2 instruction; in our tiered model, then, children who are struggling receive the instruction that they need, meeting the mandate of RTI, but other children also have some instruction in addition to their grade-level whole-class instruction. In that way, we are not trying to reduce the achievement gap between children (by capping growth of high-achieving children) but rather we are trying to ensure that all children meet the state benchmarks and all children experience at least a year's growth each year. This inclusion of the needs of high-achieving students will be new to many schools.

Some of the skills and strategies that will be targeted in small-group instruction can be predicted from a knowledge of reading development. Typically, some children in preschool, kindergarten, and grade one will need small-group instruction in phonological awareness. Planning to build alphabet knowledge and decoding is a smart bet for small groups in kindergarten, first grade, and second grade. Fluency is likely to be a necessary component after grade one. Finally, we see small-group work in reading comprehension as essential in second grade and beyond; we target listening comprehension for all students before that. In Chapter 7, when we discuss reading development across ages and stages, we explain this concept further.

We consider individual practice as an essential part of a literacy program. For vocabulary and comprehension development, individual practice comes as children read widely, listen to literature read aloud, and discuss and write about texts. Texts for vocabulary and comprehension practice include authentic children's literature, content-related trade books, high-interest books, and web-based texts. For decoding, this individual practice should focus on reading and rereading of materials that beginning readers can actually use to practice their decoding skills in context. Decoding practice usually uses little books specifically designed to highlight phonics patterns. For fluency, individual practice includes wide and repeated reading of texts that are easy for children to read; the characteristics of "easy" texts shift as children proceed through the stages of reading development.

Intervention, the focus of Chapter 9, is intensive in time and resources in a schoolwide literacy program. It occurs in addition to the regular reading block (before school, after school, in the summer, or sometimes in place of science and social studies instruction or specials). We define *intervention* as extremely targeted, aggressively paced, explicit instruction delivered by personnel with specialized training and/or through specially designed programs. Children identified for intervention need specialized curriculum resources and extended time.

Potentially, then, selection of instructional materials includes three tiers: materials for grade-level whole-class instruction, for small-group instruction, and for intervention. You may be surprised to know that we think even materials for students to use for reading practice should be selected very carefully and distributed fairly across classrooms. When you begin to think schoolwide, you see that all students (and teachers) should have what they need, regardless of their classroom placement. This makes disparities in resources (including classroom libraries) unconscionable. We provide further guidance for selecting materials later. For now, though, consider the process below.

Planning for Curriculum Selection
1. Start with your materials for whole-class instruction and reading practice.
2. Carefully consider the results of your assessments.
3. Move to your materials for small-group instruction.
4. Carefully consider the results of your assessments.
5. Move to your materials for intervention.
6. Carefully consider the results of your assessments.

ALLOCATION OF TIME

Even with an effective assessment system, a regrouping philosophy, and curriculum resources that make it easier for teachers to use research-based strategies and meet the needs of children, the challenge is still in the details. Time for instruction is key to a schoolwide effort; effective schools allocate and reallocate time thoughtfully. In this section, we focus on choices that literacy coaches have regarding time: for instruction, intervention, planning, and professional development. As in a schoolwide assessment system, the keys to organizing time effectively are to start with goals, formulate a plan that supports those goals, and monitor implementation of that plan, making adjustments as necessary.

Time for Learning

One thing is certain: All schools can benefit from an analysis of the ways they use time. Allington and Cunningham (2006) conceptualize time as minutes, hours, days, weeks, and years, which can be either used well or wasted. How many minutes can be lost in noninstructional activities (e.g., packing up, lining up, gearing up)? How many hours can be wasted in haphazard or poorly planned activities? How many days can be wasted in noninstructional programs? How many weeks can be wasted in redundant layers of assessment? Good leadership in a schoolwide program will address these issues of time.

To give just one example, consider a teacher who has not established efficient procedures for transitions involving small-group and independent activities. Let's assume that a transition should take no more than a minute, that these children require 3 minutes, and that there are three transitions. This means that 6 minutes are wasted each day. That doesn't sound like much, but over a 180-day school year, 18 hours of instructional time are lost. How much growth might have been fostered through better use of that time?

Another way to think about using time well is to consider ways to extend it. It makes sense that children with greater needs may need more time to achieve the same goals. The traditional route to extending time—retention in grade—is clearly ineffective (Allington & McGill-Franzen, 1995). There are other ways, though. Additional hours of instruction can be provided during extended-day and summer programs with clear goals and specific materials. Additional weeks of instruction can be provided during these out-of-school-time (OST) programs, again with clear goals and materials. Lauer et al. (2006) reviewed research on OST programs and concluded that both summer and after-school programs can contribute to better achievement (though no advantage was observed for one over the other), but an important factor is how targeted the instruction tends to be. Not surprisingly, assessment-based tutoring in reading was found to be especially effective. And, of course, additional *years* of instruction can be provided with preschool programs! All of these units of time are potentially malleable within a schoolwide literacy program.

Time for Teaching

Regardless of how the structural decisions about time described above are made, extended, uninterrupted time for literacy instruction every day is essential. Preschool typically has 60 minutes of dedicated time for literacy and K–5 typically has 90 minutes for reading and 30 minutes for writing. How schools schedule and use that time is related to their decisions about regrouping. We provide some models for planning this time that are related to the grouping decisions above.

Instructional time in preschool is especially precious. Typically, a PreK schedule includes a shared storybook reading for all children and exploration and language development in centers. In our experience, two additional elements vary considerably: the extent to which teachers use small groups for instruction and the extent to which all adults have specified instructional roles. We think that small-group instruction is essential in PreK *and* that all adults can provide some. In a PreK with a teacher and two assistants, children could be split into three groups, either homogeneous or heterogeneous by achievement, and those groups could move from one adult to the next. Each could have a different focus: building alphabet knowledge, building phonological awareness, or building oral language and vocabulary. If there are two adults, two of those focus areas could be addressed each day, and the third focus could always be included in centers (Beauchat, Blamey, & Walpole, 2010).

Figure 3.12 provides a beginning framework for time across grades K–5 if a schoolwide plan incorporates flexible within-class regroupings. Note that the

45 minutes	Grade-level shared reading and children's literature read-aloud		
15 minutes	Tier 2 small-group instruction	Reading practice	Writing in response to reading
15 minutes	Reading practice	Tier 2 small-group instruction	Writing in response to reading
15 minutes	Writing in response to reading	Reading practice	Tier 2 small-group instruction
30 minutes	Grade-level writing instruction		

FIGURE 3.12. Time for instruction with within-class regrouping in K–5.

teacher's focus is shaded. At first blush, you may think that it is not possible to accomplish these goals in the time allowed; we revisit the notion of instructional time (and how to use it well) in many subsequent chapters. After grade-level instruction and before writing instruction, the teacher meets with each of three small groups for 15 minutes. When children are not with the teacher, they are engaged in reading practice or in writing in response to their reading (rather than the worksheets or complex centers that characterize many classroom plans). We favor simple uses of time, and a focus on what the children are doing (practicing) rather than where they are doing it (centers or desks).

There are two ways that a coach might increase the effectiveness of this basic plan for time. First, data may indicate that there are more than three groups in a classroom. To meet their needs without extending the entire reading block, teachers may be able to shift just a few children across classrooms to end up with three groups. Second, imagine that the first group served is the lowest achieving. Rather than progressing from their group time to 30 minutes of practice, they could leave the classroom for intensive intervention (trading practice time for more instruction). In upper elementary grades, 30 minutes of intensive intervention per day might not be enough time; those students might be best served by moving from their work with grade-level instruction right into intensive intervention, leaving the classroom to work with a specialist while the teacher serves the needs of the rest of the class.

If a schoolwide program employs across-grade-level regrouping, grade-level instruction could be followed by the move to reading groups (as in Figure 3.7). Since there is essentially only one "group" in terms of achievement, the teacher can provide more instructional time—as much as 45 minutes instead of just 15. Alternatively, the teacher might divide the group in half, with each receiving a 20-minute block of instruction and 20 minutes of practice.

School-level planning for this uninterrupted time involves consideration of when children move to "specials" (physical education, art, music, computer lab, library) and when they go to lunch. That scheduling problem (and many others) is virtually solved by dividing the school into two halves and alternating their literacy blocks. For example, in a K–5 building, the kindergarten, first grade, and second grade could have their literacy block first thing in the morning, go to lunch, go to specials, have math instruction, and end the day with either science or social studies. The third, fourth, and fifth grades could start the day with specials, move to math instruction and to science or social studies, begin their literacy block with their grade-level lesson, move to lunch, and end the day with their small-group time and their writing instruction. We provide specific model schoolwide schedules in Chapter 6.

Finding time to address the entire curriculum is daunting. Social studies, science, and math educators will undoubtedly question this emphasis on time for literacy, though you will see that we encourage the integration of nonfiction related to the science and social studies curriculum into literacy time. The choice to group children within classrooms has time implications; in order for each group to meet with the teacher each day, time has to be allocated for each group. The alternative grouping decisions provide more constraints on the school-level schedule, but they relieve some of the pressure on time.

Time for Professional Development

Drafting a great assessment plan, carefully selecting instructional materials, and designing an efficient and effective school schedule will be a waste of time without a plan for professional development for the entire staff. We discuss the "what's" and "how's" of professional development in Chapter 10. Right now, we concentrate on the "who's" and the "when's."

The "who's" are easy. Schoolwide reform efforts need to involve every adult who works with children in any capacity, many of whom are not regular classroom teachers: counselors, special education teachers, paraprofessionals, librarians, art teachers, music teachers, and physical education teachers. We are not suggesting that all of these individuals share the same needs for professional development. Nevertheless, all must be embraced in the overall professional development plan.

The "when's" are not as easy. Professional development sessions after a long school day are not always conducive to learning, but it is difficult to envision a reform effort that will not include at least some after-school time. Here are some lessons we've learned about scheduling professional development:

- Consider scheduling (and funding) more preplanning days. A paid, required summer institute of three days prior to the start of the new school year provides a much better start to a reform effort.
- Establish a weekly after-school professional development day, rotating among four meeting formats: professional development for all, professional

development for the PreK–2 team, professional development for the 3–5 team, and faculty meeting for all.

- Establish common grade-level planning time during the school day, and schedule professional development with the literacy coach during that time one day each week, starting the first week of school.
- Be proactive with the district about schedules for building-level days. Often, those days are interrupted by committee meetings, and whole-staff work is impossible. Instead, propose that all committee meetings be scheduled in the afternoons, and that mornings be reserved for professional development with the entire staff.

SYSTEMS FOR TEAMWORK

Lest you should lose hope from the start, you are not alone in a schoolwide program. Successful schoolwide programs are led by strong and active leaders, many of whom rely on leadership teams. They have sound structures for decision making and transparent organizational charts. A literacy coach is part of this leadership team. In all schools, success of a schoolwide program is influenced (perhaps even controlled!) by the extent to which formal and informal power structures in schools are related. Recent leadership studies are providing evidence of what many have long suspected: teachers' perceptions of their principal's support and vision are related to their level of shared instructional purpose (e.g., Supovitz, Sirinides, & May, 2010).

Teamwork goes deeper than that. Sara Ray Stoelinga (2008) has investigated leadership networks in elementary schools and speculates that schools where perceptions of instructional leadership overlap with the formal roles for instructional leadership have healthier schoolwide programs. For coaches, a strong structural indicator of healthy schoolwide culture is the extent to which teachers seek advice about literacy instruction from the literacy coach.

Different school organizations produce different teams. In preschools, the essential unit is the individual teacher and his or her classroom assistants. Together, the classroom team decides how to serve the needs of children and how to respond to opportunities and challenges in the always-unpredictable preschool day. In elementary schools, we are convinced that the grade-level team is the essential unit. Schools with strong schoolwide programs have grade-level teams that work together, plan together, and reflect together; coaches can coach the teams rather than each teacher individually. Strong grade-level teams give up some of their individual freedom to make collective decisions; they ensure that their team provides a similar structure for instruction and has similar resources. In schools with large numbers of reading specialists and special educators, the intervention team is another powerful collaboration; they collaborate with grade-level teams to improve the quality of initial grade-level instruction and they collaborate to design tiered safety nets when that is insufficient. Once teachers begin to departmentalize (either in upper elementary or middle school), the cross-grade content team is another important addition. Successful schoolwide programs have cross-content teams that work together to coordinate instruction and assessment.

TAKING STOCK

Whether you are considering your own career as a coach in the future, or the very real needs of a particular school, your mind probably raced during this chapter. Going schoolwide is asking a lot, but you will only get there by starting. We organized this chapter in the order in which we think you should tackle its challenges. It may be that a particular school has already done many of these things, but it makes sense to check.

1. Select and schedule assessments.
2. Select instructional materials, at least for core grade-level instruction.
3. Select a regrouping approach.
4. Select a professional development time.
5. Create a schoolwide schedule for literacy blocks, specials, math, social studies, and science.
6. Establish a leadership team.

Simmons et al. (2000) subtitled their article on schoolwide reform, "No One Ever Told Us It Would Be This Hard!" They must not have asked any literacy coaches. Every coach we've ever met reports the same thing: The process of designing and maintaining a schoolwide literacy program is very hard work. Consider yourself warned. Also consider yourself invited. If you start to attend to these issues up front (assessment, grouping, instructional materials, time, and teamwork), and if you make a long-haul commitment to the adults and children at your site, there is no more rewarding job than that of a literacy coach leading a schoolwide literacy program.

CHAPTER 4

Finding and Applying Reading Research

The late Madeline Hunter argued that teaching is both an art and a science. The art of teaching involves somewhat intangible attributes, such as our emotional involvement in, and passion for, our craft and our ties to students as human beings. The science of instruction, on the other hand, involves our conscious selection of methods and materials and whether they can be expected to have the effects we desire. It is the job of researchers to undertake investigations that will help teachers and coaches plan and provide effective instruction. In this chapter, we summarize some important research findings, and also suggest strategies coaches can use to keep up with research.

It is important that a literacy coach become a prudent *consumer* of research literature, even while engaging as a *producer* of findings about the effectiveness of a particular schoolwide program. The two roles are reciprocal. Coaches who are avid consumers of research are more likely to make decisions that yield better schoolwide results. Being a consumer involves making choices about what to buy (or buy into). Imagine yourself in the produce section of your local supermarket. Before selecting, say, an avocado, you would pick it up and examine it closely. As a savvy consumer, you know what to look for: soft spots that suggest overripeness, overall shape and appearance. Being a research consumer is no different. It means knowing something about the issues involved in research—knowing what to look for. For example, not all published work is actually research. And not all published research studies are of equal merit; some are actually rather shoddy. In addition, some excellent studies are not actually meant to influence the selection of instructional methods. The research methodology varies considerably from study to study, depending on the questions an investigator chooses to pursue. In this chapter, we provide some guidance that will be useful to literacy coaches as consumers of educational research. We hope we will build your research literacy a bit here and also whet your appetite for making research a regular part of your own reading regimen.

We start with research design. An important distinction in methodology is whether the researcher has chosen a qualitative or a quantitative approach. Qualitative methods are useful for describing processes and interactions that are difficult to reduce to a set of numbers. Interchanges during class discussions, for instance, are perhaps best studied through qualitative procedures. In contrast, studies of whether or not a particular teaching technique is more effective than an alternative technique are best grounded in quantitative measures. In recent years, quantitative research has dominated policy, particularly at the federal level. There is an increasing insistence that teachers responsible for reading employ teaching methods grounded in *scientifically based reading research* (SBRR). This policy is controversial and has been attacked by those who claim that it reduces the true complexity of learning to read. But let's examine the issue briefly, and you can decide for yourself.

SCIENTIFICALLY BASED READING INSTRUCTION

Few researchers would dispute that the most powerful design possible is the *true experiment*. In such a study, children are randomly assigned to two or more treatment groups, and valid and reliable measures of each treatment's impact are obtained. Rigorous statistical procedures are employed to analyze the data collected and to arrive at defensible conclusions. Variables that might contribute to (or detract from) the impact of a treatment are carefully controlled. For example, researchers may check to see how faithful teachers have been to implementing the treatment.

Needless to say, the true experiment sets a very high standard—one that very few studies can achieve. A frequent shortcoming is the random assignment of students to treatments. Random assignment is difficult to achieve because educators in schools have their own ideas about which students are to be placed in which classes. Researchers often have to make do with preexisting, nonrandom assignments. The result is called a *quasi-experiment*—a design that can still have remarkable rigor even though it is a cut below the standard of the true experiment.

Studies designed in this way are based on *Bacon's law*. Sir Francis Bacon, founder of the scientific method, was the first to contend that a cause-and-effect relationship could not be proven unless a control group was available for which all conditions were the same except the factor being studied. (Today, these are sometimes called *contrast* or *comparison* groups.) Studies grounded in this logic are the mainstay of medical research, but they are far less common in education. In the report of the National Reading Panel[1] (National Institute of Child Health and Human Development [NICHHD]; 2000), fewer than one in 1,000 studies located by the panel represented rigorously conducted experiments or quasi-experiments. This depressing fact is perhaps the result of the pressure on researchers to publish many pieces, as well as the large number of education journals. It also may be that reaching this gold standard for evidence is very difficult to do in schools; researchers and school personnel must have very strong relationships and a set of shared goals.

EVIDENCE-BASED READING INSTRUCTION

Since the publication of the NRP report in 2000, the U.S. Department of Education has broadened its position somewhat by endorsing *evidence-based* education. We applaud this change. As Figure 4.1 makes clear, scientific research has its place within evidence-based practice, but other sources of evidence are included as well. The rationale is persuasive. Empirical evidence is needed to compare competing instructional approaches, generate cumulative knowledge, and help educators avoid fads. Professional wisdom is needed so that teachers can apply research findings to local circumstances and inform instruction in cases where research is unavailable or unclear. This delineation makes sense to us. Our only fear is that professional wisdom may be used to trump research findings that are counter to what teachers believe or are comfortable with. We hope that coaches will constantly build their own knowledge of evidence-based instruction and that they will guide teachers to do the same. You will see in the pages that follow that we are peppering our description of the empirical evidence with our own professional wisdom.

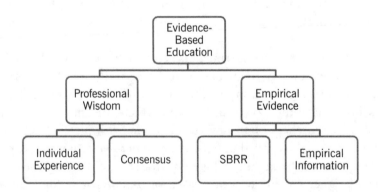

FIGURE 4.1. Evidence-based education and SBRR. Source: Whitehurst (2002).

---

[1]The entire report of the NRP is available online at *www.nationalreadingpanel.org*.

HOW MUCH DO WE KNOW?

In the first edition of this book, we used the NRP's report to give a brief summary of some findings that literacy coaches should know. The NRP was commissioned by Congress in 1997 to "assess the status of research-based knowledge, including the effectiveness of various approaches to teaching children to read" (NICHHD, 2000, p. 1-1). Its final report, released in 2000, has drawn both praise and criticism. Critics, however, have expressed concern mainly for the rigorous standards by which the panel's members excluded many available studies. Had they been less demanding, however, flawed studies might well have skewed the conclusions they ultimately reached.

Fortunately, the NRP found enough hard evidence to arrive at many useful conclusions about the nature of effective instructional approaches in the teaching of reading. At a large, programmatic level, the panel identified several components of a sound reading program in an elementary school. Key among these components are phonemic awareness, phonics, fluency, vocabulary, and comprehension. Naturally, the emphasis on each of these components varies according to grade level. In kindergarten, for example, the emphasis on phonemic awareness and phonics should be higher than it is in later years (other than for students who need additional instruction).

A problem we faced in revising *The Literacy Coach's Handbook* was how much stock to place in the panel's findings. More than a decade has passed since the publication of the report and many studies and reviews have appeared in subsequent years. We decided that the most workable approach was to start with the NRP's findings and to update them based on subsequent evidence. As a general observation, we discovered that more recent studies and summaries have not led to the rejection of the NRP's conclusions. Instead, they have resulted in more nuanced guidance for coaches.

PHONEMIC AWARENESS

Phonemic awareness is the ability to segment oral speech into its component speech sounds, or phonemes. For example, if you pronounce the spoken word *peach*, and ask a child to tell you the sounds in *peach*, a phonemically aware child will pronounce three: /p/ /ea/ /ch/. Phonemic awareness can be tricky business. Research suggests that not all students become phonemically aware without explicit instruction. Findings of note include these facts:

1. Phonemic awareness instruction must become a formal part of the reading program.
2. It is a prerequisite for effective phonics instruction.
3. The lack of it has been repeatedly tied to later reading failure.
4. It can be taught successfully to young children.

Evidence also documents the development of phonemic awareness from broader phonological awareness over five stages:

1. Rhyme recognition.
2. Sentence segmentation.
3. Syllable segmentation and blending.
4. Onset–rime blending and segmentation.
5. Blending and segmenting individual phonemes.

Instructional activities should be ordered along these lines from the simplest to the most sophisticated, and the five levels of awareness can serve as a useful guide in sequencing instruction.

NRP's Conclusions about Phonemic Awareness Instruction

Overall, the findings reviewed by the NRP showed that teaching children to manipulate phonemes in words was highly effective under a variety of teaching conditions with a variety of learners across a range of grade and age levels, and that teaching phonemic awareness to children significantly improved their reading more than instruction that lacked any attention to phonemic awareness.

Specifically, the results of the experimental studies led the NRP to conclude that phonemic awareness training was the cause of improvement in students' phonemic awareness, reading, and spelling following training. The findings were replicated repeatedly across multiple experiments, and thus they provide converging evidence for causal claims. Although phonemic awareness training exerted strong and significant effects on reading and spelling development, it did not have an impact on children's performance on math tests. This indicates that *halo* or *Hawthorne* (novelty) effects did not explain the findings, and that indeed the training effects were directly connected with and limited to the targeted domain under study. Importantly, the effects of phonemic awareness instruction on reading lasted well beyond the end of training. Children of varying abilities improved their phonemic awareness and their reading skills as a function of phonemic awareness training.

Phonemic awareness instruction also helped normally achieving children learn to spell, and the effects lasted well beyond the end of training. However, the instruction was not effective for improving spelling in disabled readers. This is consistent with other research showing that disabled readers have difficulty learning how to spell.

Programs in all of the studies provided explicit instruction in phonemic awareness. Specifically, the characteristics of phonemic awareness training found to be most effective in enhancing phonemic awareness, reading, and spelling skills included explicitly and systematically teaching children to associate phonemes with letters, focusing the instruction on one or two types of phoneme manipulations rather than multiple types, and teaching children in small groups.

Findings of the National Early Literacy Panel

Perhaps the most important realization since the NRP report is the simple caution that phonological awareness is only one part of a comprehensive emergent literacy program. The National Early Literacy Panel (NELP; 2008, p. vii) identified six preschool factors with strong predictive power for later reading achievement:

1. *Alphabet knowledge*—knowledge of the names and sounds associated with printed letters.
2. *Phonological awareness*—the ability to detect, manipulate, or analyze the auditory aspects of spoken language (including the ability to distinguish or segment words, syllables, or phonemes), independent of meaning.
3. *Rapid automatic naming (RAN) of letters or digits*—the ability to rapidly name a sequence of random letters or digits.
4. *RAN of objects or colors*—the ability to rapidly name a sequence of repeating random sets of pictures of objects (e.g., "car," "tree," "house," "man") or colors.
5. *Writing*—the ability to write letters in isolation on request or to write one's own name.
6. *Phonological memory*—the ability to remember spoken information for a short period of time.

It is important to note that the two RAN tasks and phonological memory are not developed explicitly through instruction. However, they are developed implicitly when we develop children's oral language skills. The NELP also identified concepts about print (e.g., that print runs left to right and top to bottom and that spaces are word boundaries) as a good predictor of later reading growth, but only if instructional contexts supported and built on those concepts. An emerging method of developing concepts about print in young children is through print referencing during shared storybook reading (Justice & Piasta, 2011). This practice "involves systematically guiding children to engage with print during shared reading interactions to help them learn more about its forms and functions" (p. 211). For example, a teacher or parent might ask a question like, "Where is the first letter on this page?" (p. 208). Print referencing has been shown to be effective in developing concepts of print and can easily be mingled with interactions designed to develop vocabulary and comprehension.

As these building blocks are implemented in the classroom, teachers should keep in mind several cautions. First, as the NELP findings stress, phonemic awareness training does not constitute a complete reading program. Rather, it provides children with essential foundational knowledge in the alphabetic system. It is one necessary instructional component within a complete and integrated reading program. Children learning to read and write must acquire several other competencies as well. Second, there are many ways to teach phonemic awareness effectively. In implementing phonemic awareness instruction, teachers need to evaluate the methods they use against measured success in their own students. Third, the motivation of both students and their teachers is a critical ingredient of success.

You will see the findings of both the NRP and NELP influence our plan for instructional tasks and procedures in Chapter 7 and also our review of reading materials in Chapter 8.

PHONICS

Few people dispute the importance of phonics, given that we are all readers of an alphabetic language (one that uses letters to represent sounds). However, the debate continues over how and how much phonics should be taught. In Jeanne Chall's (1967, 1996) classic book *Learning to Read: The Great Debate*, she produced the first synthesis of the available research on the question of phonics instruction. Chall's chief conclusion was that research clearly favors a systematic approach in which teachers teach letter sounds directly. More recent studies, elegantly summarized in Marilyn Adams's (1990) *Beginning to Read: Thinking and Learning about Print*, have reinforced Chall's initial conclusion. An excellent (and far shorter) overview is that of Stahl, Duffy-Hester, and Stahl (1998).

The NRP examined five different approaches to phonics instruction. Its classification is a useful one. The approaches are as follows:

1. *Analogy-based phonics*—Teaching students unfamiliar words by analogy to known words (e.g., recognizing that the rime segment of an unfamiliar word is identical to that of a familiar word, and then blending the known rime with the new word onset, such as reading *brick* by recognizing that *-ick* is contained in the known word *kick*, or reading *stump* by analogy to *jump*).
2. *Analytic phonics*—Teaching students to analyze letter–sound relations in previously learned words to avoid pronouncing sounds in isolation. For example, children might first be taught words like *red*, *run*, and *rat* as whole words. The teacher would then call the children's attention to the initial sound of all of these words without actually trying to pronounce the sound in isolation.
3. *Embedded phonics*—Teaching students phonics skills by embedding phonics instruction in text reading. This is a more implicit approach that relies to some extent on incidental learning. In embedded phonics instruction, a teacher might use the shared-book experience to present a big book to a small group or to the entire class. The text in the big book might then be used to teach phonics skills. The teacher might focus on rhyming words, for example.

4. *Phonics through spelling*—Teaching students to segment words into phonemes and to select letters for those phonemes (i.e., teaching students to spell words phonemically).

5. *Synthetic phonics*—Teaching students explicitly to convert letters into sounds (phonemes) and then to blend the sounds to form recognizable words. In a synthetic approach, children might first learn the sound represented by the letters *r, a* (its short sound), and *t*. They would then be taught to blend these sounds from left to right to make (synthesize) the word *rat*.

The NRP's Conclusions about Phonics Instruction

The NRP produced many useful conclusions about phonics instruction. Systematic phonics instruction—instruction with a clear set of instructional procedures and a clear and sequential set of lessons—produced significant benefits for students in kindergarten through sixth grade and for children having difficulty learning to read. The ability to read and spell words was enhanced in kindergartners who received systematic beginning phonics instruction. First graders who were taught phonics systematically were better able to decode and spell, and they showed significant improvement in their ability to comprehend text. Older children receiving phonics instruction were better able to decode and spell words and to read text orally, but their comprehension of text was not significantly improved.

Systematic synthetic phonics instruction had a positive and significant effect on disabled readers' reading skills. These children improved substantially in their ability to read words, and they showed significant (albeit small) gains in their ability to process text as a result of systematic synthetic phonics instruction. This type of phonics instruction benefited both students with learning disabilities and low-achieving students who were not disabled. Moreover, systematic synthetic phonics instruction was significantly more effective in improving alphabetic knowledge and word-reading skills for children of low socioeconomic status (SES) than instructional approaches that were less focused on these initial reading skills.

Across all grade levels, systematic phonics instruction improved the ability of good readers to spell. The impact was strongest for kindergartners and decreased for children in later grades. For poor readers, the impact of phonics instruction on spelling was small, perhaps reflecting the consistent finding that disabled readers have trouble learning to spell.

Although conventional wisdom has suggested that kindergarten students might not be ready for phonics instruction, this assumption was not supported by the data. The effects of systematic early phonics instruction were significant and substantial in kindergarten and first grade, indicating that systematic phonics programs should be implemented at those age and grade levels.

The NRP's analysis indicated that systematic phonics instruction is ready for implementation in the classroom. The findings of the NRP regarding the effectiveness of explicit, systematic phonics instruction were derived from studies conducted in many classrooms with typical classroom teachers and typical American or English-speaking students from a variety of backgrounds and SES levels. Thus the results of the analysis are indicative of what can be accomplished when explicit, systematic phonics programs are implemented in today's classrooms. Systematic phonics instruction has been used widely over a long period of time with positive results, and a variety of systematic phonics programs have proven effective with children of different ages, abilities, and SES backgrounds.

These facts and findings provide converging evidence that explicit, systematic phonics instruction is a valuable and essential part of a successful classroom reading program. However, there is a need to be cautious about giving a blanket endorsement of all kinds of phonics instruction.

It is important to recognize that the goals of phonics instruction are to provide children with key knowledge and skills, and to ensure that they know how to apply that knowledge in their reading and writing. In other words, phonics teaching is a means to an end. To be able to make use of letter–sound information, children need phonemic awareness. That is, they need to be able to blend sounds together to decode words, and they need to break spoken words into their constituent sounds to spell words. Programs that focus too much on the teaching of letter–sound relations and not enough on putting them to use are unlikely to be very effective in the long run. In implementing systematic phonics instruction, educators must keep the end in mind: They must ensure that children understand the purpose of learning letter sounds, and that they are able to apply these skills accurately and fluently in their daily reading and writing activities.

Of additional concern is the often-heard call for "intensive, systematic phonics instruction." Usually the term *intensive* is not defined. How much is required to be considered intensive? This is not a question that we can answer from research. In addition, it is not clear how many months or years a phonics program should continue. If phonics has been systematically taught in kindergarten and first grade, should it continue to be emphasized in second grade and beyond? How long should single instructional sessions last? How much ground should be covered in a program? Specifically, how many letter–sound relationships should be taught, and how many different ways of using these relationships to read and write words should be practiced for the benefits of phonics to be maximized? These questions remain for future research.

Another important area is the role of the teacher. Some phonics programs showing large effect sizes require teachers to follow a set of specific instructions provided by the publisher; although this may standardize the instructional sequence, it also may reduce teacher interest and motivation. Thus one concern is how to maintain consistency of instruction while still encouraging the unique contributions of teachers. Other programs require a sophisticated knowledge of spelling, structural linguistics, or word etymology. In view of the evidence showing the effectiveness of systematic phonics instruction, it is important to ensure that the issue of how best to prepare and support teachers to carry out this teaching effectively and creatively is given high priority.

Knowing that all phonics programs are not the same brings with it the implication that teachers must themselves be educated about how to evaluate different programs, so that they can determine which ones are based on strong evidence and how to use these programs most effectively in their own classrooms. It is therefore important that teachers be provided with evidence-based preservice training and ongoing inservice training to select and implement the most appropriate phonics instruction.

A common question with any instructional program is whether "one size fits all." Teachers may be able to use a particular program in the classroom, but may find that it suits some students better than others. At all grade levels, but particularly in kindergarten and the early grades, children vary greatly in the skills they bring to school. Some children will already know letter–sound correspondences, and some will even be able to decode words, while others will have little or no letter knowledge. Teachers should be able to assess the needs of the individual students and tailor instruction to meet specific needs. However, it is more common for phonics programs to present a fixed sequence of lessons scheduled from the beginning to the end of the school year. In light of this, teachers need to be flexible in their phonics instruction in order to adapt it to individual students' needs.

Children who have already developed phonics skills and can apply them appropriately in the reading process do not require the same level and intensity of phonics instruction provided to children at the initial phases of reading acquisition. Thus it will also be critical to determine objectively the ways in which systematic phonics instruction can be optimally incorporated and integrated into schoolwide reading programs. Part of this effort should be directed at preservice and inservice education to provide teachers with decision-making frameworks to guide their selection, integration, and implementation of phonics instruction within a schoolwide reading program.

Teachers must understand that systematic phonics instruction, like phonemic awareness, is only one component (though a necessary component) of a total reading program; systematic phonics instruction should be provided along with other reading instruction in phonemic awareness, fluency, vocabulary, and comprehension strategies to create a complete reading program. Although most teachers and educational decision makers recognize this, there may be a tendency in some classrooms, particularly in first grade, to allow phonics to become the dominant component—not only in the time devoted to it but also in the significance attached to it. It is important not to judge children's reading competence solely on the basis of their phonics skills, and not to devalue or discourage their interest in books because they cannot decode with accuracy. It is also critical for teachers to understand that systematic phonics instruction can be provided in an entertaining, vibrant, and creative manner.

Systematic phonics instruction is designed to increase accuracy in decoding and word-recognition skills. Experience decoding words creates a large sight vocabulary, which in turn facilitates comprehension. However, it is again important to note that fluent and automatic application of phonics skills to text is another critical skill that must be taught and learned to maximize oral reading and reading comprehension. This issue again underscores the need for teachers to understand that although phonics skills are necessary in order to learn to read, they are not sufficient in their own right. Phonics skills must be integrated with the development of phonemic awareness, oral reading fluency, and reading comprehension skills.

Trends in Phonics Since the NRP

The most controversial of the NRP's findings concerned the conclusion that systematic phonics instruction is more effective than other approaches to phonics. Several reanalyses of the data, however, have confirmed the NRP finding but with an important addition: "Comprehensive programs that integrate reading and language arts and provide tutoring to increase intensity are more effective than programs that isolate these elements. This is a constructive way to view balanced reading instruction" (Foorman & Connor, 2011, p. 138).

Based on a review of 11 carefully controlled studies of interventions used at K–3, Weiser and Mathes (2011) concluded that effective interventions shared these elements: They identified students early, provided explicit decoding instruction, included word study, and allowed students ample time to manipulate sounds and spell them. Moreover, the relative gains were in both reading and spelling.

Is an early phonics focus enough to ensure success? Research has consistently demonstrated that decoding instruction is necessary but not sufficient to accomplish the kind of growth in reading we desire. Robert Slavin and his colleagues (Slavin, Lake, Chambers, Cheung, & Davis, 2009) concluded that "Whereas phonics appears necessary in reading instruction, adding a phonics focus is not enough to increase reading achievement" (p. 1453). A balance of the principal components of reading development is called for. You will see that we take this advice to heart in our planning.

FLUENCY

Fluency entails word recognition that is, except in rare instances, unconscious and automatic. The fluent reader reads aloud with proper phrasing, intonation, and expression (characteristics that are often called *prosody*). Until a reader achieves fluency (usually in second or third grade), comprehension is apt to suffer, because too much conscious attention must be directed at word identification and too little attention can be paid to comprehending what is read.

An issue of usage has arisen that may cause some confusion. The term *fluency* can refer to any process in which an individual has achieved a high level of proficiency. A child might be described as fluent in the naming of letters or in letter writing, for example. For our purposes, the word *fluency* refers to oral reading fluency, unless otherwise noted.

The NRP's Conclusions about Fluency Instruction

On the basis of a detailed analysis of the available research that met the NRP's methodological criteria, the panel concluded that guided repeated oral reading procedures (i.e., procedures that included guidance from teachers, peers, or parents) had a significant and positive impact on word recognition, fluency, and comprehension across a range of grade levels. These studies were conducted in a variety of classrooms in both regular and special education settings with teachers using widely available instructional materials. This suggests the classroom usefulness of guided oral reading and repeated reading procedures. These results also applied to all students—good readers, as well as those experiencing reading difficulties. Nevertheless, there were important gaps in the research. In particular, the NRP could find no multiyear studies providing information on the relationship between guided oral reading and the emergence of fluency.

There has been widespread agreement in the literature that encouraging students to engage in wide, independent, silent reading increases reading achievement. Literally hundreds of correlational studies have found that the best readers read the most and that poor readers read the least. These correlational studies suggest that the more children read the better their fluency, vocabulary, and comprehension will be. However, these findings are correlational in nature, and correlation does not imply causation. No doubt, it could be that the more that children read, the more their reading skills improve—but it is also possible that better readers simply choose to read more.

In order to address this issue of causation, the NRP examined the specific impact of encouraging students to read more on fluency, vocabulary development, and reading comprehension. The studies that were identified as addressing this issue were characterized by three major features. First, the studies emphasized silent reading procedures in which students read on their own with little or no specific feedback. Second, the studies did not directly assess fluency or the actual increase in the amount of reading due to the instructional procedures. Rather, only changes in vocabulary and/or comprehension were typically measured as outcomes, rather than increases in fluency that could be expected from the increased reading practice. Third, very few studies that examined the effect of independent silent reading on reading achievement could meet the NRP research review methodology criteria ($n = 14$), and these studies varied widely in their methodological quality and the reading outcome variables measured. Thus a meta-analysis could not be conducted. Rather, the 14 studies were examined individually and in detail to identify converging trends and findings in the data.

With regard to the efficacy of having students engage in independent silent reading with minimal guidance or feedback, the NRP was unable to find a positive relationship between programs and instruction that encouraged large amounts of independent reading and improvements in reading achievement, including fluency. In other words, even though encouraging students to read more is intuitively appealing, there is still not sufficient research evidence obtained from studies of high methodological quality to support the idea that such efforts reliably increase how much students read, or that such programs result in improved reading skills. Given the extensive use of these techniques, it is important that such research be conducted.

These findings do not negate the positive influence that independent silent reading may have on reading fluency; nor do the findings negate the possibility that wide independent reading significantly influences vocabulary development and reading comprehension. Rather, there are simply not sufficient data from well-designed studies capable of testing questions of causation to substantiate causal claims. The available data do suggest that independent silent reading is not an effective practice when used as the only type of reading instruction to develop fluency and other reading skills, particularly with students who have not yet developed critical alphabetic and word-reading skills. In sum, methodologically rigorous research designed to assess the specific influences that independent silent reading practices have on reading fluency and other reading skills and the motivation to read has not yet been conducted.

Trends Since the NRP: Prosody and Wide Reading

The NRP had little to say about prosody (the naturalness of oral reading), but researchers since the NRP report have stressed its importance as "the third component of fluency" (Rasinski, Reutzel, Chard, & Linan-Thompson, 2011, p. 295). In their very readable review of research, Kuhn and Stahl (2003) conclude that prosody instruction is an important element of good fluency instruction. They conclude that "Given that fluent oral reading is considered to be expressive as well as quick and accurate and that prosodic features are, to a large extent, responsible for such expression, it is important to consider a definition of fluency that encompasses more than rate and accuracy" (p. 18).

A popular approach to fluency building in the elementary grades is wide reading. Consequently, the NRP finding that there was little research supporting its encouragement was quite controversial (Rasinski et al., 2011). It may be true that turning students loose to read independently may assume too much about their abilities to do so without support. Nevertheless, many need help in transferring what has developed as an oral skill set to silent reading. Evidence compiled since the report suggests that with guidance students can begin to successfully transfer their fluency skills to silent reading (e.g., Hiebert, 2006). We note also that one of the most effective approaches to fluency building in second grade, fluency-oriented reading instruction (Stahl & Heubach, 2005) has an independent reading component.

VOCABULARY

Vocabulary development represents one of the single greatest challenges to American educators. There is clearly a "vocabulary divide" that separates proficient and struggling readers and that grows larger over time. Hart and Risley (1995) have documented this trend in arresting terms. They teach us that those children whose vocabularies are richest when they start school also expand their vocabularies more quickly. Unfortunately, research has done more to reveal the problem than to solve it. The conclusions of the NRP summarize how SBRR has illuminated this area of reading instruction. Note that the NRP deftly avoids a long-standing (though friendly) debate about whether vocabulary should be taught *directly*, through planned lessons, or *incidentally*, through ensuring that students are exposed to words in many contexts. Both are important.

The NRP's Conclusions about Vocabulary Instruction

The studies reviewed by the NRP suggest that vocabulary instruction does lead to gains in comprehension, but that methods must be appropriate to the age and ability of the reader. The use of computers in vocabulary instruction was found to be more effective than some traditional methods in a few studies. Computer-based instruction is clearly emerging as a potentially valuable aid to classroom teachers in the area of vocabulary instruction. Vocabulary can also be learned incidentally in the context of storybook reading or of listening to others. Learning words before reading a text is helpful, too. Techniques such as task restructuring and repeated exposure (including having the student encounter words in various contexts) appear to enhance vocabulary development. In addition, substituting easy words for more difficult words can assist low-achieving students.

The findings on vocabulary yielded several specific implications for teaching reading. First, vocabulary should be taught both directly and indirectly. Repetition and multiple exposures to vocabulary items are important. Learning in rich contexts, incidental learning, and use of computer technology all enhance the acquisition of vocabulary. Direct instruction should include task restructuring as necessary and should actively engage the student. Finally, dependence on a single instructional method will not result in optimal learning.

Although much is known about the importance of vocabulary to success in reading, there is little research on the best methods or combinations of methods of

vocabulary instruction, or on the measurement of vocabulary growth and its relation to instructional methods.

Trends Since the NRP: The Earlier the Better

The rate at which vocabularies diverge from the most- to the least-proficient children has occasioned calls for early intervention in order to bridge the gap. Marulis and Neuman (2010) reviewed 67 studies of PreK and kindergarten children
and concluded that vocabulary interventions indeed tend to be effective, especially
when a combination of implicit and explicit instruction is provided by well-trained
teachers and is "followed by meaningful practice and review" (p. 325). Surprisingly, they found no advantage for small-group vocabulary instruction over whole-
class approaches. Though powerful, the interventions they reviewed were not able
to close the vocabulary gap.

The NELP (2008) identified vocabulary knowledge as a good predictor of later
reading growth, but again only if instructional contexts supported and built on that
knowledge. Unfortunately, supportive contexts are not the rule. The importance
of vocabulary development is often underestimated in PreK, kindergarten, and
first grade because the demands of the texts children encounter are low (Biemiller,
2006). By the time children reach third grade, the vocabulary gap becomes all too
apparent, but it is hard to bridge. "Average children acquire approximately 6,000
root-word meanings by the end of second grade. Children in the lowest quartile
acquire roughly 4,000 root-word meanings" (p. 44). Although there is no national
vocabulary list to be taught year by year, Biemiller recommends that teachers use
their own judgment about which words to teach and that the source of these words
should be stories shared in interactive read-alouds.

Vocabulary as Common Denominator

Vocabulary instruction seems to have emerged as a common element across many
segments of a schoolwide program, assisting literacy development in several areas.
First, and perhaps most obviously, vocabulary instruction is easily linked to comprehension during read-alouds. However, this link must be cultivated through professional development, and the coach's role is pivotal. Mol, Bus, and deJong (2009)
found that teacher training is especially important for effective vocabulary instruction delivered through interactive read-alouds for PreK and kindergarten children.
They noted in particular that adults working at these levels tended to experience
difficulties in conducting the read-alouds in the intended manner.

Less apparent is the link between vocabulary instruction and phonological
awareness. The power of explicit instruction in phonological awareness has long
been documented, but more recently another avenue has emerged. The strong relationship between vocabulary knowledge and phonological awareness suggests that

a focus on vocabulary development may have the effect of developing phonological awareness at the same time (Metsala, 2011). The evidence is largely correlational, but it suggests yet another reason to target vocabulary growth in preschool and kindergarten.

Basic Principles for Building Vocabulary

Based on the limited amount of research on building children's vocabulary prior to kindergarten, Neuman and Dwyer (2009) distilled four principles that should guide instruction. These principles might take the form of any number of instructional strategies, and we believe they are equally relevant throughout the elementary years.

1. Be systematic and explicit, providing children with plenty of opportunities to use words in classroom transactions.
2. Involve a good deal of practice that is active, guided, and extensive.
3. Incorporate periodic review.
4. Include observation and progress-monitoring assessments to inform further instruction. (pp. 385–386)

A coach and teachers might brainstorm approaches that reflect these principles— and possibly reevaluate practices that do not. To these four principles, we might add a fifth, also suggested by Neuman (2006). She suggests a useful distinction between vocabulary and knowledge. Though related, they are not the same, and she warns of a growing knowledge gap "between the 'information haves' and the 'information have-nots'" (p. 29). And so, our additional principle would be simply this:

5. Do not overrely on vocabulary instruction alone to build prior knowledge. More may be needed.

Vocabulary Instruction through Morphology

New insights to vocabulary instruction have come through examining the power of teaching children about the units of meaning (morphemes) contained in words. Their importance, however, often takes a backseat to decoding instruction. But attention to morphology (affixes, base words, compounds, etc.) can be effective as early as PreK. Bowers, Kirby, and Deacon (2010) reviewed studies conducted with students PreK–8 that examined the effectiveness of teaching children about morphology. They concluded that such instruction was beneficial for older and younger students alike, that it was best when integrated with other literacy activities rather than taught in isolation, and that it was more effective for less-able readers.

COMPREHENSION

Reading comprehension is a vast area, complicated from the outset by differences in definition and perspective. When we look for research on effective instructional techniques, for example, do we mean *effective* in the sense of helping students comprehend a specific selection, or *effective* in the sense of making students better comprehenders in general? And when we look at how studies measure comprehension, are we content with questions that have only one correct answer, or do we adopt the constructivist view that such questions dangerously oversimplify the process of bringing meaning to text? Such questions are important to literacy coaches as they enter the morass of findings on comprehension instruction. We define *comprehension* as creation of a personal mental representation of the meaning of text. How to measure it and teach it is another matter—one open to intense debate. A good starting place is the NRP report. The conclusions of the NRP address the matters of how comprehension ability develops and the evidence underlying specific instructional approaches as well.

The NRP's Conclusions about Comprehension Instruction

Comprehension is enhanced when readers actively relate the ideas represented in print to their own knowledge and experiences, and when they construct mental representations of these ideas in memory. The rationale for the explicit teaching of comprehension strategies is that comprehension can be improved by teaching students to use specific cognitive procedures or to reason strategically when they encounter barriers to understanding what they are reading. Readers acquire these strategies informally to some extent, but explicit or formal instruction in the application of comprehension strategies has been shown to be highly effective in enhancing understanding. The teacher generally demonstrates such strategies for students until the students are able to carry them out independently.

In its review, the NRP identified 16 categories of text comprehension instruction, of which seven appear to have a solid scientific basis for conclusions that they improve comprehension in nonimpaired readers. Some of these types of instruction are helpful when used alone, but many are more effective when used as part of a multiple-strategy method. The types of instruction are as follows:

1. Comprehension monitoring, where readers learn how to be aware of their understanding of the material.
2. Cooperative learning, where students learn reading strategies together.
3. Use of graphic and semantic organizers (including story maps), where readers make graphic representations of the material to assist comprehension.
4. Question answering, where readers answer questions posed by the teacher and receive immediate feedback.

5. Question generation, where readers ask themselves questions about various aspects of a text.

6. Story structure instruction, where students are taught to use the structure of the story as a means of helping them recall story content, in order to answer questions about what they have read.

7. Summarization, where readers are taught to integrate ideas and generalize from the text information.

In general, the evidence suggests that teaching a combination of reading comprehension techniques is the most effective. When students use them appropriately, they assist in recall, question answering, question generation, and summarization of texts. When used in combination, these techniques can improve results in standardized comprehension tests.

Nevertheless, many questions remain unanswered. More information is needed on ways to teach teachers how to use such proven comprehension strategies. The literature also suggests that teaching comprehension in the context of specific academic areas—for example, social studies and science—can be effective. If this is true of other subject areas, then it might be efficient to teach comprehension as a skill in all content areas.

Questions also remain as to which strategies are most effective for which age groups. Moreover, further research is necessary to determine whether the techniques apply to all types of text genres (including narrative and expository texts), and whether the level of difficulty of the texts has an impact on the effectiveness of the strategies. Finally, it is critically important to know what teacher characteristics influence successful instruction of reading comprehension.

Teaching reading comprehension strategies to students at all grade levels is complex. Teachers not only must have a firm grasp of the content presented in text but also must have substantial knowledge of the strategies themselves, of which strategies are most effective for different students and types of content, and of how best to teach and model strategy use.

Research on comprehension strategies has evolved dramatically over the last two decades. Initially, investigators focused on teaching one strategy at a time; later studies examined the effectiveness of teaching several strategies in combination. However, implementation of this promising combined approach has been problematic. Teachers must be skillful in their instruction and be able to respond flexibly and opportunistically to students' needs for instructive feedback as they read.

The initial NRP search for studies relevant to the preparation of teachers for comprehension strategy instruction provided 635 citations. Of these, only four studies met the NRP research methodology criteria. Hence the number of studies eligible for further analysis precluded meta-analysis of the data derived from these investigations. However, because there were only four studies, the NRP was able to review them in detail. The studies investigate two major approaches: *direct explanation* and *transactional strategy instruction*.

The direct explanation approach focuses on the teacher's ability to explain explicitly the reasoning and mental processes involved in successful reading comprehension. Rather than teach specific strategies, teachers help students (1) to view reading as a problem-solving task that necessitates the use of strategic thinking, and (2) to learn to think strategically about solving comprehension problems. For example, teachers are taught that they can teach students the skill of finding the main idea by casting it as a problem-solving task and reasoning about it strategically.

Transactional strategy instruction also emphasizes a teacher's ability to provide explicit explanations of thinking processes. Furthermore, it emphasizes the ability of teachers to facilitate student discussions in which students collaborate to form joint interpretations of text and acquire a deeper understanding of the mental and cognitive processes involved in comprehension.

The four studies (two studies for each approach) demonstrated that teachers could be instructed in these methods. Teachers required instruction in explaining what they were teaching, modeling their thinking processes, encouraging student inquiry, and keeping students engaged. Data from all four studies indicated clearly that in order for teachers to use strategies effectively, extensive formal instruction in how to teach reading comprehension is necessary, preferably beginning as early as preservice training.

More research is needed to address the following questions: Which components of teacher preparation are most effective? Can reading comprehension strategies be successfully incorporated into content-area instruction? How can the effectiveness of strategies be measured in an optimal manner? Can strategies be taught as early as grades 1 and 2, when children also are trying to master phonics, word recognition, and fluency? How can teachers be taught to provide the most optimal instruction?

Trends Since the NRP: Nonfiction, Content, and Read-Alouds

Taffy Raphael and her colleagues (Raphael, George, Weber, & Mies, 2009) provide a useful history of research over the past few years into how best to teach comprehension. During the 1980s, researchers focused on teaching individual strategies; during the 1990s, attention turned to teaching multiple strategies rather than approaching them one by one. During the first decade of the present century (after publication of the NRP report), the focus shifted again, this time to how schools can orchestrate their efforts to build proficiency and "support high-level instruction across grade level and school subject areas to create a coherent literacy curriculum" (p. 449). Raphael et al. do not challenge the NRP findings. On the contrary, they tell how the findings have been extended into schoolwide contexts. There have been several reasons for this shift in research. One is the body of evidence concerning how to bring about lasting change in schools. Another is the pressure to show growth across the board and to meet the challenges posed by new and more rigorous standards. They describe one of the initiatives that have shown promise, the Standards-Based Change Process (Au, 2005; Raphael, Goldman, et al., 2006), and there may be lessons in this and similar initiatives that will prove useful to schoolwide inquiry guided by a coach.

They also identify four key issues that now confront both individual teachers and the schools in which they serve. One of these issues involves the best ways to integrate technology into comprehension instruction. Reading in digital settings requires that students apply strategies without counterparts in print, such as navigating purposefully through Internet sites (Duke, Schmar-Dobler, & Zhang, 2006). A second issue entails approaches to motivate children to read. A third is the formation of communities of students through collaboration. Finally, they stress the need for comprehension opportunities that students find relevant. These four issues can be related in various ways, such as collaborative Internet projects (e.g., Miller, 2003).

Since the NRP report, strides have been made in better understanding the role of discussion and questioning in fostering comprehension. Almasi and Garas-York (2009), in reviewing the large body of research in this area, conclude that teachers play a vital role from the earliest grades onward. They are positioned not only to check factual understanding but to scaffold children through open-ended questions as they interpret facts. Teachers are also in a position to facilitate peer interaction. Through activities such as Idea Circles (Guthrie & McCann, 1996), Questioning the Author (Beck & McKeown, 2006; Beck, McKeown, Sandora, Kucan, & Worthy, 1996), and Collaborative Reasoning (Clark et al., 2003), elementary students' ability to comprehend has been shown to improve. An important by-product of peer interactions like these is students' social and affective growth (Almasi et al., 2004).

Nonfiction and Genre Knowledge

In our view, two of the most important issues revealed by research conducted after the NRP report are the limited amount of nonfiction encountered by elementary students (Duke, 2000) and, in consequence, an inadequate focus on genre. Saul and Dieckman (2005) have offered research-based guidance for integrating information trade books, and Duke (2003) has produced a book-length discussion that would be an excellent choice for teacher study. Correcting the imbalance between fiction and nonfiction has also led to suggestions for read-aloud choices and small-group work (Walpole & McKenna, 2009a; Walpole, McKenna, & Philippakos, 2011). A difficulty facing coaches is that teachers may harbor biases against conducting read-alouds with information trade books. Donovan and Smolkin (2001), for example, interviewed elementary teachers about the choices they make for read-alouds and text sets in science. They discovered that these choices are often based on two faulty assumptions: that science is boring and that information books are inappropriate for reading aloud.

Content versus Strategies

The NRP report placed comprehension strategy instruction at center stage. But how much instruction is required? Willingham (2006–2007) has warned that strategy instruction, though desirable, is a one-time boost and that a more important goal of schooling from kindergarten on should be to build content knowledge. It is a lack of prior knowledge, he warns, that causes most of the reading difficulties students experience as they move beyond the elementary grades. We believe that a balance between strategy and content instruction is possible—namely, through an interactive read-aloud of a nonfiction text. During a read-aloud, a teacher can quickly review a strategy and then use the text as a springboard for learning new ideas and word meanings. In fact, we believe that all five recommendations of a recent research review of K–3 comprehension instruction can be accomplished through skillfully delivered read-alouds:

1. Teach students how to use comprehension strategies.
2. Teach students to identify and use the text's organizational structure to comprehend, learn, and remember content.
3. Guide students through high-quality discussion of the meaning of text.
4. Select texts purposefully to support comprehension development.
5. Establish an engaging and motivating context in which to teach reading comprehension. (Shanahan et al., 2010, p. iii)

Predictors of comprehension in the elementary grades are now much better understood, and our growing understanding has implications for instruction. Specifically, foundational skills (phonological awareness, phonics, and fluency) are predictive of comprehension during the primary years, but in the upper elementary grades language development and content knowledge are far more powerful (Duke & Carlisle, 2011).

Read-Alouds as a Means of Tying It All Together

Reading aloud to children is universally heralded as a beneficial approach, and the research support is indeed compelling. In their review of the preschool literature, Zucker and Landry (2010) noted that the "accumulated evidence shows that high-quality classroom read-alouds are a critical component of daily instruction because this activity can have substantial, positive effects on two foundational aspects of children's literacy development: oral language and print knowledge" (p. 78). The report of the NELP (2008) supported the practice of shared reading as a means of fostering oral language development of young children.

Before going further, however, we need to consider whether shared reading is the same as reading aloud. A. E. Cunningham and Zibulsky (2011) provide a useful distinction to help coaches and teachers understand best practice. They begin with the difference between reading *to* children and reading *with* them. Imagine a continuum of possibilities, with a dramatic read-aloud (little interaction) at one end and a big book (with opportunities for print concepts and other foundational skills) at the other. In between are read-aloud options that include questioning, predicting, think-alouds, vocabulary development, inferring, and other embedded activities. Figure 4.2 depicts this continuum of possibilities. Except for dramatic read-alouds, everything on the continuum is a form of shared reading, and *all* have a good basis in research.

Clearly we have moved beyond the fundamental question of *whether* teachers should conduct read-alouds. The questions that now confront coaches involve what types of texts should be included, how frequently read-alouds should occur, whether the same book should be read aloud more than once, which grade levels should conduct them, and how they should be conducted.

What Types of Texts Should Be Read Aloud?

Coaches should strive to ensure a balance between literary texts (fiction and poetry) and nonfiction. The main battle may be to overcome the tendency to rely mostly on fiction, particularly in the primary grades (Duke, 2000). Reading aloud information texts, however, has a number of advantages that coaches can share with teachers. First, they can be tied to curricular objectives in science and social studies. Second, nonfiction read-alouds are, perhaps surprisingly, no less appealing to children than fiction. Third, nonfiction supplies students with the prior knowledge they will need to read further on the same topics. Fourth, nonfiction exposes children to a variety of text structures, notably those they will encounter again and again in content-area reading. Fifth, read-alouds of nonfiction will positively influence children's writing.

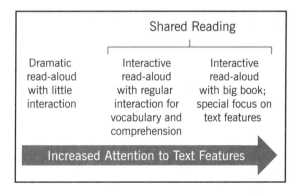

FIGURE 4.2. Read-alouds and shared reading.

At Which Grade Levels Should Teachers Conduct Read-Alouds?

Our belief is that read-alouds should be part of the daily schedule from PreK through grade 5. Teachers in the upper-elementary grades may balk at this idea, but the power and flexibility of read-alouds can make their lives easier. The challenge in coaching is to make them realize this. By reading aloud nonfiction selections, teachers can build background for science and social studies lessons. By reading aloud fiction, they can involve all children in meaningful discussions and build general vocabulary knowledge. Although most of the research on read-alouds has focused on preschool and the primary grades, the benefits extend throughout elementary school. Speaking broadly, Smolkin and Donovan (2002) concluded that "Research has almost universally supported the idea that reading aloud to children leads to improved reading comprehension" (p. 144).

How Frequently Should Teachers Read Aloud?

A. E. Cunningham and Zibulsky (2011) echoed the NELP's conclusion in support of shared reading, but they sounded a note of caution concerning balance: "It is important to note that in addition to engaging in shared reading experiences, more formal instruction in alphabetic knowledge and decoding is necessary to facilitate early reading development" (p. 408). The notion of balance is important simply because the time required to conduct a read-aloud must be subtracted from the time available for other activities during a literacy block. Our belief is that there should be multiple read-alouds every day. This recommendation may at first seem to contradict the call for balance. However, we argue that multiple daily read-alouds are feasible for two reasons. First, read-alouds can be brief—as little as 10 minutes—and they can be interrupted to accommodate schedules and picked up again later. Second, read-alouds of information books can be a part of the time allocated for science and social studies. In the upper elementary grades, they might even include interactive read-alouds of selections from the textbook.

How Frequently Should the Same Book Be Read Aloud?

An issue related to the frequency of read-alouds is whether the same book should be repeatedly read aloud. The answer may depend on grade level. In their review of research, McGee and Schickedanz (2007) support three readings of the same book in kindergarten and first grade, each time altering the focus slightly. Morrow (2007) tells of a particularly compelling study about the effectiveness of repeated read-alouds with 4-year-olds:

> One group listened to three repeated readings of the same story, and the other group listened to three different stories. After the stories were read, the discussions consistently revealed that the children in the repeated-reading group increased the number,

kind, and complexity of responses made.... The repeated-reading group's responses became more interpretive, and they began to predict outcomes and make associations, judgments and elaborative comments. (p. 152)

We suspect that in the upper grades, breadth rather than depth assumes greater importance because of the need for growth in vocabulary and background knowledge.

How Should Read-Alouds Be Conducted?

Although there is a broad consensus that read-alouds are effective, the devil is in the details. Ongoing research is being conducted to identify the most effective approaches, and there are many articles and books that would make good selections for teacher study groups. Although studies have not yet identified all of the specifics concerning how to plan and deliver an interactive read-aloud, the basic ingredients are known. In Figures 4.3 and 4.4, we list the best-researched components of interactive read-alouds using fiction and nonfiction selections, respectively. These components, we believe, can be the basis of professional development, either through group study or individual coaching.

Coaching for Better Read-Alouds

There is clearly much to consider in thinking about how to help teachers improve the effectiveness of their read-alouds. Beauchat, Blamey, and Walpole (2009) offer guidance in the form of practical rubrics. These break down read-aloud delivery into its basic components and provide a tool for gauging a teacher's status in numerous dimensions. They can help focus the efforts of a coach on specific aspects of read-aloud delivery and set reasonable goals for improvement.

WRITING

In federally funded schoolwide initiatives, such as Reading First and Reading Excellence, writing received scant attention. It is not mentioned in the NRP report. This neglect is particularly important given the close ties between reading and writing development. Instruction in one is helpful to the other. This mutually beneficial relationship is well established and has been called "the reading–writing connection."

Fortunately, the NELP (2008) has helped to turn the spotlight on writing. The panel stressed the importance of writing development in young children, though their conclusion from the available research was understandably modest. They concluded that children be able to write their own names and to write individual letters when prompted. This ability during preschool has strong predictive

---

Before reading

- Select a text that is within your students' conceptual grasp. You will be able to support their comprehension as you read, but your support can only go so far. Compare what the author assumes they know with what you believe they actually know.
- Decide how to briefly introduce the author and illustrator along with a quick overview of the book.
- Decide whether the author assumes readers have had experiences your students may not have had. Plan how to boost prior knowledge of such experiences.
- Do not preteach Tier 2 words and do not do a picture walk.
- Choose between introducing a skeletal story map or reviewing a comprehension strategy to reinforce. There may not be time to do both.

During reading

- Decide where to stop and engage students. Look for points at which interesting predictions can be made, inferences reached, visual images formed, questions generated by students, and so forth. Your choice will depend in part on whether or not it is the initial read-aloud. For example, the first read-aloud might include a question like "What do you think will happen next?" At the same point in the second read-aloud you might ask, "Do you remember what happens next?"
- Guide students toward analyzing the story, not just noting the sequence of events.
- Include opportunities for every-pupil response in order to achieve high levels of engagement (e.g., thumbs up if you think . . ., turn and share with a partner).
- Decide which words students might not know but that can be fast mapped (defined as an aside without distracting the students).
- Look for places to conduct think-alouds. These are places where information may be at odds with prior understanding.

After reading

- Ask a few inferential questions. Those beginning with *why* are especially effective.
- If you began the read-aloud with a blank story map, complete it together with the input of children.
- Select two or three Tier 2 words from the text. For each, provide a brief, kid-friendly definition. Return to text and reread the sentence that contains the word. Then offer another sentence context of your own.
- Consider providing a writing prompt based on the read-aloud.

FIGURE 4.3. Best practices for planning a fiction read-aloud.

---

power for subsequent growth in reading and writing as long as subsequent school experiences are high quality. The Common Core State Standards Initiative (2010) extended this focus to students in grades K–12.

Development of Spelling and Writing

One of the most fascinating aspects of teaching young children to write is watching their written products evolve from what appear to be mere pictures to recognizable letters and words. Novice teachers may not be able to interpret their children's earliest written products but it is important that they afford their children

Before reading
• Select a text that is related to a current content objective in science or social studies. As with fiction, the text must be within your students' conceptual grasp. Consider what your students already know based on previous content.
• Provide a quick overview of the selection.
• Decide on a method of introducing key content terms (e.g., concept of definition, semantic map or another type of diagram, feature analysis, or another kind of chart. You are only introducing these words. Do not worry about teaching them to mastery.
• Choose between reviewing a comprehension strategy or the text structure. There may not be time to do both.

During reading
• Decide where to stop and engage students. Look for points at which interesting predictions can be made, inferences reached, questions generated by students, and so forth.
• Remember to discuss text features that are not part of the linear text (e.g., sidebars, diagrams, graphs, pictures, photos). Remind students that reading involves thinking about these features.
• Include opportunities for every-pupil response in order to achieve high levels of engagement (e.g., thumbs up if you think . . ., turn and share with a partner).
• Although you have pretaught a cluster of words, decide which *other* words students might not know but that can be fast mapped (defined as an aside without distracting the students).
• Look for places to conduct think-alouds. These are places where information may be at odds with prior understanding.

After reading
• Summarize the content. In the process, review the words you pretaught, referring back to the graphic.
• Ask a few inferential questions. Those beginning with *why* are especially effective.
• Consider providing a writing prompt based on the read-aloud.

FIGURE 4.4. Best practices for planning a nonfiction read-aloud.

From *The Literacy Coach's Handbook, Second Edition*, by Sharon Walpole and Michael C. McKenna. Copyright 2013 by The Guilford Press. Permission to photocopy this figure is granted to purchasers of this book for personal use only (see copyright page for details).

opportunities to explore. The progress from drawing to writing, which Patricia Cunningham calls "driting," is natural (P. M. Cunningham & Allington, 2010). An example of this development appears in Figures 4.5–4.8. Writing samples of Sharon Walpole's son Kevin (now an adult), collected over a year's time, capture the obvious trend from drawing to writing. In their development as writers, children in preschool and kindergarten explore spelling and phonics at the same time (Invernizzi, 2003).

Schickedanz and Casbergue (2004) offer a useful summary of this gradual evolution:

[Preschoolers] begin trying to write words by using the letters in their names and copying letters from the environment. Until children figure out that letters are mapped to speech, their words are mock words, nonphonemic letter strings. As children make the connection between sounds and letters, they first represent very few of the sounds

Tyrannosaurus rex

FIGURE 4.5. Kevin's writing in October of kindergarten.

they hear, often only the first sound in a word. Gradually, however, they begin to isolate or hear more and more sounds in words they say, and to include more and more
letters in their writing to represent this increased phonemic awareness. Finally, but
usually not until kindergarten or first grade, children are able to represent most of the
sounds that actually make up words. (p. 43)

Although this account accurately captures the general process, the instructional
issues concern the pace at which these developments should occur, whether coaches
and teachers should attempt to accelerate that pace, whether exploration and dis-
covery are superior to explicit instruction, and how to help those children who
are not progressing as we would like. We anticipate that as more and more states
enact the Foundational Skills in Reading from the Common Core State Standards
(*www.corestandards.org*), there will be more consensus on these issues of pacing.

In addition to the idea that spelling and writing progress through stages,
Boscolo (2008) points out two additional conclusions reached by researchers. One
is the fact that children's written products tell only part of the story. The *process*
of arriving at a final *product* is just as central to understanding their development
as writers and helping them along that path. The other insight is the importance of
viewing writing as a social activity, as a means of communicating. When teachers

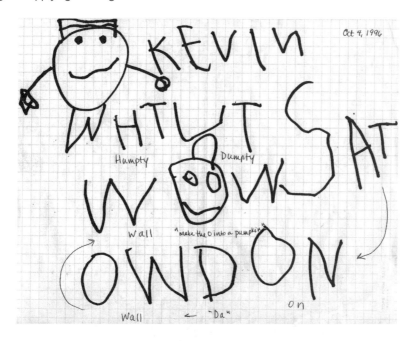

HTUT SAT NO DWO WOW

"Humpty Dumpty sat on a wall

(and I made the O into a pumpkin!)"

FIGURE 4.6. Kevin's writing later in October of kindergarten.

provide children with opportunities to write for the purpose of conveying ideas, the activities tend to be more effective than writing prompts.

The notion of process writing remains very popular in elementary schools. *Process writing* is a generic term used to refer to instruction that guides children through a series of steps ending in a finished product. These steps generally include prewriting, drafting, revising, editing, and publishing. Moore (2012) traces the origin of process writing instruction to Emig (1971). Since then, many specific versions have appeared, such as workshop approaches. Workshops engage children systematically in the steps of the process, during which they receive individual support. Writer's Workshop (Atwell, 1987) is probably the best-known workshop approach to process writing instruction, but it is not the only one. Boscolo (2008) describes the basic features of process writing instruction:

> First, lectures are minimized and small-group work is valued, with an emphasis on concrete materials, problem solving, and students' engagement in writing. Second, children should be allowed to choose the topics on which to write, at least in elementary school, as this is believed to have a motivating effect. Third, the teacher is not an evaluator, but an audience who gives feedback through conferences with students.

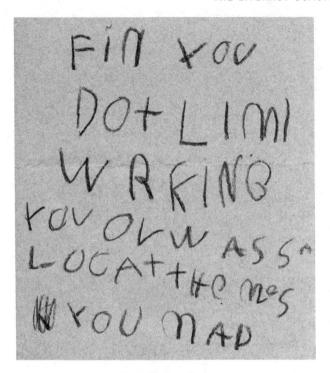

Fin you dot limi wrking
you ovwas s locat the
mes you mad

"Fine. You don't like my working.
You always say look at the
mess you made."

FIGURE 4.7. Kevin's writing, summer between kindergarten and first grade.

Through conferences, he or she shows how to write by posing questions that help planning, by reformulating children's ideas when writing, and by soliciting a new development of a story or new information for a report. Thus, the teacher is a facilitator and a model. Fourth, the social dimension of writing is emphasized, because students often work in small groups, and what they write is a product that is made available to other children. (p. 299)

Research into the effectiveness of the process approach is not extensive. In an early review, Hillocks (1986) concluded that process writing instruction is most effective when a teacher uses structured materials and activities to guide students. Two of the difficulties we associate with process writing are the amount of time it requires and the prevailing notion that the process occurs in lockstep. Editing, for example, follows revising. Moore (2012) points out that the steps are now seen as recursive in nature. Editing and revising may alternate, for instance. Nevertheless,

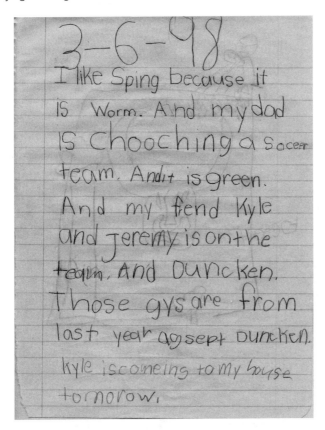

"I like spring because it is warm. And my dad is coaching a soccer team. And it is green. And my friends Kyle and Jeremy are on the team. And Duncan. Those guys are from last year, except Duncan. Kyle is coming to my house tomorrow."

FIGURE 4.8. Kevin's writing, March of first grade.

the basic steps of planning, drafting, revising, editing, and publishing occur more or less in that order.

Whether a teacher adopts a process approach or takes a more explicit route, there is a question of what children should be taught to do. It is easy to say, "Plan first, then write a draft," for example, but how exactly is a child to do these things? For example, research evidence suggests that children do not intuitively know how to plan; the process must be modeled for them (McCutchen, 2006). Indeed, a growing body of evidence supports the idea of teaching a small number of specific strategies that are useful before, during, and after writing. The idea is similar to teaching comprehension strategies. The best-known approach is self-regulated strategy development (SRSD), developed by Harris and Graham (1996). SRSD involves the use of minilessons through which strategies are modeled and discussed. The strategies are often applied during revising (MacArthur, Graham, & Harris, 2004). In one study, for example, elementary students with learning disabilities were successfully taught to inspect their persuasive writing for the number of arguments they included and how clearly these were expressed (Graham & MacArthur, 1988). We expect that this emphasis on persuasive writing will be bolstered by its emphasis in the Common Core State Standards.

There is little doubt that instructing children in specific writing strategies can be effective. In a recent meta-analysis of studies that involved students from grades 2 to 12, Graham (2006) reported large effect sizes for strategy instruction. On the other hand, for writing instruction to be effective, adequate time must be devoted to it. In a national survey of teachers in grades 4 to 6, Gilbert and Graham (2010) found that an average of just 15 minutes per day are devoted to writing instruction. A similar national survey conducted in grades 1 to 3 (Cutler & Graham, 2008) yielded similar results, prompting the researchers to call for increased time for writing as well as targeted professional development. Perhaps the scant attention to writing across the elementary grades lies in the fact that a majority of these teachers reported feeling underprepared to teach writing effectively. Depending on the situation in a particular school, this finding suggests that writing could be an important focus for coaching.

An important area where reading and writing development overlap is that of genre. Genres are the major forms of writing typically encountered as we read or seek to produce as we write. Genres "exist to provide orientations for both readers and writers" (Tardy & Swales, 2008, p. 565), and there is evidence that even preschoolers pick up an early sense of genre and apply it to their writing (Rowe, 2008). You can think of a genre as a skeleton, an organizing structure that helps children organize their thoughts as they write or see more easily how a writer's thoughts are organized as they read. Teaching children about genres is useful for two reasons. Knowing the purpose and structure of a genre (e.g., the difference between a persuasive piece and a narrative) enables children to better comprehend each genre when they encounter it, but it also positions them to write their own examples of a given genre. In teaching children to write in various genres, it is important to convey the idea that a genre is more than "an empty structure" (Boscolo, 2008, p. 304) with certain features. That structure is just the beginning; many choices must be made as children put flesh on the bones.

In their extensive research review, Donovan and Smolkin (2006) reached several useful conclusions about children's genre knowledge. Such knowledge is emergent. It is fostered by repeated reading of the same book. The features of a genre can be taught to preschoolers. Exposing children to a variety of genres and pointing out their key features is desirable. Nell Duke and her colleagues have produced an excellent resource that suggests many opportunities for developing children's concept of genre through both reading and writing (Duke, Caughlan, Juzwik, & Martin, 2011).

Motivation is a key issue in writing instruction, perhaps more so even than in reading (Hidi & Boscolo, 2006). To be sure, children face formidable obstacles as they write. Their prior knowledge may be inadequate, the feedback they receive is delayed, and they may lack the effort needed to persist. Even famous writers have voiced their frustration. Samuel Johnson, one of the greatest British writers, once remarked that writing was for him "an effort of slow diligence, to which the mind is dragged by necessity or resolution." Dragged! Where does that leave the rest of us? It is not surprising that first graders' attitudes toward writing are slightly negative and then generally worsen throughout elementary school (Kear, Coffman, McKenna, & Ambrosio, 2000). Hidi and Boscolo (2006) suggest that when classroom activities are viewed by students as meaningful, motivation to write is improved. The challenge, of course, is to discover such activities. Pajares and Valiante (2006) identify self-efficacy (the perception that one is able to write well) as another factor that can be influenced by teachers. That is, when proficiency is fostered, motivation may follow. Pajares and Valiante also point out the gender difference in motivation that favors girls, a trend that Kear et al. likewise observed. Pajares and Valiante argue that writing is viewed by many students as a feminine activity, as opposed to science and math. Efforts to promote a willingness to write, they suggest, should reflect an awareness of this imbalance.

Not surprisingly, students with learning disabilities find writing filled with challenges. Their written products are often shorter than those of their more proficient classmates, and they are characterized by poor organization, and both mechanical and grammatical errors (Troia, 2006). They tend not to plan, preferring "to rely on a knowledge-telling tactic for many writing tasks, generating content in an associative, linear fashion" (p. 325). Consequently, their compositions are more likely to contain irrelevant material. They tend to spend less time in truly revising, spending their time instead on matters of mechanics and usage (editing). Based on his review, Troia concludes that effectively meeting the needs of children with learning disabilities requires that teachers apply modified versions of the techniques useful with other children. They should stress "the equal importance of form, process, and meaning, but their instruction should emphasize those aspects that are most problematic for any given student" (p. 330). They should present writing tasks that are meaningful and challenging, and strike a balance between narrative and expository writing. They should establish a predictable routine that includes the major components of process writing. They must devote sufficient time to teaching transcription skills such as spelling. Troia notes that assistive technology, such as spelling and grammar checkers, is not the panacea one might suspect because its use requires that a student be able to apply strategies for planning and revising in the first place.

SPELLING

Many of the teachers we know view spelling as little more than a technical aspect of writing—a matter of mechanics to be taught and mastered by rote drill. The basal spellers that dominated most of the twentieth century, with their "list of the week," reflected this view. It may surprise you to learn that teachers in the nineteenth century held a very different view. They believed that reading and spelling should be taught together, for by learning to *spell* words the child can at the same time learn to *decode* them (Zutell, 2007).

In the late twentieth century, this idea was rediscovered. Careful observation of children's invented spellings, like the examples in Figures 4.5–4.8, revealed that children typically pass through discernible stages en route to standard spelling. McCutchen (2006) summarizes the research usefully:

> Despite controversies about specific stages and strategies, a general picture emerges from the research on children's spelling. After an initial period of "play" with letter-like symbols, children's early spelling attempts are supported by their awareness of phonological information, followed by increasingly sophisticated awareness of the relationships among phonology, orthography, and morphology. (p. 120)

Although the exact nature of these stages is not totally agreed upon, we support the stage idea as the most practical approach to planning instruction.

Researchers have discovered that (1) short, group-administered assessments can reliably determine a child's developmental spelling level; (2) providing instruction at that level results in optimal gains in spelling proficiency; and (3) such instruction reinforces decoding ability.

The best spelling instruction is that which leads the student to the next developmental level. The most effective way of accomplishing this goal is not to ask children to memorize a series of lists but to engage them in studying the orthographic patterns that are shared by certain words. Sorting words by orthographic feature and discussing similarities and differences is an effective activity for building the proficiency needed to progress to the next stage (Bear, Invernizzi, Templeton, & Johnston, 2011).

The link from decoding to spelling is strong but slightly delayed. Because it is easier to decode a word that appears in print than to spell that same word, decoding instruction should be a step ahead of spelling. Spelling instruction should confirm children's decoding knowledge, in addition to making them better spellers. What, then, are the lessons for literacy coaches? What kind of spelling instruction should be encouraged? We believe the following principles now have a solid grounding in research:

- Spelling instruction should be based on a child's stage of development.
- Spelling instruction should involve the child in comparing and contrasting orthographic features.
- Spelling instruction should follow and reinforce decoding instruction.

We also believe that ignoring these principles can exacerbate the problems children experience with spelling. In a recent national survey (Graham et al., 2008), teachers in grades K–3 reported that, on average, 27% of their students experienced problems with spelling. However, 42% of the teachers reported making few if any adaptations to the spelling instruction they provided. We argue that the principles we have just outlined are the key to differentiating spelling instruction and tying it meaningfully to growth in decoding.

HOW CAN WE KEEP UP?

"Knowledge is of two kinds," remarked Samuel Johnson some two and a half centuries ago. "We know a subject ourselves, or we know where we can find information upon it." It is unrealistic for a literacy coach, working alone, to be able to synthesize and summarize the existing research evidence related to reading instruction one study at a time. Fortunately, there's an easier approach. The abundance of evidence has led in recent years to the publication of research summaries on particular topics. These summaries attempt to synthesize what researchers have found and distill its lessons. We believe that it is the job of a literacy coach to understand the findings of these research reviews as they relate to instruction, and to develop strategies to keep up with new findings. Research summaries can be instrumental in wrestling with the issues affecting school reform. They can be tackled by an individual coach, by a collegial group of coaches, or by teacher study groups guided by a coach. Particularly powerful syntheses include those listed in Figure 4.9.

Handbooks

Complementing the research syntheses listed in Figure 4.9 are handbooks of research. A *handbook* is a somewhat encyclopedic edited volume that can double as a doorstop when not in use. A handbook consists of chapters devoted to specific subjects and authored by experts in those subjects. Each chapter contains an extensive review of research, and often ends with an overview of where the research community stands and what remains to be learned. Like an actual encyclopedia, a handbook is not intended to be read from cover to cover but to be used topically as the occasion warrants. Major handbooks are listed in Figure 4.10. Note that new *volumes* are added to many popular handbooks. These are not the same as new *editions* of a book. A new volume contains its own distinct set of topics, and although some may be similar to the topics addressed in previous volumes, they are not intended to be revisions.

Journal Articles

Reading research journals sometimes publish articles that summarize the research on a topic, especially those topics that are multifaceted or involve major

Synthesis	Summary	Source
Snow, Burns, and Griffin (1998)	Broadly reviews research on literacy development, including parenting	The book is listed in the reference section. You can actually download this book free at *www.nap.edu/catalog.php?record_id=6023*.
National Reading Panel (National Institute of Health and Human Development, 2000)	Reviews SBRR on major dimensions of elementary reading programs; established the "five pillars"	Free download available at *www.nationalreadingpanel.org*.
National Literacy Panel on Language-Minority Children and Youth (2006)	Reviews research on English language learning	Published in book form; see August and Shanahan (2006) in reference list. Download executive summary free at *www.cal.org/projects/archive/nlpreports/executive_summary.pdf*.
National Early Literacy Panel (2008)	Reviews research on literacy development, birth through K	Free download available at *http://lincs.ed.gov/earlychildhood/NELP/NELP09.html*.
Review of Educational Research	Comprehensive research reviews on a range of education topics	Journal published quarterly by the American Educational Research Association. Examine contents and abstracts for literacy-related topics here: *http://rer.sagepub.com*.
Literacy Information and Communication System (LINCS)	USDOE source for literacy research summaries and other tools	Free downloads available at *http://lincs.ed.gov*.
Institute of Education Sciences (IES)	USDOE reviews of research and interventions in variety of areas	Free downloads available at *http://ies.ed.gov/ncee/wwc/publications_reviews.aspx*.
Center on Instruction	One of five USDOE national content centers. Wide range of tools, including research reviews	Free downloads available at *www.centeroninstruction.org*.

FIGURE 4.9. Useful research syntheses available online.

controversies. Some journals, such as the *Review of Educational Research*, publish nothing but research reviews (see Figure 4.9). Of course, the opening portion of any research report published in the journal contains a review of the literature, but this is likely to be highly focused on the question being investigated in that particular study. We heartily recommend the following journal articles, which present summaries that are both rigorous and readable for these topics: decoding instruction for students at risk (Weiser & Mathes, 2011), fluency instruction (Kuhn & Stahl, 2003), morphology (Bowers et al., 2010), RTI (Mesmer & Mesmer, 2008), vocabulary interventions (Marulis & Neuman, 2010), read-alouds (Mol et al., 2009), and effective reading programs (Slavin et al., 2009). Although the journal articles were once available only through subscription or the library, you will see that access to an individual important article is now possible through the publisher for a modest fee.

Books

In a few cases, entire books have been devoted to sifting through the research on a broad topic, summarizing the results, and arriving at recommendations regarding instructional planning and practice. Such books usually make excellent selections for teacher study groups, and they are a must in the personal library of any literacy coach. Opinions will differ on which books to include in a "short list," but this has not stopped us from developing our own. In Figure 4.11 we have updated the list from the first edition. These are books that we have found to be especially useful.

Handbook of Reading Research (Vol. 1), 1984

Handbook of Reading Research (Vol. 2), 1991

Handbook of Reading Research (Vol. 3), 2000

Handbook of Reading Research (Vol. 4), 2010

Handbook of Research on Reading Comprehension, 2008

Handbook of Reading Interventions, 2011

Handbook of Learning Disabilities, 2005

Handbook of Reading Disability Research, 2010

Handbook of Research on New Literacies, 2008

Handbook of Research on Literacy and Diversity, 2010

Handbook of Research on Teaching the English Language Arts (3rd ed.), 2010

Handbook of Early Childhood Literacy, 2003 (British)

Handbook of Early Literacy Research (Vol. 1), 2001

Handbook of Early Literacy Research (Vol. 2), 2007

Handbook of Early Literacy Research (Vol. 3), 2011

International Handbook of Literacy and Technology, 2006

Handbook of Research in Second Language Teaching and Learning, 2005

Handbook of Research on Teaching (4th ed.), 2001

Handbook of Research on Multicultural Education (2nd ed.), 2003

Handbook of Research on Writing, 2008

Handbook of Writing Research, 2006

FIGURE 4.10. Handbooks of research related to literacy.

Phonological awareness	*Phonological Awareness: From Research to Practice (Gillon, 2004)*
Word recognition	*Teaching Word Recognition: Effective Strategies for Students with Learning Difficulties (O'Connor, 2007)*
Spelling	*Words Their Way: Word Study for Phonics, Vocabulary, and Spelling Instruction (5th ed.) (Bear, Invernizzi, Templeton, & Johnston, 2011)*
Fluency	*The Hows and Whys of Fluency Instruction (Kuhn, 2008)*
Vocabulary	*Teaching Word Meanings (Stahl & Nagy, 2005)* *Bringing Words to Life: Robust Vocabulary Instruction (Beck, McKeown, & Kucan, 2002)* *Creating Robust Vocabulary: Frequently Asked Questions and Extended Examples (Beck, McKeown, & Kucan, 2008)*
Comprehension	*Explaining Reading: A Resource for Teaching Concepts, Skills, and Strategies (2nd ed.) (G. G. Duffy, 2009)*
Leadership	*Best Practices of Literacy Leaders (Bean & Swan Dagen, 2011)*
Writing	*Best Practices in Writing Instruction (Graham, MacArthur, & Fitzgerald, 2007)*
Common Core	*Teaching with the Common Core Standards for English Language Arts (Morrow, Shanahan, & Wixson, 2013a, 2013b) (PreK–2; Grades 3–5)*
General	*Best Practices in Literacy Instruction (4th ed.) (Morrow & Gambrell, 2011)*

FIGURE 4.11. Suggested books for teacher study.

Sharing the Burden

The sources we have listed here may seem overwhelming. A literacy coach can only do so much to keep up with current research and still meet other job expectations. In Chapter 10, we discuss the idea of creating study groups among teachers to examine the research available in a particular area. Danielson (2002) recommends that teachers choose specific sources for which they are responsible—perhaps journals to which they subscribe or in which they have an interest. When these sources are straightforward, such as journal articles, this is probably a feasible plan. It may be harder to convince your colleagues to read a voluminous handbook chapter, however, let alone an entire hefty book. On the other hand, all of these sources should be read selectively and strategically, with specific questions in mind. This mindset makes a remarkable difference.

What If There Are No Answers?

Is it possible, given the thousands of research reports currently available, that there remain instructional issues that have not been put to rest? Unfortunately, such issues abound. In a sense, of course, even questions that are very well settled may still be issues for a particular teacher, school, and instructional setting. For example, the effectiveness of graphic organizers as an instructional tool has been established through many studies, but does this mean that they will be likely to work well for teacher X in school Y? Even the most rigorous of research studies cannot answer this question definitively, and yet previous findings can give us a road map that will allow a literacy coach to give teacher X informed advice.

Unfortunately, there are also a host of issues that are poorly informed by previous research. Should a first-grade reading group ideally consist of four members? Six? Eight? What is the optimal number of teacher read-alouds for third grade? Is parallel block scheduling the best way to accommodate individual reading levels? Is it worthwhile to provide an uninterrupted block of time for silent reading each day? Should incentive programs be instituted that reward children for the number of books they read? These questions (and many others like them) either are poorly addressed or have produced conflicting results in the research literature. When literacy coaches come to the planning table, they may well be asked to give informed opinions on such issues. Such an experience is likely to be outside their comfort zone, especially because they may feel obligated, in the words of one, to "know just about everything."

Our advice is simple. The most important thing to remember is that when an issue has not been resolved by research, other research findings can sometimes be useful. For example, a vast body of research supports the fact that learning is related to the amount of time spent on task. It is a short jump to conclude that activities that engage children for longer periods of time are likely to be more effective than those that allow or invite off-task behavior. Like us, literacy coaches will have to learn to say, "I don't know of research that answers that question directly. Maybe we can look at a related area." Other important things are to answer evidence-based questions with evidence-based answers, to recognize (and admit) that many questions have no answer in the research, and to develop strategies to keep up with new evidence.

Research on Commercial Products

Literacy coaches are often asked about the likely effectiveness of particular commercial products. Can this question be researched? The answer is "It depends." It is rare to find an effectiveness study related to a particular product and conducted by researchers who are independent of the company. A company often makes available its own effectiveness studies, ostensibly conducted by outside experts, but research that is sponsored by a company in order to document the effectiveness of its own product must be viewed with a certain amount of skepticism. Studies like these may be completely unbiased and ethical, of course, but one never knows. We know of one company that rejected an investigation conducted by an outside expert with whom the company had contracted. The company simply did not like the results of the report and had no interest in disseminating it. It is a sure bet that any research report provided by a company, either in print form or online, will be supportive of the product in question.

Finding a research study that is completely independent of a company that has produced a product may not be easy. Professional journals have long discouraged "*Consumer Reports*" studies of this kind, though the attitudes of some editors may be changing. For example, two journals have published controlled studies of the Waterford Early Reading Program (Cassady & Smith, 2005; Paterson, Henry, O'Quin, Ceprano, & Blue, 2003). The second of these extended the findings of the first.

A more frequent approach to evaluating the effectiveness of a commercial product is to conduct a component analysis. That is, the activities and methods embodied in the product are evaluated one by one, with a rubric used to rate the research behind each. For example, we know that certain teaching methods tend to be effective in developing phonemic awareness, and we would expect to see those methods embraced within a commercial product designed to develop such awareness. For example, the *Guidelines to Review Comprehensive Core Reading Programs* is a rubric developed at the Florida Center for Reading Research to break a core into bite-size morsels that can be sized up one at a time (downloadable at *www.fcrr.org/fcrrreports/guides/CCRP.pdf*). Although intended to be comprehensive across all of the major dimensions of reading, this rubric can also be used to evaluate products that target only one of the essential elements of a comprehensive reading program.

It may also be useful to keep one finger on the pulse of the experiences of similar schools. What are the opinions of teachers there who have actually implemented a particular commercial product? What benefits and pitfalls have they encountered? Does snooping of this kind count as research? Of course it does. It may or may not be ironclad, but such inquiries may result in better-informed decisions.

IES Practice Guides

The U.S. Department of Education's Institute of Education Sciences (IES) offers convenient publications in the form of practice guides. These are recommendations for best practice based on the available evidence. New guides are continually added to this wonderful library of resources. Many of the guides focus on literacy, and they offer one efficient means of staying current. You can access the guides at *http://ies.ed.gov/ncee/wwc/publications_reviews.aspx*.

Google Scholar

Research at your fingertips is available through Google Scholar. This tool allows you to simultaneously search numerous electronic databases and compile a list of potential sources. You can find Google Scholar by going first to *google.com* and using the pull-down menu labeled More. Then select Even More and scroll to Scholar. You can use Google Scholar just like the ordinary Google search engine, but we advise clicking on Advanced Scholar Search. Once you have arrived, bookmark or make a favorite of this page so that you can return to it conveniently. At the top of the screen, enter words and/or phrases to focus your search. Note that you can specify where key words appear and that you can also specify words you do not want included. For example, if you wanted recent sources on differentiated reading instruction at the elementary level, you might enter these words, separated by commas, in the top box (labeled "with **all** of the words"):

differentiated, reading, elementary

To be sure your search included only sources about reading at the elementary level, you might go to the box labeled, "**without** the words," and enter:

math, "middle school"

The phrase "middle school" is placed in quotation marks to signal that it should be regarded as an intact phrase.

Keep in mind that Google Scholar is not limited to education. Start each search by making sure you select only Social Sciences, Arts, and Humanities. In most cases, it is also a good idea to specify a range of years. The sources your search generates are rank ordered by factors such as how often an article is cited by others. When you click on a source listing, you may or may not be able to access the full text. However, you can usually get enough information (e.g., an abstract) to decide whether you want to pursue the source.

Bullets Can Be Dangerous

The sheer number of research reports, findings, and summaries available these days makes the task of sorting out what we know daunting indeed. There is a clear temptation to cut through all of the complications and simplify the lessons of research into a few bullets that crystallize our knowledge about effective practice. We empathize. And we by no means wish to discourage you from referring to bulleted conclusions as a way of contending with the myriad conclusions afforded by research. That's what they're intended for, after all. At the same time, however, we caution you about relying on those bullets alone. A bulleted finding typically represents a result reported in numerous studies, but there is no guarantee that it will apply to any specific context. Moreover, the nature of the research that underlies a bulleted conclusion needs to be carefully considered. Here is an example (melded from a variety of sources) of the kind of bulleted finding that could be a real boon to coaches on the go:

- Explicit instruction in phonological awareness is causally related to decoding development.

True enough, but how can we use this information to inform our decisions as coaches? Does every child require such instruction? How much is enough? What are the best methods of providing it? Some districts have responded to bullets similar to this one by mandating that every kindergarten teacher spend 30 minutes a day providing instruction in phonological awareness. That amounts to 90 hours over the course of the year. But the NRP actually concluded that an average of about 18 hours is sufficient for most children (NICHHD, 2000). This qualification was frequently lost sight of, however, by administrators and policymakers desperate to find solutions.

The lesson here is that a coach must understand research at a level deeper than the bullet. We are by no means suggesting that encyclopedic knowledge is required, but if findings are to be used as the basis of working with teachers, they must be grasped in sufficient detail for a coach to provide informed guidance. Imagine reading only headlines to get an idea of what's happening in the world. It's better than nothing, but your knowledge would be superficial indeed. It's only by reading the stories that follow those headlines that you are able to grasp their real significance. And there's no need to go it alone. Exploring the story behind a bullet can be an engaging focus for study groups. We invite you to join us in a career of finding and using answers from research to inform work in schools.

CHAPTER 5

Reading Assessment

Reading assessment serves a variety of purposes, and the literacy coach is connected to all of them. We begin this chapter with a description of the major kinds of tests and the role that each plays in a comprehensive reading program. A working knowledge of these kinds of assessments and their different functions is essential to prudent decision making. A literacy coach is likely to be charged with selecting some or all of the assessments to be used in the building, with training teachers to give the assessments, with interpreting and summarizing the assessment data, and with planning programmatic changes based on trends in the assessments.

TYPES AND USES OF TESTS

Tests can be categorized in various ways. We often speak of the differences between formal and informal tests, norm-referenced and criterion-referenced tests, and so forth. We focus here on the *uses* that are made of tests. From this perspective, it is helpful to categorize tests in four ways.

Screening Tests

Screening tests are quick assessments designed to alert teachers to the presence of a problem in a specific area. Good examples are the subtests in the Dynamic Indicators of Basic Early Literacy Skills (DIBELS Next) battery. Each DIBELS Next subtest requires only about 3 minutes to give, but can provide a valuable "heads-up" about a student's progress in a particular area of reading development. We mention the DIBELS Next subtests as popular examples, but many other available assessments can be used for screening purposes, such as Phonological Awareness Literacy Screening (PALS) and AIMSweb. Screening tests are like colanders: They are designed to separate a group of children who need additional testing from the rest of the cohort, so that schools and teachers can focus their additional assessment time and resources on the children who need them.

Diagnostic Tests

A *diagnostic test* is one that is administered after a problem has been identified. Such measures are almost always individually administered, and they are designed to identify specific instructional needs. As a matter of best practice, a screening measure would first identify the presence of a problem, and the diagnostic test would then provide detailed information needed for effective planning to address the problem. For example, the Nonsense Word Fluency subtest of the DIBELS Next battery might signal a problem in the general area of decoding. An individually administered inventory of phonic skills would then be needed before a teacher could plan appropriate instruction.

Progress Monitoring Tests

After the screening–diagnostic one–two punch has identified a teachable target area, instruction can accelerate the student's growth in that area. To determine if the instruction is having the desired impact, it is a good idea to monitor the student's progress from time to time. *Progress monitoring tests* are quick measures designed to be administered periodically with little disruption of classroom practice. The DIBELS Next measures, for example, can serve both as screening and as progress monitoring tests. Progress monitoring tests must be very closely matched to the content of instruction; they must test what has been taught. A school-level assessment plan provides systematic procedures and tools for gathering this information. Considered together, the system of screening, diagnostic, and progress monitoring tests operates to ensure that instruction targets children's needs. In this system, instructional planning is sometimes described as "assessment driven" (e.g., McKenna & Walpole, 2005).

Outcome Tests

The type of test that is likely to have the least direct utility for a classroom teacher is an *outcome test*. Such measures are indicators of long-term growth and include the high-stakes tests that have been the source of so much scrutiny. Outcome measures are not always high-profile assessments, however. For example, a DIBELS Next subtest used for screening purposes might also be used to gauge trends from fall to spring. More often, outcome measures include nationally normed group achievement tests and state-developed competency tests aligned with the state curriculum.

If outcome measures have any real purpose for teachers, it lies in their potential use as screening measures. A student's standardized test scores from the previous spring, for example, might be used to make tentative judgments about the student's proficiency in the fall. Such a use has two major problems, however. First, group measures of this kind are not designed for this purpose. The measurement error associated with them tends to be prohibitive, though it also tends to "wash out" when the scores of large numbers of students are averaged. A second problem lies in the fact that some students do not take such tests seriously. They may be frustrated by reading to begin with, and may passively refuse to expend much effort in a group setting where their noncompliance will not be recognized for months to come (if ever). A third problem is the shelf life of group achievement tests. A test taken in March or April can hardly be expected to have high predictive value in August or September, even if the first two problems do not apply. In short, group achievement measures are no substitutes for individually administered screening tests, and their frequent use for placing children in homerooms is highly questionable.

Multitasking with Tests

These four categories provide a convenient means of pigeonholing assessments, but they can constrain our thinking as well. To be clear, when we place a test in one of the categories we have just described, we are thinking of its principal use. But tests are tools, after all, and many tools can be used for multiple purposes. With a hammer we can pound or pull nails. The same can be said about many of the reading assessments in common use today. We have already mentioned how a DIBELS Next subtest can be used both to screen (its main function) and to monitor progress. It can also be used as an outcome measure when a coach aggregates results across the course of a semester or year. Similar examples include inventories of decoding and high-frequency words. Such measures are, first and foremost, diagnostic assessments, but they can be readministered periodically to track a student's progress in acquiring the skills a teacher has targeted. To us, multiple uses like these make perfect sense. As our thinking has evolved, we believe it is more accurate to view tests in terms of their uses rather than type. This perspective helps avoid the perplexities of trying to force fit a given test into a particular box and never to let it out. Thinking in terms of how a test can be used is much more reasonable.

AN ASSESSMENT STRATEGY

Tests are useful tools for delivering appropriate instruction and for determining its effectiveness. However, like all tools, they must be used strategically, with a sense of purpose. Reading is a highly complex process, and without an overall strategy for conducting an assessment, it is often difficult to determine the best way to

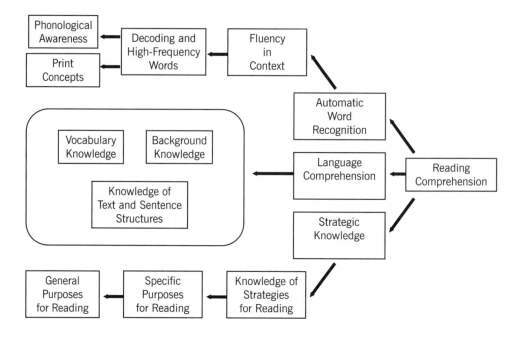

FIGURE 5.1. The cognitive model of reading assessment. Adapted from McKenna and Stahl (2009, p. 8). Copyright 2009 by The Guilford Press. Adapted by permission.

proceed. McKenna and Stahl (2009) have proposed a model of reading assessment that is driven by a sequence of strategic questions. These questions correspond to Figure 5.1. They encourage the coach to work backward, beginning at the far right with the most basic issue of whether a reading problem actually exists. If a child can read grade-level texts independently and with strong comprehension, there is no need for more information. For children who cannot do that, the questions progress from general to specific in three broad areas:

1. Is the child able to read texts at grade placement with automatic word recognition and adequate expression?
   - Does the child make use of previous text to monitor his or her decoding accuracy?
   - Does the child read at an adequate rate?
   - Does the child have adequate knowledge of high-frequency words?
   - Does the child have adequate knowledge of decoding strategies?
   - Does the child have adequate phonemic awareness?
2. Is the child able to comprehend the language of the text?
   - Does the child have an adequate vocabulary for his or her age and grade?
   - Does the child have the background knowledge necessary to understand the particular passage that he or she is reading?
   - Is the child able to use common text structures and sentence structures to aid in comprehension?

3. Does the child have adequate knowledge of the purposes for reading and possess strategies available to achieve those purposes?
   - Does the child have a set of strategies that can be used to achieve different purposes in reading?
   - What does the child view as the goal of reading in general?

If the answer to any of the three broad questions is yes, the questions related to it may be skipped. If the answer to any of them is no, the related questions may help to pinpoint a problem area. These questions are deceptively simple. They provide a useful framework for thinking diagnostically, but they require dependable data to answer. The results of screening and diagnostic tests can provide such data, as can less formal classroom measures.

Adapting the Cognitive Model for Beginning Readers

As an overall assessment strategy, the cognitive model begins, reasonably enough, by considering whether a child can read and comprehend grade-level texts. If so, we don't need to go further because there is no problem to solve. We think this is a prudent approach for late first grade and beyond, but what exactly does it mean to read and comprehend grade-level texts at the kindergarten level or the beginning of first grade? After all, we do not typically expect children to be reading conventionally prior to the middle of grade one. Fluency benchmarks are unavailable prior to that point and in some systems they are not presented before the end of first grade. For these reasons, we think the cognitive model must be modified for kindergarten and the beginning of first grade. Two of the three strands (automatic word recognition and language comprehension) still apply, but our expectations are different. We suggest that a modified set of questions is more appropriate for beginning readers:

1. Is the child learning the phonological awareness and decoding skills taught so far?
   - To answer this question, we can screen first in decoding and then, if necessary, in phonological awareness, and we can follow up with appropriate diagnostics. This process is related to curriculum, although we see growing consensus in the importance of early decoding mastery. After all, we do not want to hold any child accountable for skills that have not yet been introduced.
2. Is the child able to comprehend text that is read aloud by the teacher and that age peers are likely to understand?
   - Under these circumstances, the "heavy lifting" of decoding is done by the teacher, so that the child is free to attend to the meaning of texts. Making judgments about language comprehension in this way is a subjective business, to be sure, but when read-alouds are truly interactive and are delivered at least once a day, a teacher can gather useful information

about whether comprehension appears to be hindered by vocabulary, background knowledge, or syntactic familiarity.

INTERPRETING OUTCOME SCORES

Outcome measures are designed to provide teachers with long-term indications of growth. Although such measures can be thought of in relation to an individual student, coaches can aggregate the results to get an idea of how a classroom, grade level, or school has progressed. Outcome measures are often high stakes because the results might be tied to whether a school has made AYP, a requirement of No Child Left Behind. But some outcome measures are of a lower profile, such as end-of-year DIBELS Next or AIMSweb tests.

Our perception is that the use of group norm-referenced achievement measures (e.g., the Iowa Tests of Basic Skills) is giving way to criterion-referenced outcome measures. These measures generally place a student's performance in one of three categories relative to two criteria: a benchmark for acceptable performance and a higher criterion denoting high proficiency. We are naturally most concerned about the lower benchmark indicating acceptable performance.

Figure 5.2 illustrates the year-end percentages of students who met the state benchmark for third, fourth, and fifth grades at Morristown Elementary for three consecutive years. The question facing a coach is how to interpret these numbers. Let's assume it is now year 3 and we can use the results for years 1 and 2 to help identify trends. One way to interpret these data is to note that the percentages have fallen at all three grade levels compared with the previous year. A problem with that conclusion is that the results are for different cohorts of children. A different perspective is possible when we note that this year's fifth graders were last year's fourth graders, and so forth. From this point of view, we can see that the percentage from third to fourth rose from 80 to 81; likewise, from fourth to fifth grade it rose from 82 to 83. Going back 2 years, we see that the percentage of third graders benchmarking in year 1 rose from 78 to 83 in year 3 when they were in fifth grade.

When student mobility is high, even a cohort approach can be problematic. Comparing this year's third graders with last year's second graders only makes

	Year 1	Year 2	Year 3
Grade 3	78	80	79
Grade 4	80	82	81
Grade 5	86	84	83

FIGURE 5.2. Percentages of students meeting the benchmark at Morristown Elementary.

sense when they are mostly the same children. The soundest comparison is limited to children who have spent the entire year enrolled at your school and for whom both pre- and posttest scores are available. In some schools, this may result in surprisingly small numbers of children. One of the large urban K–5 schools with which we work serves many struggling families. Such schools experience very high student mobility. We once tracked the children who began attending this school as kindergartners and who were still enrolled at the end of fifth grade. There were only five! Nevertheless, there will always be enough children to make a 1-year cohort comparison worthwhile, provided that scores are available every year.

Common Core Assessments

Because most states have adopted the Common Core State Standards, the state criterion-referenced outcome measures must adjust to reflect the change. In the near term, states must modify their assessments on a state-by-state basis. As we write, however, new computer-adaptive assessments are being developed that are geared to the Common Core. These assessments will provide outcome (summative) results and also formative results potentially useful in differentiating instruction. The state-specific criterion-referenced measures will eventually be replaced with assessments that are shared across states.

Most states have joined one of two assessment consortia. One is the Partnership for Assessment of Readiness for College and Careers (PARCC; *www.parc-conline.org*); the other is the Smarter Balanced Assessment Consortium (*www.smarterbalanced.org*). We encourage coaches to visit the site for their state and keep abreast of the developments in the new measures.

We would like to sound a note of caution concerning the use of the new Common Core measures. Although we are hopeful that they will constitute a new generation of assessments, we suspect that much of the information needed to inform day-to-day instruction will continue to come from the screening and diagnostic measures that teachers can administer quickly and easily. These are likely to remain the best means of using the cognitive model to form small groups, plan intensive intervention, and monitor progress.

Lexiles: A Promising Metric

Most group achievement tests now report scores in Lexiles, in addition to the more common scores. A Lexile is a scale score ranging from 200 to 1700 (in units of 10). It can be used to estimate a student's reading comprehension proficiency, on the one hand, and the complexity of a text on the other. This means that Lexiles provide a means of matching a student with an appropriate book because, as Figure 5.3 illustrates, both the book and the student can be gauged on the same scale. There are older methods for making this same judgment, of course. We can compare the readability level of a text (expressed as a grade level) with a child's

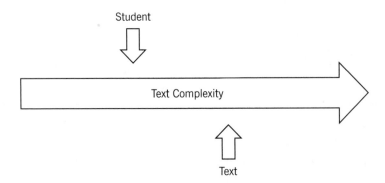

FIGURE 5.3. A common metric to assess proficiency and texts.

instructional reading level, or we can use a leveled book system such as those commonly used in Reading Recovery or Guided Reading. Lexiles, however, are far more flexible because they have already been used to determine the difficulty level of the vast majority of books in print, and they will also be useful in middle and high school. You can access these levels free at *www.lexile.com*. Another advantage of Lexiles is that they are embraced by the Common Core State Standards, and for that reason alone their use will become even more widespread.

At the Lexile website you can download the most current version of the Lexile map, a chart that correlates Lexiles with approximate grade levels and lists examples of books corresponding to each Lexile (e.g., *Play Ball, Amelia Bedelia* is rated at 220L, *The Giver* at 770L, and *Bud, Not Buddy* at 950L). These popular books are listed in order to provide a frame of reference for teachers and coaches. We warn you that the Lexile chart may strike you as vague. There are deliberate overlaps with grade levels to stress the fact that these are only estimates. We noted such overlaps to produce the quick reference chart that appears in Figure 5.4.

Lexile	Grade level	Fountas and Pinnell
	K	A–C
220L–410L	1	C–I
420L–490L	1–2	I–J
450L–790L	2–3	J–P
770L–980L	4–5	Q–W
955L–1155L	6–8	X–Z+

FIGURE 5.4. Lexile comparison chart. Sources: *www.lexile.com*; Common Core State Standards Initiative (2010), Appendix A; Weaver (2000).

We encourage you to take to heart the fact that Lexiles are mere estimates. They are useful estimates, to be sure, but you should be prepared to overrule a Lexile if your experience with a book suggests otherwise. Lexiles present the illusion of precision but they account for only a limited number of factors associated with text difficulty, such as sentence length and word frequency. Other sources of difficulty include theme and levels of meaning. In our view, however, Lexiles are proving to be an excellent tool for coaches and teachers.

MULTIPLE ASSESSMENT HATS OF THE LITERACY COACH

An effective literacy coach may be called upon to serve in a variety of assessment capacities. Official job descriptions will differ, of course, but we describe here the typical expectations related to assessment.

Coach as Tester

Depending on the available demands at the beginning of school, the literacy coach may be called upon to conduct screening assessments in order to identify deficits. Such tasks are arguably in the domain of the classroom teacher, but the coach may have to jump-start the process or lend a hand during time crunches. Some schools now use a SWAT approach, in which a coach joins forces with reading specialists and special educators to conduct screenings in short order. The coach may also be in a position to select assessments, or at least to have a major say in which assessments will be used. Literacy coaches need to learn how to find information on the validity and reliability of assessment instruments and on their utility for screening, diagnosis, progress monitoring, and evaluation. A good place to start is the National Center on Response to Intervention (*www.rti4success.org*), which offers ratings of available assessments. For literacy coaches, there are also contextual factors to consider in selecting an instrument:

- How much time does it take to administer?
- How much and what kind of information does it provide?
- How much does it cost?
- What sort of training will be needed to administer it effectively?

Coach as Interpreter

It may well fall to a literacy coach to help interpret group achievement test results when they arrive. The knowledgeable coach will conduct a cohort analysis, contrasting last year's scores with the present year's, as we have discussed. Assistance may be available in the form of consultants to the school. For example, state-funded regional service agencies may have the expertise needed to help with test score analysis. University professors may be called upon as well, and teachers who are enrolled in graduate coursework in the area of research and measurement may be able to glean advice by asking professors to inspect group achievement results.

Arriving at a reasonable interpretation of testing results is a necessary first step. It is also a good idea to help with public relations. A letter to parents can be drafted, a press release can be sent (particularly when explanations are called for), and presentations can be made to parent groups.

Coach as Profiler

One of the most important tasks confronting the literacy coach is ensuring that instruction in the school is informed by data. Results of screening and progress monitoring measures should be profiled for classroom teachers. One way of doing so is to provide each teacher with a class roster on which results of screening measures are briefly presented. Updates of this profile can be shared periodically during conferences. Such conferences can be held with individual teachers or with all of the teachers at a particular grade level. In the latter case, a grade-level profile will be needed in order to apprise the teachers of general areas where a more intense instructional focus is called for.

The coach can also be instrumental in using screening results and other information to identify children who need diagnostic assessments. Whether or not this identification is actually carried out by the coach, the coach should share the results with the teachers responsible for these children. In the case of struggling readers, for whom diagnostic assessments have been administered, communication with teachers must center around instructional techniques. That is, it is not enough to identify areas of weakness. This information needs to be translated into instructional strategies that will help accelerate the progress of a particular child.

The actual means of preparing class profiles typically involve simple computer applications. For example, an Excel file can be created for each teacher in such a way that grade-level reports can also be generated. If the school administers DIBELS Next and chooses to pay for data management, then class rosters are routinely generated. These results can supplement a homemade Excel file, or they can be incorporated into it. We urge literacy coaches to create and maintain a data set at the school, so that they can incorporate all data available into one file that can be sorted and analyzed. Such customizable longitudinal data systems are now much more commonly provided by states; there is still much to learn about their actual use in schools.

A sample class profile for Ms. Ellis, our fictional second-grade teacher, appears in Figure 5.5. It is especially helpful if the information in the profile can be tracked over time, so that the growth (or lack of it) of a particular child in a given area can be monitored. When a student's ID number is included, an Excel report can be generated across a span of years, displaying the child's progress. Notice also

	A	B	C	D	E	F	G	H
1	Student name	Student ID no.	Teacher	Grade	State CRT comprehension last spring	August DORF level	August DORF WCPM	August DRA level
2	Beck, Joe	66578	Ellis	3	Failed	Low risk	52	18
3	Chase, Fred	33412	Ellis	3	Failed	Some risk	36	16
4	Chatham, Sue	87609	Ellis	3	Competent	Low risk	48	20
5	Dodd, Kareem	45239	Ellis	3	Failed	Some risk	30	16
6	Flood, Lakesha	54890	Ellis	3	Failed	At risk	15	4
7	Good, Johnny B.	45124	Ellis	3	Proficient	Low risk	67	30
8	Hall, Monte	65409	Ellis	3	Competent	Low risk	60	20
9	James, Nancy	67845	Ellis	3	Failed	At risk	22	12
10	Keeshan, Jack	67567	Ellis	3	Competent	Some risk	28	16
11	Louis, Joe	87098	Ellis	3	Competent	Low risk	45	16
12	Newman, Fred	67121	Ellis	3	Competent	Low risk	55	20
13	Perez, Juan	43567	Ellis	3	Failed	At risk	8	3
14	Power, Tyrone	67543	Ellis	3	Proficient	Low risk	80	40
15	Rogers, Fred	87692	Ellis	3	Competent	Low risk	61	20
16	Rudd, Sarah	67545	Ellis	3	Failed	At risk	19	12
17	Smith, Raneesha	56780	Ellis	3	Failed	At risk	17	16
18	Tuttle, Wylie	90045	Ellis	3	Failed	Some risk	39	16
19	Vincent, Jim	56749	Ellis	3	Competent	Low risk	54	20
20	Wade, Trey	87496	Ellis	3	Competent	Low risk	59	20
21	Wilson, William	45671	Ellis	3	Competent	Low risk	47	18
22	Yopp, Hallie	34518	Ellis	3	Competent	Low risk	45	18
23	Young, Robert	87947	Ellis	3	Competent	Low risk	56	20
24	Avery, Steve	74859	Jones	3	Competent	Low risk	62	20
25	Baker, Joe	49824	Jones	3	Failed	At risk	15	12

CRT, criterion-referenced test; DORF, DIBELS Next Oral Reading Fluency; WCPM, words correct per minute; DRA, Developmental Reading Assessment

FIGURE 5.5. Sample Excel profile for a second-grade classroom, around September.

that the profile of the next second-grade teacher's class follows immediately after that of Ms. Ellis (see lines 24 and 25). This arrangement makes it easy to generate grade-level profiles.

A further advantage of using Excel is that columns can be added where needed, even for individual children. For example, in the case of Sarah Rudd, a poor score on the DIBELS Next Oral Reading Fluency (DORF) subtest warrants administering progress monitoring DORF tests on a weekly or biweekly basis. These scores could be built into the database for Sarah and others being monitored (though they could be tracked in other ways as well). It is possible to include progress monitoring columns for every child, even those not assessed; however, many of the cells would remain blank, and the grid would soon become unwieldy.

Finally, adding formulas permits automatic calculations of averages and other descriptive statistics. The time required to enter data into an Excel file is often offset by the time saved in computation. Without a doubt, a literacy coach with expertise in Excel is in a position to create many useful applications.

Coach as Cheerleader

Good literacy coaches look for the positive aspects of assessment results. This is not to say that they should ignore bad news, but it must be presented in perspective. There is often a silver lining in an ominous cloud. For example, in one of our schools, a cohort analysis indicated that the percentage of children at risk in the area of oral reading fluency at the beginning of second grade had risen slightly by the beginning of third grade. This was certainly not good news for the second-grade teachers. On the other hand, they were happy to learn that the average number of words correctly read per minute had risen considerably during the year. Of course, it had not risen sufficiently to bring the worrisome children out of danger, but the teachers' initial reaction was that no growth whatsoever had occurred. The assessment data led them to understand that their efforts had facilitated some improvement, but not enough; they knew they would have to increase attention to this area of the curriculum.

A literacy coach is in a unique position to stimulate achievement by working with individual teachers and groups. Depending on the circumstances, the coach will be in a position to encourage, energize, reassure, counsel, and console.

Coach as Booster

The literacy coach may be called upon to lead efforts to improve scores on high-profile, high-stakes tests. This is serious business because of the demands related to AYP, still a requirement of No Child Left Behind. Not surprisingly, many schools have developed creative and sometimes ingenious approaches to improving achievement scores. In the next section, we present several of the strategies commonly used to accomplish this goal. We want literacy coaches to consider these sugges-tions with a grain of salt; none of them will matter at all unless systematic, explicit instruction has supported children's literacy growth so that they can read the test.

IMPROVING GROUP ACHIEVEMENT SCORES

Standardized testing is a burden that most teachers bear resentfully. Such testing often has an undue influence on planning and it can detract considerably from the time available for instruction. It is a source of anxiety and frustration for teachers and administrators alike. Its validity is suspect, and its results can occasionally provoke unjustified criticism. For all of their shortcomings, however, standardized group achievement tests are not likely to be scrapped any time soon. A literacy coach can help a school make the most of a bad situation.

The suggestions offered here are made with this reality in mind. Most have been collected through interviews with practicing educators. Others come from the research literature. Together, they constitute what might be called a "survivor's guide" to high-stakes testing. Although there is no magic bullet that we can use to raise scores to the levels we'd like, there are nevertheless actions we can take to help ensure that scores reflect what students are capable of doing. The literacy coach can be instrumental in facilitating these actions.

Steps for Curriculum Alignment

If children are tested over knowledge and skills they have not been taught, the validity of the test is low, and scores will suffer accordingly. Making certain that the test reflects what actually happens in the classroom is the surest way to improve scores. This process of comparing the objectives covered by the test with those tar-geted by teachers is called *curriculum alignment*.

Fenwick English (2011), a long-time authority on how schools can narrow the gap between what is tested and what is taught, suggests that not one but three curricula are present in any school. The first is the *written curriculum*, the official set of objectives approved by authorities such as the district administration, the school board, or the state department. The second is the *taught curriculum*, those objectives actually targeted by teachers as they plan their instruction. The third is the *tested curriculum*, the objectives reflected in the group achievement test that students will eventually take.

The three-way Venn diagram presented in Figure 5.6 illustrates how these three curricula can dramatically diverge. When this occurs, the result will be depressed test scores—that is, scores that are lower than the true achievement levels of the students. To put this another way, their scores would have been higher had they been assessed with a properly aligned test. A curriculum that is well

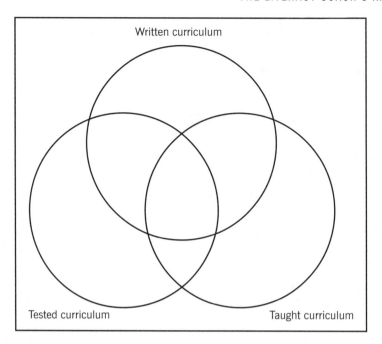

FIGURE 5.6. The three curricula to be aligned.

aligned will focus teacher effort and energy into the shared portion of the diagram, where what is tested reflects what is taught. Note that aligning two of the three curricula has been attempted in producing the state criterion-referenced tests and is a key goal of the new Common Core assessments being developed by PARCC and Smarter Balance.

Evaluating the Curriculum

Effective curriculum alignment is a two-step process. First, the written and tested curricula must be painstakingly contrasted. Objectives that are tested and yet have no counterparts in the official curriculum must be identified. At the same time, objectives that are embraced by a district but that are not tested must be rethought, at least in terms of the emphasis teachers are encouraged to place upon them. There is a danger in this process that the test will, in effect, "drive" instructional decision making. Of course it will. This is a reality with which educators have lived for years. Our purpose here is not to debate the wisdom of this reality but to offer ways of coming to terms with it. Bringing the written curriculum and the tested curriculum into alignment by identifying where the two do not overlap is the initial action we must take in doing so.

It is important to note that in the case of a test created by a state department of education—such as Florida's Comprehensive Assessment Test, Georgia's Criterion

Referenced Competency Test, or Virginia's Standards of Learning Test—this step is unnecessary. This is because the same authorities who establish the written curriculum have also constructed (or overseen) the assessment instrument. However, for states embracing the Common Core State Standards and then the new tests, the curriculum must be evaluated from scratch.

The second step in curriculum alignment is to contrast the tested curriculum with the taught curriculum. This is done by making a long-term commitment to ensure that what is tested at the end of the year is what was taught during the year. The suggestions that follow will help to accomplish this goal.

Creating Curriculum Maps

A *curriculum map* is a chart that begins with an objective to be tested, includes activities that might be incorporated into lessons, and suggests how the objective might be assessed by a classroom teacher. Perhaps no single teacher can create a comprehensive curriculum map for his or her own subject or grade level, but teams of teachers working together can construct such maps. The literacy coach can lead or facilitate these teams.

We caution, however, that it is not enough to create a curriculum map. If it languishes on the shelf, as we have often observed, the entire exercise will have been in vain. Teachers must use such maps in writing daily lesson plans, and the maps must be periodically reviewed and revised. They must become living, organic documents that actually inform instruction. If they are not, then the process is ineffectual and pointless—a waste of precious time that could have been put to better use.

Checking Curriculum Maps

A literacy coach should encourage teachers to acquire the habit of using the curriculum map to plan daily lessons. Each teacher should indicate the objective(s) to be targeted and should consider the activities and instructional techniques suggested by the mapmakers. Planning instruction, like planning a trip, is generally more successful when we use a map. Otherwise, we might not reach our destination.

Watching the Calendar

As the test date approaches, remind teachers to take stock of the objectives that have yet to be addressed in class. Because testing is usually done in March or April, there may be a number of tested objectives that will not be taught in time. Every teacher should make a "hurry-up" plan to touch on these objectives, even if they cannot be taught to mastery.

Steps for Making Sure Students Are "Test-Wise"

McKenna and Robinson (2012) distinguish between two types of test-wiseness. Evidence of the positive variety is seen when students use strategies that enable them to put their best foot forward, so that test results reflect what they are capable of. Negative test-wiseness, in contrast, involves taking steps to inflate scores so that they overestimate true proficiency. The suggestions that follow are intended to promote positive test-wiseness.

We encourage literacy coaches to share the following dos and don'ts with their teachers. They pertain specifically to reading comprehension subtests based on passages and questions.

"Don't Read the Questions First!"

Do not encourage students to read the questions first. They tend to make little sense without the context of the passage.

Stressing Inferential Questions

Make sure students understand that many answers cannot be located in the passages. Inferential questions are by far the dominant type used in standardized assessments, so getting this point across is critical. The passage will always contain the basis of an answer, even if the answer itself is not explicitly stated.

What to Do about Hard Words

When reading a passage on a comprehension subtest, students must avoid becoming bogged down on individual words. This is especially true of proper names. Tell them to keep reading and to try to get the gist of a sentence. Laboring over one or two unfamiliar words can cause frustration and may well prevent a student from correctly answering those test items that do not concern these words.

Going Back and Forth

When answering questions about a reading passage, students should go back to the passage actively. Make them realize that the idea is not to test their memories. It's "fair" to go back and ferret out answers.

Modeling the Process

Try modeling this process by using a document camera to project a passage along with one or more multiple-choice questions. Use a pointer or marker to indicate portions of the passage that pertain to each question.

Steps for Making Sure Students Give Their Best Effort

Discussing How the Results May Be Used

Test results are generally a factor in instructional placements, especially as students get older. A literacy coach might discuss the implications of doing one's best in terms of these prospects. Students who do their best will be rewarded by placements that are appropriate for them.

Counseling Individual Students

Identify students who scored extremely poorly last year, but whose ability as indicated by other data is clearly higher. Counsel these students prior to the next standardized test administration. If it is permissible, test them in small groups with direct supervision.

Providing Snacks

Provide juice or milk before testing and during breaks. It can be dispensed at a table in the hall. If possible, provide breakfast, but without syrup, doughnuts, or other sugary foods. Try getting one of your school's business partners to contribute the goodies.

Encouraging Students to Review Answers

Teachers should tell students that if they finish before time is called, *they are not through!* They should spend the remaining time reviewing their answers. Everyone should be working from start to finish.

Sending a Parent Letter

Make sure a letter goes home to parents prior to testing. It should stress making sure that children get plenty of sleep and have a good breakfast. A version you might use as a model appears in Figure 5.7. Keep the letter short; the longer it is, the less likely parents are to read it. Use a large type size and paper of an unusual color to attract attention. Sign the letters individually. Add handwritten notes where appropriate. Such a letter should also include the days of testing and the subjects to be tested.

A FINAL WORD

There is an old saying that you cannot fatten a cow by weighing it. Ironically, America's preoccupation with testing may actually threaten achievement by

Dear Parent,

    Next week we will begin our yearly testing. It is important for all children to do their best. You can help make this happen! Here's how:

    ✓ Make sure your child gets to bed early. A good night's sleep is important.

    ✓ Every child should eat a good breakfast. It takes energy to perform well!

    ✓ Have a talk with your child the night before the test. Stress the importance of trying hard.

                                   Sincerely,

                                  Your friendly literacy coach

FIGURE 5.7. Sample letter to parents.

causing us to devote too much time to test preparation and too much worrisome attention to the scales we use to "weigh" our students. It is for this reason that we offer some of the preceding suggestions about standardized testing half-heartedly. It is, of course, only natural to look for Band-Aid approaches to such testing—approaches that appear to hold the promise of improved results at little or no cost. And it does make sense for a literacy coach to lead the effort to revisit the school's policies concerning how this type of testing is conducted. However, screening, diagnostic, and progress monitoring assessments should not be viewed in that way; they must become essential to everyone in the school community to understand the needs of students and address them in instruction. Bear in mind that there is only one satisfactory remedy for low achievement scores in literacy: increasing literacy achievement. Teachers who are focused on this goal, and who employ instructional strategies known to be effective in attaining it, can be confident that test scores will take care of themselves. It is up to the literacy coach to help maintain this focus.

CHAPTER 6

Instructional Schedules

In this chapter, we present some sample schedules that educators at real schools have constructed to facilitate teaching and learning. Schedules are constrained by building-level realities, such as the number of classroom teachers, the number of intervention teachers, and the number of teachers for "specials" (e.g., physical education, art, music). It is unlikely that any one school's schedule can be transported directly into another setting. However, it is possible that elements of these schedules might be useful in crafting a schedule that improves opportunities for teachers and children.

Several issues must be considered prior to designing a schedule. None of these can be decided through examination of research; they are all potentially good decisions if they are right for the setting. One is the total length of the literacy block. We have worked with schools reserving anywhere from 2 to 3 hours for literacy instruction. Another is the flexible grouping strategy that will be used to differentiate instruction to address children's needs. As we mentioned in Chapter 3, we have worked with schools grouping within the classroom, within each grade level, or across the grade levels. All of these grouping plans can work; all have an effect on the master schedule. Another decision to make up front is what time will be used for intervention—the type of intervention that actually provides additional instruction in literacy for students with serious literacy deficits. Some schools choose to provide intervention during regular school hours, and they interrupt instruction in other content areas; other schools choose to extend time, either by creating after-school programs or by adding days to the school year. Finally, a decision has to be made about the ideal time and place for professional development and collaboration. Again, some schools choose to do these things during the regular school day, and others choose after-school hours. We frame our presentations of model schedules around the answers to these questions.

REPRESENTATIVE SCHEDULES

Fortunately or unfortunately, researchers have not identified a single best schedule, nor are they likely to. There are too many factors to consider related to the local context. In this section we offer some exemplary schedules developed in a few of the schools where we have worked. In Chapter 3, we identified the important considerations that should inform your school's policy about assigning children to homerooms and forming small groups for targeted instruction. The examples that follow are based on several assumptions:

- Every classroom teacher will teach reading during a protected block of time, though how long the block is and whether it is uninterrupted will vary.
- Instruction during the block will entail a combination of whole-class instruction and small-group differentiated instruction.
- Every classroom teacher will instruct children at more than one level of proficiency.

We will next examine two types of schedules, at the classroom and grade level. A coach must consider a number of issues related to each.

Classroom Schedules

We believe that the literacy block must contain a combination of whole-class and small-group work. Figure 6.1 illustrates this arrangement for kindergarten. We suggest sandwiching small-group work between whole-class segments. We have advocated for this arrangement elsewhere (Walpole et al., 2011) because it tends not to overtax the attention spans of kindergartners.

By grades 3–5, the instructional diet has changed. Phonological awareness has no place in whole-class or small-group instruction, although intensive intervention for a few students may be required. Decoding instruction is brief and limited to multisyllabic words except for small-group work provided for children who are still struggling. Figure 6.2 shows an example of a third-grade teacher's schedule in which an hour of whole-class instruction is followed by an hour for small groups. A 15-minute whole-class session devoted to writing instruction concludes the block. Another difference in the upper grades is more time for content subjects. In this example, note that afternoon periods for science and social studies are scheduled. We include them as literacy-related instruction because of the opportunities for children to read and write nonfiction and to study content-specific vocabulary.

Grade-Level Schedules

No classroom operates in a vacuum. Even when no interclass regrouping occurs (so that teachers serve only their homeroom children throughout the day), the

	Whole class
8:30–9:00	Calendar, morning message, interactive read-aloud Provide writing prompt tied to read-aloud Core selection
	Small groups
9:00–9:15	Teacher works with middle group Low group works with push-in intervention provider High group does independent work, responds to writing prompt
9:15–9:30	Teacher works with low group Middle group does independent work, responds to writing prompt High group does independent work
9:30–9:45	Teacher works with high group Middle group does independent work Low group does independent work, responds to writing prompt
	Whole class
9:45–10:30	Writing instruction

FIGURE 6.1. Kindergarten schedule that begins the block with small-group instruction.

Time	Classroom teacher	Time	Dimension
9:00–10:00	**Whole-class instruction**		
	Read-aloud	15 min.	Vocabulary/comprehension
	Core story	30 min.	Vocabulary/comprehension
	Multisyllabic decoding	15 min.	Spelling (Mon.)
	Spelling	15 min. (Mon.)	Decoding (Tues.–Fri.)
10:00–11:00 (60 min.) 15–20 min. each group	**Small-group instruction** (teacher) Core-based leveled readers	**Small-group instruction** (special ed. teacher) Phonics skills Sight words Decodable books	**Literacy work stations** (2 to 3 students to a station) Various reading and writing activities
11:00–11:15	**Whole-class instruction**	15 min.	Writing
1:00–1:45	**Science**	45 min.	Vocabulary/comprehension Content-area writing
1:45–2:30	**Social studies**	45 min.	Vocabulary/comprehension Content-area writing

FIGURE 6.2. Third-grade schedule with small-group instruction between whole-class segments.

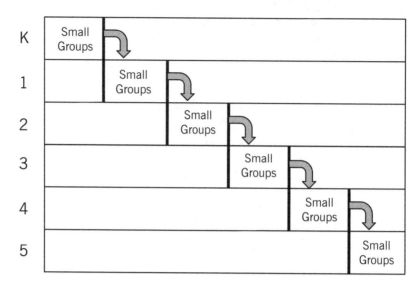

FIGURE 6.3. General leapfrog approach to the use of specialists.

schedule must account for the services of shared personnel, such as instructional assistants and intervention providers, for specials, and for lunch. We focus here only on the services of other personnel. In the case of intervention providers (reading specialists, special educators, English-as-a-second-language teachers, etc.), their availability is limited and they typically leapfrog from room to room on strict schedules of their own. Pull-out approaches present the same scheduling complications, of course. Figure 6.3 shows the general leapfrog schedule as specialists move from classroom to classroom. It assumes, for purposes of illustration, that the specialists will make visits of equal duration to all six grades. Their availability will determine when small-group work occurs within the block.

Figure 6.4 presents a first-grade schedule depicting how six classrooms share the services of one specialist and two assistants using a leapfrog model. The length of the block is the same for all five teachers (135 minutes for this school), but two of the teachers, with input from the coach, have decided to allocate more time for small-group instruction. Children have been assigned to the five homerooms using a controlled heterogeneous system. This means that there is a range of ability in each but clustering has limited that range to make it manageable. Teacher 1 has a gifted cluster and is the only teacher who does not receive the services of a specialist. Teachers 4 and 5 serve slightly more of the lower-achieving children and they have decided to devote more time to small-group work.

Figure 6.5 presents a similar example for second grade. As in the first-grade example, the length of the block is 135 minutes. Likewise, because of clustering, some of the teachers have less need of the specialist's services. Unlike the first-grade example, these teachers have no assistants. Note that Teachers 4–6 are the only adults present during the small-group time. When children are not in the

Time	Teacher 1	Teacher 2	Teacher 3	Teacher 4	Teacher 5	Teacher 6
8:15–9:00	Whole-class literacy	Whole-class literacy	Whole-class literacy	Whole-class literacy	Differentiated instruction (2 Assistants)	Differentiated instruction (1 Specialist)
9:00–9:45	Differentiated instruction (2 Assistants)	Whole-class literacy	Whole-class literacy	Differentiated Instruction (1 Specialist)	Whole-class literacy	Whole-class literacy
9:45–10:30	Whole-class literacy	Differentiated instruction (1 Assistant)	Differentiated instruction (1 Assistant)	Whole-class literacy	Whole-class literacy	Whole-class literacy

FIGURE 6.4. First-grade schedule for six classrooms.

From *The Literacy Coach's Handbook, Second Edition*, by Sharon Walpole and Michael C. McKenna. Copyright 2013 by The Guilford Press. Permission to photocopy this figure is granted to purchasers of this book for personal use only (see copyright page for details).

Time	Teacher 1	Teacher 2	Teacher 3	Teacher 4	Teacher 5	Teacher 6
8:15–9:00	Differentiated instruction (1 Specialist)	Whole-class reading	Whole-class reading	Whole-class reading	Whole-class reading	Whole-class reading
9:00–9:45	Whole-class reading	Differentiated instruction (1 Specialist)	Whole-class writing	Whole-class writing	Whole-class writing	Whole-class writing
9:45–10:30	Whole-class writing	Whole-class writing	Differentiated instruction (1 Specialist)	Differentiated instruction	Differentiated instruction	Differentiated instruction

FIGURE 6.5. Second-grade schedule for six classrooms.

From *The Literacy Coach's Handbook, Second Edition*, by Sharon Walpole and Michael C. McKenna. Copyright 2013 by The Guilford Press. Permission to photocopy this figure is granted to purchasers of this book for personal use only (see copyright page for details).

group with which the teacher is working at a particular time, they are engaged in independent work.

From these examples of scheduling possibilities, we now provide more detailed descriptions of several schools. It is important for a coach to understand how the local school context must affect the process of scheduling. In all of the schools we have visited, we have yet to find two identical schedules either at the classroom or grade level. There are simply too many factors at play. Our hope is that these extended examples will raise your awareness of how these factors can be accounted for in crafting optimal schedules for your own school.

PORTER HIGHLAND SCHOOL

Our first school schedule was designed by a team working at Porter Highland School (all school schedules are real, but the names are pseudonyms) to reform the curriculum of a fairly small school with very generous resources. This school had four classrooms at each grade level, kindergarten through fourth grade. Together, the team members made decisions that supported literacy teaching and learning by drastically changing their master instructional schedule. The first decision they made was that they would allocate 90 minutes each day for whole-class and differentiated instruction for all children, and then 30 additional minutes each day for students performing below grade level.

The team members realized that 90 minutes was not a lot of time, and this consideration influenced their decisions about grouping. In the kindergarten and first-grade classrooms, teachers had paraprofessionals who received professional development alongside them and who worked as instructional partners. Because a teacher and paraprofessional could work with two groups at once, the team members decided that within-class grouping was preferable at these grade levels.

In the second and third grades, paraprofessional partners were not available. Because of the short time allotted for literacy instruction, the team members chose a within-grade-level regrouping plan for these grades. Each teacher would spend 1 hour with a group comprising children with similar literacy profiles, from any of the homeroom classes. Three reading specialists would join each grade-level team, taking the three lowest-performing instructional groups in the grade level. After that hour, the children would have 30 minutes of fluency practice in their heterogeneous homeroom classes, and also a whole-class read-aloud to develop comprehension strategies later in the school day.

The school assessment profile showed that large numbers of children required intervention: Their initial literacy achievement was below grade level, so they were unlikely to achieve literacy acceleration without drastic measures. The team decided that kindergarten and first-grade children should have daily small-group intervention time, and that this should come during science and social studies time, protecting math instruction for all. For the second and third grades, the team decided that intervention should come during the school day for those with the largest deficits; again, it would come from science and social studies time, when the curriculum materials were too difficult to serve these children's needs well. They would not sacrifice all of their science and social studies content, though. The team members decided that intervention could only come three times each week, and that they would use content-area trade books matched to the state standards for science and social studies in their read-alouds. In addition, they decided to provide intervention opportunities for those children who were only slightly below grade level. They organized a late bus schedule for two after-school sessions each week to serve these children.

The team members were committed to learning together during the school day through team planning and with their literacy coach. They decided that they wanted to spend some of their professional development time in grade-level teams and some of their time as a whole faculty. Grade-level meetings were scheduled during the day, with each grade-level meeting weekly at a different time while children were in specials. The team members modified their weekly work schedule so that they could leave earlier several days each week, in order to make up for an hour of planning time devoted to professional development. They alternated this planning time with two sessions each month to work with the literacy coach and two sessions to work on curriculum mapping with a gifted education special- ist. Through grant funds, the school was able to set aside money to pay the teachers and paraprofessionals to stay for an additional hour three times each month; this time was reserved for whole-school professional development led by the literacy coach.

Figure 6.6 presents the master schedule for Porter Highland School. One aspect to notice is that the lunch schedule at this school was the same for all, because there was no cafeteria. All students ate in their rooms. Because of the decisions described above, creating the schedule was like solving a jigsaw puzzle. All the pieces must fit together. The team members started by considering the weekly professional development time. In order for that to work, each grade level had to have an hour of specials at the same time one day each week, and of course these times could not overlap because of the personnel. The specials began in third grade, first thing in the morning, and then moved down through the grades. Sec- ond graders went next, first graders were third, and kindergartners had their spe- cials at the end of the day.

Once the specials were planned, the focus was on creating the literacy block time. To allow the intervention team (three teachers in all) to work effectively as part of team-reading instruction, this block had to allow for different instruc- tional times in second and third grades. To trace the work of a single intervention teacher, then, the schedule enabled her to teach one small group at second grade for an hour, and then to teach another group at third grade for an hour. During the reading practice times, all children were back in their homerooms, which were heterogeneous in terms of achievement.

Finally, the team planned the intervention time. Since the intervention provid- ers were already teaching groups from 9:00 to 11:00, interventions could not begin until after that time. The three teachers assumed different responsibilities. One spent her afternoon with consecutive groups of kindergartners. Another spent her time with first graders. The third spent her time with struggling second and third graders, and also managed the after-school program for those two grade levels.

This schedule was a huge departure from "business as usual" at this school. In fact, in order to use time and personnel in more carefully planned and coordinated ways, all teachers gave up autonomy about when they taught what. The sacrifice of

Time	K	1	2	3
9:00–10:00	Reading block (teacher and assistant)	Reading block (teacher and assistant)	Team reading instruction	Specials
10:00–10:30	Reading block	Reading block	Reading practice	Team reading instruction
10:30–11:00	Recess	Recess	Specials	Read-aloud and writing
11:00–12:00	Math	Math	Read-aloud and writing	Reading practice
12:00–12:30	Lunch	Lunch	Lunch	Lunch
12:30–1:00	Intervention, science, or social studies	Specials	Intervention, science, or social studies (three/week)	Math
1:00–1:30	Intervention, science, or social studies	Writing	Intervention, science, or social studies (three/week)	Math
1:30–2:00	Specials	Intervention, science, or social studies	Math	Intervention, science, or social studies (three/week)
2:00–2:30	Centers	Intervention, science, or social studies	Math	Intervention, science, or social studies (three/week)
2:30–3:00	Intervention or centers	Intervention, science, or social studies	Writing	Writing
3:00–4:15	Writing	Writing	After-school session (two/week)	After-school session (two/week)

FIGURE 6.6. Schedule for Porter Highland School.

this freedom was worthwhile. The adults in the school learned to build a program by putting the needs of children first. The school attained full accreditation after 2 years.

McMILLAN ACADEMY

McMillan Academy, also a small school (18 classrooms, three each in kindergarten through fifth grade) made different decisions, and these decisions drove the

Time	K	1	2	3	4	5
8:15–9:15	Whole-class literacy	Whole-class literacy	Whole-class literacy	Whole-class literacy	Specials	Whole-class literacy
9:15–10:15	Differentiated instruction	Differentiated instruction	Differentiated instruction	Differentiated instruction	Whole-class literacy	Specials
10:15–11:15	Social studies/ science Lunch	Math	Specials	Math	Differentiated instruction	Differentiated instruction
11:15–12:15	Differentiated instruction	Science/Social Studies Lunch	Lunch Science/Social Studies	Specials	Math	Science/Social Studies
12:15–1:15	Math	Specials	Math	Lunch Differentiated instruction	Writing Lunch	Math
1:15–2:00	Specials	Differentiated instruction	Differentiated instruction	Science/Social Studies	Science/Social Studies	Lunch
2:00–2:30	Writing	Writing	Writing	Writing	Differentiated instruction	Writing

FIGURE 6.7. Schedule for McMillan Academy.

creation of a different master schedule. First, the team members decided to devote 3 hours each day to reading and writing. They made arrangements for after-school professional development (again by paying teachers overtime). Since their literacy block was long, they chose a within-classroom grouping strategy, with 20 minutes of teacher instruction for each group while the other group engaged in reading and writing practice. Most groups had a morning and afternoon session. Finally, they decided to use extended time options (intersessions in their modified calendar, as well as summer school) to provide intervention, rather than building it into the school day. The schedule they devised is presented in Figure 6.7.

BRADENTON ELEMENTARY

The team at Bradenton Elementary, a much larger school with seven sections at each grade level (kindergarten through fifth grade), made different basic decisions and created a different master schedule; this is presented in Figure 6.8. At Bradenton, time for literacy instruction included 90 minutes of differentiated time and 60–90 minutes of whole-class time. As a result, there was little time for other

Time	K	1	2	3	4	5
8:00–8:30	Opening	Writing	Writing	Writing	Writing	Writing
8:30–9:00	Literacy block	Differentiated reading instruction	Cross-grade-level regrouping	Cross-grade-level regrouping	Cross-grade-level regrouping	Cross-grade-level regrouping
9:00-9:30						
9:30-10:00						
10:00–10:30	Specials	Whole-class literacy instruction	Whole-class literacy instruction	Whole-class literacy instruction	Whole-class literacy instruction	Science/Social Studies
10:30–11:00	Lunch					Specials
11:00–11:30	Science/Social Studies	Lunch			Specials	Whole-class literacy instruction
11:30–12:00		Math	Lunch	Specials	Lunch	
12:00–12:30	Recess		Math	Lunch	Math	
12:30–1:00	Writing			Math		Lunch
1:00–1:30	Math	Science/Social Studies	Specials		Science/Social Studies	Math
1:30–2:00		Specials	Science/Social Studies	Science/Social Studies		
2:00–2:30	Read-aloud	Read-aloud	Read-aloud	Read-aloud	Read-aloud	Read-aloud

FIGURE 6.8. Schedule for Bradenton Elementary.

work: 60 minutes for math, 30 minutes for science or social studies, and 30 minutes for a content-area read-aloud.

Like the team at Porter Highland, the Bradenton team members chose different grouping strategies for different grade levels. They chose within-class strategies for the kindergartners and the first graders. For the older children, though, they chose cross-grade regrouping. They did this because they had such large groups of children functioning 2 or more years below grade level, and they had to serve them all with extended time and limited personnel. Taken together, the weakest-performing fourth and fifth graders had skills similar to those of an existing group of third graders. All of these children could be served in the same group, and then regrouped and moved as their skills improved. At the same time, these struggling older children needed to learn grade-level vocabulary and comprehension strategies; they did this during whole-class literacy instruction.

This huge commitment to literacy instruction made further intervention time during the school day impossible; extending the school year for struggling children was a more viable option. For teachers, scheduling professional development time during the day was impossible. Instead, the principal contracted with a group of seven substitutes to spend time learning a set of curriculum practices at each grade level, and to come to substitute on the same day every week. They spent the first 3 hours of that day at one grade level, while those teachers collaborated and had time for staff development with their literacy coach; in the afternoon, the substitutes moved to another grade level. In this way, each grade-level team had a 3-hour block of professional development time every 3 weeks. The fact that the substitutes were there every week integrated them into the school team. Doing so also cut down on wasted time and reduced the number of behavior problems. Less tangibly, it provided a loyal and experienced cadre of substitutes to address the need for substitutes on other days.

WHITE OAK SCHOOL

The principal and literacy coach at White Oak School had a big-school problem in a small-school setting: Their instructional day was so fragmented that teaching and learning were compromised. In this kindergarten-through-fourth-grade school, intervention providers (including Title I teachers, special educators, physical therapists, psychologists, and counselors) traveled between two schools, each with an independent schedule. This arrangement created a scheduling nightmare for the front office and a sense of helplessness for teachers trying to set up instructional schedules. The principal made a bold decision. He decided that all literacy instruction would happen at the same time—8:20 to 11:20—and that no interruptions would be permitted. He scheduled whole-class instruction, differentiated instruction, and intervention with reading specialists during those 3 hours, and asked all other intervention providers to use their morning hours at the other school. Although this plan was controversial at first and ruffled a few feathers during implementation, it was better for both sites in the end.

Another significant change came in the physical education schedule. The school had no resources for art or music; physical education was the only special. Each classroom was traditionally scheduled for 30 minutes in the gym twice each week. With no interruptions before 11:20, this would not be possible. Also, the tenured gym teacher would have nothing to do in the mornings. The gym teacher took matters into his own hands. He enrolled in a reading endorsement program through a local university and joined the intervention team in the morning literacy block. Then he doubled up in his own schedule, meeting two classes at a time instead of one, so that the children still had physical education twice each week. Because he was an excellent manager, the principal told us that the gym program ran just as before, and the children who worked in reading interventions with the gym-teacher-turned-interventionist were highly motivated.

TIME FOR TEACHING

The work that these (and many other) schools did at the school level made a difference in the instruction provided at the classroom level. Here is a snapshot. The schedules that follow (Figures 6.9–6.12) are displayed outside the doors of classrooms at Christiansberg Elementary School. Here there is a direct connection between the literacy coach's and principal's efforts to focus attention on using time wisely and the teachers' instructional schedules. School-level efforts make it easier for teachers to implement evidence-based instructional approaches. In Chapter 7, we describe instructional procedures that teachers at these grade levels would use in these precious minutes.

7:45–8:00	Announcements, pledge, calendar
8:00–8:30	Read-aloud (whole class) Writing in response to reading (small groups)
8:30–9:05	Phonemic awareness activities (whole class) Phonemic awareness activities (small groups)
9:05–9:30	Shared reading (whole class)
9:30–10:00	Recess
10:00–10:45	Math
10:45–11:15	Lunch
11:20–11:50	Science/social studies
11:50–12:30	Phonics (whole class) Reading decodable texts (small groups)
12:30–1:30	Literacy rotation and intervention (small groups)
1:30–2:10	Activity period
2:15	Dismissal

FIGURE 6.9. Kindergarten daily schedule: Christiansberg Elementary.

Kindergarten

The instructional team in kindergarten at Christiansberg includes a teacher and a paraprofessional partner. The two work together to divide the class into two instructional groups as often as possible (for writing, for phonemic awareness, for reading decodable text, and during the literacy rotation). The schedule, reproduced in Figure 6.9, allows the children to move both physically and mentally from whole-class activities to small-group activities. In the afternoon literacy rotation, the groups are even smaller. The intervention teacher comes into the classroom for an hour to work with children who are struggling, and therefore three adults meet with groups at the same time.

First Grade

The first-grade teachers have the support of paraprofessionals through 10:40, so that is when they do the bulk of their literacy work (see Figure 6.10). Compared with the kindergarten team, the first-grade team devotes more time to writing. As with the kindergartners, the school schedule allows an intervention teacher to come into the classroom for 1 hour—the hour used for fluency groups. During that hour, the weakest-performing children work together with the intervention provider, and the rest of the class rotates among the teacher, the paraprofessional, and independent reading practice.

7:45–8:00	Partner reading (take-home books)
8:00–8:30	Phonics and reading decodable books (whole class, small groups)
8:30–9:00	Shared reading (whole class)
9:00–9:40	Writer's workshop (whole-class mini-lesson, individual writing)
9:40–10:40	Fluency groups and intervention (small groups)
10:45–11:15	Lunch
11:20–11:45	Science/social studies
11:45–12:45	Math
12:45–1:25	Activity period
1:25–1:45	Recess
1:50–2:10	Read-aloud
2:15	Dismissal

FIGURE 6.10. First-grade daily schedule: Christiansberg Elementary.

7:45–8:00	Partner reading
8:00–9:00	Math
9:00–9:30	Phonics and reading practice
9:30–10:15	Writer's workshop
10:15–11:15	Fluency groups and intervention
11:15–11:45	Lunch
12:00–12:40	Activity period
12:45–1:15	Shared reading/read-aloud
1:15–1:45	Content-area reading
1:50–2:10	Recess
2:15	Dismissal

FIGURE 6.11. Second-grade daily schedule: Christiansberg Elementary.

Second Grade

In order to accommodate the rest of the school's needs, the second-grade teachers begin the day with math instruction. The schedule is presented in Figure 6.11. The second two blocks, phonics instruction/reading practice and a writer's workshop, are run by the teachers working alone. The fluency groups, which start next, are linked to the intervention time; again, an intervention provider comes into the room and spends that entire time working with the weakest-performing children. The teacher rotates the rest of the children through work with her and independent reading. Afternoon literacy time in second grade is whole-class, and the focus is on comprehension instruction, both in narrative texts and in information texts that reflect the focus on content-area reading strategies.

Third Grade

The third-grade team has the support of an intervention provider first thing in the morning, so that is the time for fluency groups (see Figure 6.12). As in second grade, the weakest-performing children spend the whole block with the intervention teacher, while the rest of the children engage in independent reading. There is still time for shared reading, when all children are working with the teacher from the third-grade basal anthology. Because many children have decoding needs, decoding and spelling are built into the daily plan. Science and social studies time may include text, either with leveled sets of texts on the same topic or with read-alouds from appropriate information text.

7:45–8:00	Partner reading
8:00–9:00	Fluency groups and intervention
9:00–9:30	Shared reading
9:30–10:00	Phonics and spelling
10:05–10:45	Activity period
10:45–11:45	Math
11:45–12:15	Lunch
12:20–1:10	Writer's workshop
1:10–1:30	Recess
1:30–2:10	Social studies/science
2:15	Dismissal

FIGURE 6.12. Third-grade daily schedule: Christiansberg Elementary.

Fourth and Fifth Grades

In order to make the best use of their limited resources, Christiansberg developed a staggered schedule for grades 4 and 5. Each of the two grades devotes 90 minutes to literacy and 60 minutes to math. The literacy time is divided equally between whole-class and small-group differentiation (45 minutes each). Figure 6.13 shows how the fourth-grade teachers begin their reading block at 9:00 and the fifth-grade teachers at 10:00. This arrangement allows the same specialist to provide interventions for students at both grade levels. Remember that the number of students whom we predict will need this instruction is very small.

Time	Fourth-grade classroom teachers	Intervention specialist	Fifth-grade classroom teachers
9:00–9:45	Whole-class instruction	Serving other grade levels	Math instruction
9:45–10:00	Differentiated reading instruction	Fourth-grade intervention	
10:00–10:30			Whole-class instruction
10:30–11:15	Math instruction	Fifth-grade intervention	Differentiated reading instruction

FIGURE 6.13. Fourth- and fifth-grade daily schedule: Christiansberg Elementary.

	Teacher-centered plan	Collaborative plan
First block	Whole-group shared storybook reading and writing	Whole-group shared storybook reading and writing
Second block	Small-group teacher instruction, with classroom assistants monitoring center explorations for other children	Small-group adult interactions, with all adults working in a specific center directly with children

FIGURE 6.14. Alternatives for PreK general scheduling.

PreK

Christiansberg's PreK classes have schedules that are distinctly different from those at kindergarten and above. Literacy experiences are of shorter duration and are scheduled throughout the day. Schedules ensure time for whole-class storybook reading and for guided practice in one-on-one and small-group settings. They also include time for play and other peer interaction, and they make it possible for all adults to engage directly with children as much as possible. Beauchat et al. (2010) offer two options for achieving these scheduling goals (see Figure 6.14). The first is teacher-centered; assistants help only with tasks and procedures. During small-group time, their task is not to instruct but to ensure that children are engaged and that they move efficiently among centers. The teacher alone provides language and literacy instruction to small groups. Consequently, there is not enough time for all of the children to receive small-group instruction. In contrast, the collaborative plan assumes that every adult functions as a "center." Christiansberg Elementary opted for this approach in its PreK classrooms because it exposes children to far more oral language experiences. This alternative also makes it possible to have more than one small group. Figure 6.15 demonstrates how each Christiansberg PreK classroom manages small-group time as the teacher and two assistants all take part.

	Teacher: Phonological awareness and alphabet knowledge	Assistant: Oral language and comprehension	Assistant: Writing	Centers: Creative play
15 minutes	Group 1	Group 4	Group 3	Group 2
15 minutes	Group 2	Group 1	Group 4	Group 3
15 minutes	Group 3	Group 2	Group 1	Group 4
15 minutes	Group 4	Group 3	Group 2	Group 1

FIGURE 6.15. Possible small-group rotation for three adults.

	Teacher: Phonological awareness and alphabet knowledge	Assistant: Oral language and comprehension	Assistant: Writing	Centers: Creative play
15 minutes	Highest achieving	Mixed levels	Mixed levels	Choice
15 minutes	Lowest achieving	Mixed levels	Mixed levels	
15 minutes	Middle achieving	Mixed levels	Mixed levels	
15 minutes	Middle achieving	Mixed levels	Mixed levels	

FIGURE 6.16. Possible small-group rotation for skills-based groups.

Of course, this rotation only works if the children are grouped in a logical way. Again, Beauchat et al. (2010) offer principal alternatives. One is to group them heterogeneously so that they move from one station to another as a group, regardless of assessed needs. The alternative is to differentiate based on skill needs. In this case, as shown in Figure 6.16, the majority of children play at centers while the teacher calls together a succession of groups with similar needs. Both planning and scheduling are more complex in this differentiated alternative, but Christiansberg Elementary elected to install it in all of its PreK classrooms.

A WORD TO THE WISE

Scheduling is important to teaching and learning. Seeing beyond the current schedule into all of the possible schedules is not easy. Visiting other schools, especially schools where decisions that affect the schedule (length of the literacy block, grouping strategies, times for intervention and for professional development) have been different, can open up possibilities. In the end, though, the realities of time, space, and personnel and curriculum in a particular building are what set the scheduling parameters. Investigating scheduling options is a fall task, making a new schedule is a spring task, and implementing a new schedule is once again a fall task.

In Figure 6.17, we restate the important questions that might guide your work. Answers to each question are important. If you have a very long literacy block, then a within-class regrouping scheme is easier to accomplish; there is ample time for both differentiated instruction for each group and grade-level instruction for all. If you have a shorter literacy block, consider the potential benefits of within-grade or across-grade regrouping. That way, you can provide differentiated instruction for all groups at the same time. If you will have intervention teachers moving into classrooms during the literacy block, consider stacking the blocks so that these teachers can work efficiently. If you want to provide intervention and professional

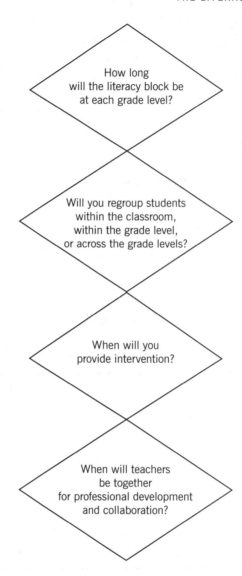

FIGURE 6.17. Scheduling guide.

development and collaboration during the day, then either stack your enrichment or specials so that teachers have planning at the same time at least once each week, or arrange for substitutes to be trained and working in classrooms on a regular schedule.

Take the time to think the schedule through, and do not consider the matter closed once it is implemented in the fall. Regard every schedule as a work in progress and realize that no matter how well conceived, it is sure to have rough edges. Being alert to how well the schedule is working is the only way to make meaningful improvements.

CHAPTER 7

Instructional Tasks and Procedures

In this chapter, we take the evidence-based instructional ideas from Chapter 4 and the assessments from Chapter 5 and use them to provide grade-level-specific snapshots. Many literacy coaches have been excellent classroom teachers, but few have experience at all of the grade levels they will coach; we paint the PreK–5 years here in broad strokes. We also briefly review stage theories in learning to read and spell. We do this here, before we discuss the selection of commercial materials in the next chapter. One of the difficulties literacy coaches tend to face at the start of their work is the large numbers of very low-performing readers in the upper grades. Stage theories are important because the only way to accelerate literacy growth for children who are behind is to acknowledge their needs—needs that are likely to be quite inconsistent with grade-level instructional materials.

We take the position here that literacy coaches should support teachers in providing some grade-level instruction to the whole class and some small-group instruction to groups formed and reformed by achievement. Although it may seem counterintuitive to say so, many teachers are uncomfortable providing direct instruction to small groups of children. Part of the reason for this may be that core program materials typically address whole-class instruction only, with very little attention to grouping or small-group instruction. In fact, in a review of seven basal series, researchers found fewer than 200 directions to teachers for leading small groups themselves and over 1,000 each for employing student-led groups or paired formats (Moody, Schumm, Fischer, & Jean-Francois, 1999). This same study, if repeated today, might find slightly different results; the most current editions of major core programs do make provisions for small groups. However, to our eyes, those groups are not targeted enough to truly address children's needs. Teachers may also shy away from small groups because they lack managing strategies. A vision of what should happen in whole-class settings and in small-group settings is essential to the literacy coach.

STAGE THEORIES IN READING AND SPELLING

What are *stages*? What does it mean to be in one stage or another? There are actually some specific conditions that must be met in order for any developmental trajectory to be characterized by stages. We must be able to identify a specific set of indicators that are found in all individuals in that stage; there must be a watershed break that separates one stage from another; and the differences between stages must be qualitative—individuals in a higher stage have to do something different, rather than just do something better or faster (Bjorklund, 1995). This is not to suggest that stages are so sharply delineated that a child may be in one stage on Tuesday and the next on Wednesday. Nevertheless, the distinctions are real, and a literacy coach's ability to anticipate and recognize progress from one stage to the next is crucial. Understanding the indicators is central to actually developing a program that both serves children's current needs and accelerates growth for those who are struggling.

Connie Juel (1991) has reviewed stage theories in beginning reading. There are some minor differences in the stage descriptions, but there is remarkable consistency across the theories. The general progression is this: Children move from attending to some aspect of the physical shape of words to processing some of the letters to processing all of the letters to recognizing most words automatically. At first, when children begin to read words, they focus their attention on only one salient aspect of the word (e.g., the picture or font as in reading environmental print, or some part of the shape of the word). They leave this stage when they have enough phonemic awareness and enough alphabet knowledge to focus on partial alphabet cues—typically, initial and final consonants. They leave this stage when they know and are able to use letter sounds, including the vowels in the middle, to decode words. Finally, they recognize familiar words automatically, with no need for decoding.

These stages are much easier to see in children's spelling. In Chapter 4, we showed you a selection of Kevin Walpole's early combinations of drawing and writing (or "driting"). You can also see his growing understanding of spelling. Bear and Templeton (1998) have identified four stages in beginning spelling. In the *prephonemic* stage, children engage in pretend writing, theorizing that writing represents meaning directly with no reference to sound. With rudimentary phonemic awareness and some alphabet knowledge, they are in the *semiphonemic* stage—theorizing that writing does represent sound, but lacking the skills to fully analyze words. At this stage, they might spell *monster* as "M" or "MR." With additional development, they move into the *letter name alphabetic* stage. At this stage, they use what they know about letter names (rather than sounds) to spell. They spell *wet* as "YAT," confusing the letter name *Y* with the letter sound /w/, the letter name *A* with the letter sound /e/, and correctly representing the letter sound *T*, because its name contains its sound. By the fourth stage, *within-word pattern*, they spell single-syllable, short vowel words conventionally and struggle with choosing correct long vowel markers.

Understanding these basic stage theories is essential to crafting a building-level program. We have focused our attention on developing knowledge of spelling stages as the foundation of our work with literacy coaches, because spelling stages are easy to see in children's work. We did this through a study group with the book *Words Their Way: Word Study for Phonics, Vocabulary, and Spelling Instruction* (Bear et al., 2011). Literacy coaches then introduced stage theories to their teachers by asking them to give and score a developmental spelling assessment (Ganske, 2000). The power of this type of data collection in exposing teachers to the very real instructional needs of their children should not be underestimated. Neither, though, should the fact that they may panic. In the sections that follow, we offer examples of particular instructional methods appropriate for readers at different ages and stages. As you read, consider the grade-level organization as the goal, but the developmental level as the potential reality. For example, when we describe instructional procedures appropriate for developing decoding in first grade, those same procedures are also appropriate for third graders whose decoding development is at the first-grade level—those children in your intervention programs. Also remember that although basic skills develop fairly sequentially, higher-order skills do not. Figure 7.1 represents this fact. Therefore, while we target basic skills directly, we also provide a context of rich language and read-alouds to develop oral language, vocabulary, comprehension, and structures for writing.

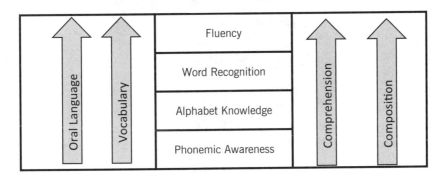

FIGURE 7.1. Sequential and continuous development of reading and writing skills.

INSTRUCTIONAL EMPHASES

Literacy programs involve days and minutes devoted to specific activities. Time matters for children (and teachers). Before we address specific instructional procedures, we want to provide an overview of how they might work together to provide a healthy diet of literacy instruction for children at different ages and stages. The new food plate (replacing the old food pyramid) is a graphic representation of our need to make choices about food. In case you're not yet familiar with the plate, the U.S. Department of Agriculture representation is provided in Figure 7.2. You can see that fully half of your day's plate should be filled with fruits and vegetables.

Instructional diets are similar. In our notion of a healthy instructional diet, we are influenced by researchers who got their start at the McGuffey Reading Center at the University of Virginia (e.g., Mary Abouzied, Donald Bear, Janet Bloodgood, Kathy Ganske, Tisha Hayes, Marcia Invernizzi, Darryl Morris, and Shane Templeton). They have long recommended that reading instruction be based on choices that together constitute a healthy diet for children. The components of this diet should shift as children's literacy skills increase.

Before we describe the particular instructional procedures we see as essential to literacy development at various ages and stages of reading development, we need to contextualize them within the broader structure of the literacy program. Figure 7.3 provides a preview of what we see as the major attention getters (fruits and vegetables) for instructional design at each grade level. You'll notice that the only element common to all grades is vocabulary. There are many ways to make vocabulary a priority, such as read-alouds and content-area instruction, and we take to heart the warning of Andrew Biemiller (2004). "Vocabulary levels diverge greatly during the primary years," he points out, "and virtually nothing effective

FIGURE 7.2. The USDA food plate (see *www.choosemyplate.gov* for more information).

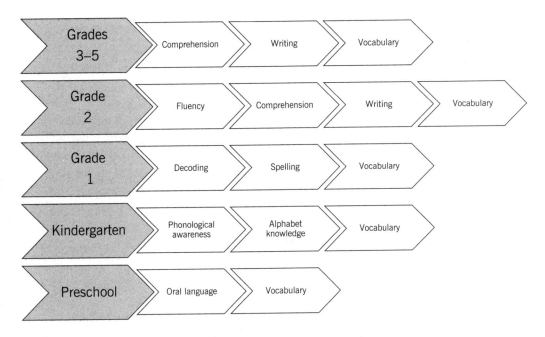

FIGURE 7.3. Important focus areas for each grade level.

is done about this in schools" (p. 29). It is often up to coaches to place vocabulary on every teacher's plate.

As on the balanced plate in Figure 7.2 though, all food groups except the most basic must be represented at all grade levels. The realities of classrooms and schools (as well as what we know about development of vocabulary and comprehension) demand that we situate some aspects of instruction in undifferentiated, whole-class settings. The realities of children's literacy needs demand that we situate other aspects of instruction in differentiated, small-group settings. We use our understanding of development to anticipate those choices.

In the sections below we provide our own "instructional diets." We have used pie charts so that you can see how things *should* change over time. Note that these proportions are not hard and fast, but they do anticipate the changes in children's needs over time. Think about them as big ideas and trace them across the grade levels. Does emphasis on oral language increase or decrease? When is decoding most important? How about fluency? Vocabulary is always important, but how can teachers think of its relative importance over time? Because time is a limited resource, we must make choices.

In the sections that follow, we provide our "short list" of instructional procedures especially useful in each grade level and also our predictions about what might be best tackled during whole-class instruction and what is more likely to require small-group attention. We can't be exhaustive here, but we can give you a flavor of how instruction must change over time. We use these criteria for assignment: If children at different levels of achievement can benefit from the same basic procedures, we assign the instruction to whole-class time; if children's achievement is likely to demand very different procedures, we assign the instruction to small groups. Note that children whose achievement is not near their grade level will benefit from a different diet, just as a person whose weight is outside normal limits may require a specialized food diet. A second grader functioning like a kindergartener needs more time in basic skills; a second grader functioning like a fourth grader needs less time in fluency. The way that we maximize growth for all is to be strategic about our emphasis during whole-class time and targeted during small groups.

INSTRUCTION FOR PRESCHOOL READERS AND WRITERS

The Common Core State Standards do not include preschool, and we must therefore rely on experience and research for guidance. There is much to do! Figure 7.4 presents an instructional diet that addresses the needs of these youngsters. Half the instructional time is devoted to vocabulary and oral language. Next comes writing and comprehension, followed by alphabet knowledge and phonological awareness.

Whole-Class Activities

Language- and literacy-rich preschool classrooms are organized around shared storybook reading, typically of big books. As we discussed in Chapter 4, these

FIGURE 7.4. Instructional diet for preschool.

literacy events provide a venue for print referencing, basic comprehension strategy use, and vocabulary development. Shared reading is the perfect time for developing concepts about print, as teachers physically mark their progress across the printed page and invite their young readers to join them.

Not all shared storybook readings are alike. The best ones provide children with a steady diet of oral language opportunities. Researchers have provided PreK teachers with two instructional routines to help ensure that focus. Teachers use CROWD questions (completion, recall, open-ended, *wh*-prompts, and distancing) to keep children talking (Whitehurst et al., 1994). As they read the same book multiple times in a dialogic reading format, they seize every chance to elicit language from children and to build on it. The PEER sequence (prompt, evaluate, expand, repeat) provides a structure. Teachers ask questions, listen to student responses, then use the PEER sequence to make their language more sophisticated (Crain-Thoreson & Dale, 1999; Dale, Crain-Thoreson, Notari-Syverson, & Cole, 1996).

Small-Group Activities

Preschool writing can be encouraged and scaffolded more easily in small groups. Preschoolers can sign their artwork, eventually learning to write their name. They can combine drawing and writing, using letterlike forms and then real letters. They can write pretend letters to friends and relatives. Teachers who engage with PreK children while they write are able to reinforce that writing is a communication form with a particular audience, and it is different from drawing.

Preschool phonological awareness can be fostered in whole-class poems, songs, and language play, but the real work is simpler to accomplish in small groups. Phonological awareness activities focus attention on the sounds of words rather than their meaning. With the help of manipulatives (blocks or chips or pictures) children can learn to segment and blend syllables, and onsets and rimes. They can sort pictures by beginning sounds. They can sort pictures of objects with names that rhyme.

INSTRUCTION FOR KINDERGARTEN READERS AND WRITERS

Kindergarten children enter the world of reading and writing, sometimes for the first time, in their classroom communities. They are eager to learn to read and write, but they come with very different entry-level skills.

Whole-Class Activities

Figure 7.5 displays the basic skills portion of the Common Core State Standards for kindergarten. Figure 7.6 presents an instructional diet for kindergarten students that will help them meet these standards.

| **Print concepts** |
| Demonstrate understanding of the organization and basic features of print. |

a. Follow words from left to right, top to bottom, and page by page.
b. Recognize that spoken words are represented in written language by specific sequences of letters.
c. Understand that words are separated by spaces in print.
d. Recognize and name all upper- and lowercase letters of the alphabet.

| **Phonological awareness** |
| Demonstrate understanding of spoken words, syllables, and sounds (phonemes). |

a. Recognize and produce rhyming words.
b. Count, pronounce, blend, and segment syllables in spoken words.
c. Blend and segment onsets and rimes of single-syllable spoken words.
d. Isolate and pronounce the initial, medial vowel, and final sounds (phonemes) in three-phoneme (consonant–vowel–consonant, or CVC) words. (This does not include CVCs ending with /l/, /r/, or /x/.)
e. Add or substitute individual sounds (phonemes) in simple, one-syllable words to make new words.

| **Phonics and word recognition** |
| Know and apply grade-level phonics and word-analysis skills in decoding words. |

a. Demonstrate basic knowledge of one-to-one letter–sound correspondences by producing the primary or many of the most frequent sounds for each consonant.
b. Associate the long and short sounds with common spellings (graphemes) for the five major vowels.
c. Read common high-frequency words by sight (e.g., *the, of, to, you, she, my, is, are, do, does*).
d. Distinguish between similarly spelled words by identifying the sounds of the letters that differ.

| **Fluency** |
| Read emergent-reader texts with purpose and understanding. |

FIGURE 7.5. Kindergarten basic skills portion of the Common Core State Standards (2010).

Kindergartners should surely spend some of their instructional day in whole-class activities. Ideally, teachers will ensure that those activities are *active*—allowing kindergarten readers and writers both the space and the opportunity to respond physically and orally, and to read and write together.

Shared reading in kindergarten is even more targeted than in preschool. For kindergarten readers, learning to track print is essential to later success in decoding (Morris, 1981). Kindergartners learn to track print by reading text that they have already memorized. For example, they may learn to sing a simple song, then learn to touch the words as they sing it. They can also learn to track print in specially designed texts with repeated sentences or phrases and/or with extremely supportive pictures. This type of reading of predictable text is easy to accomplish in whole-class settings by using big books or chart-paper poems and stories.

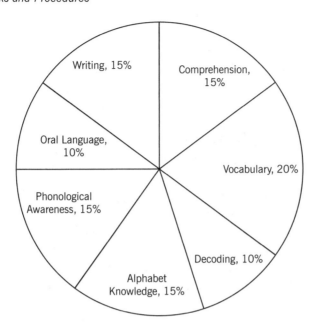

FIGURE 7.6. Instructional diet for kindergarten.

Vocabulary development is absolutely essential in the kindergarten classroom. Vocabulary development in kindergarten must not be confused with development of word recognition: Kindergarten children might learn to read the word *run*, but they might also learn the meanings of *prance, wobble, slink,* and *tiptoe*—words that they cannot yet read. The best source of words to teach children is the authentic children's literature that they hear read aloud. Beck et al. (2002) present an instructional framework for such vocabulary development:

1. After choosing a word from a story, write it and say it.
2. Ask children to repeat the word.
3. Explain the meaning of the word in terms familiar to the children.
4. Refer to the sentence context in the story as an example of how the word is used.
5. Provide another sentence context, outside of the story.
6. Support children as they generate their own contexts.
7. Ask children to say the word again and remind them of its meaning.

This simple procedure embeds what we know about vocabulary learning, reviewed in Chapter 4, within an essential component of the kindergarten day—the interactive read-aloud.

Interactive read-alouds are also the perfect place to develop comprehension and address the Common Core Standards in Reading for key ideas and details, craft and structure, and integration of knowledge and ideas. The key is to select excellent texts and then to plan for interaction (before, during, and after reading). After reading, retellings allow young children to develop their oral language skills, as well as the rudimentary knowledge of story structure that is so important to comprehension. Retellings are personal oral representations of text that has been read (and perhaps reread) aloud. For kindergartners, retellings must be scaffolded by the teacher (Morrow, 1984). Temporal prompts (such as beginning, middle, and end) or narrative prompts (such as who, when, and where) help children to formulate retellings that develop their comprehension skills.

Kindergarten children usually come to school without the alphabet knowledge necessary for writing, but they develop that knowledge over the course of the year. This does not mean that they should wait to write. At the beginning of the year, shared writing experiences (where teachers transcribe children's oral language, transforming talk into text) help children to learn the conventions of writing and to become engaged in the process. These shared writing experiences are also opportunities to develop phonemic awareness and alphabet knowledge, as teachers segment words and spell them.

Small-Group Activities

We have designed a set of small-group lessons for kindergartners to develop their initial word-recognition skills and the phonemic awareness necessary to read and spell (Walpole & McKenna, 2009a). The lessons last 15 minutes (well within the attention span of 5-year-olds). Figure 7.7 presents an overview of how they progress.

To develop basic alphabet knowledge, we are long past the days of a letter a week. Children need to learn to sing and track the full alphabet. They need to develop automaticity with letter names and sounds, presented in sets rather than one at a time. They also need to segment and blend the sounds that they are working with; we accomplish this by sorting pictures with a small set of beginning sounds, an initial sounds phonemic segmentation task. Finally, to ensure that these emergent readers develop a firm concept of word in text, they memorize and fingerpoint read a sentence.

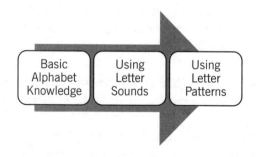

FIGURE 7.7. Small-group lessons for kindergarten.

Once children know their letter sounds, they have to learn to use them to read and spell. Full phonemic awareness (the ability to segment and blend individual speech sounds) is required. We develop this capacity through an approach called Say It and Move It (Blachman, Ball, Black, & Tangel, 1994). Once they have worked through sounds orally, with the support of manipulatives, we support their first decoding efforts, first modeling and then having them practice sounding and blending consonant–vowel–consonant (CVC) words. We also help them to read and spell those high-frequency words that they will need, regardless of their regularity.

Children who can segment and blend phonemes, and who can read simple words by sounding them out, phoneme by phoneme, are ready to learn letter patterns. They learn patterns by learning that sound and spelling are related (Bear et al., 2011); words that sound alike are spelled alike. For these children, we focus on spelling for sounds. Given words dictated by the teacher, children learn to use their sounds to produce their spellings.

There are many kindergarten children who can advance beyond using simple letter patterns, but we do not recommend acceleration of decoding. If you do have kindergartners with very strong alphabet knowledge, phonemic awareness, and decoding, we recommend that you spend time on spelling and writing. Those tasks are always challenging and allow kindergartners to enhance their understanding of the alphabetic system without going too far in the decoding curriculum.

INSTRUCTION FOR FIRST-GRADE READERS AND WRITERS

The first-grade year is the watershed opportunity for developing the essential foundational skills that underlie future literacy success. In order for the curriculum to ensure maximum success, every moment counts. Planned use of time and groupings is essential. Figure 7.8 presents the basic skills portion of the Common Core State Standards for first grade. Figure 7.9 presents a first-grade literacy diet.

Whole-Class Activities

Progress in reading in first grade can range from steady, incremental increases to huge stalls and leaps. Whole-class activities in first grade lay the foundation for many children's successful move to conventional reading and writing.

First graders must develop the knowledge and skills to understand and use the alphabetic principle to read and spell. Their decoding instruction, then, must target developing this knowledge and using it to read and spell words. The scope and sequence of instruction are both important; instruction must be clear, direct, and progressively more challenging. Unfortunately, research does not tell us exactly what the ideal sequence should be. Rather, it tells us that it must be explicit and systematic. Some characteristics of the ideal scope and sequence can be inferred

Print concepts
Demonstrate understanding of the organization and basic features of print.
a. Recognize the distinguishing features of a sentence (e.g., first word, capitalization, ending punctuation).

Phonological awareness
Demonstrate understanding of spoken words, syllables, and sounds (phonemes).
a. Distinguish long from short vowel sounds in spoken single-syllable words. b. Orally produce single-syllable words by blending sounds (phonemes), including consonant blends. c. Isolate and pronounce initial, medial vowel, and final sounds (phonemes) in spoken single-syllable words. d. Segment spoken single-syllable words into their complete sequence of individual sounds (phonemes).

Phonics and word recognition
Know and apply grade-level phonics and word-analysis skills in decoding words.
a. Know the spelling–sound correspondences for common consonant digraphs. b. Decode regularly spelled one-syllable words. c. Know final -e and common vowel team conventions for representing long vowel sounds. d. Use knowledge that every syllable must have a vowel sound to determine the number of syllables in a printed word. e. Decode two-syllable words following basic patterns by breaking the words into syllables. f. Read words with inflectional endings. g. Recognize and read grade-appropriate irregularly spelled words.

Fluency
Read with sufficient accuracy and fluency to support comprehension.
a. Read on-level text with purpose and understanding. b. Read on-level text orally with accuracy, appropriate rate, and expression on successive readings. c. Use context to confirm or self-correct word recognition and understanding, rereading as necessary.

FIGURE 7.8. First-grade basic skills portion of the Common Core State Standards.

from developmental research. It must include review of letter sounds from the kindergarten curriculum, a focus on reading and spelling short-vowel sounds correctly, mastery of r-controlled vowels, and work with long-vowel patterns. At the same time, first graders must learn to recognize and spell many high-frequency words with uncommon spelling patterns (e.g., *love*). The focus of the decoding curriculum must be on (1) using letter sound and spelling pattern knowledge to recognize unknown words and (2) building an essential sight-word vocabulary.

The decoding curriculum must include attention to the strategies that good readers use. The tricky issue is the role of context. The fact is that struggling readers do use context to guess what words might be; often they are correct when they guess. They use context to compensate for their lack of proficiency in decoding.

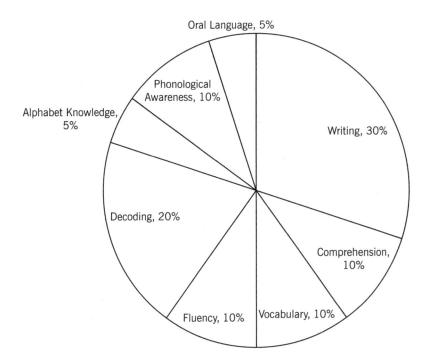

FIGURE 7.9. First-grade literacy diet.

As they become more skillful, context will be used chiefly to infer the intended meanings of multiple-meaning words. As proficient adult readers, we use context for this purpose alone, and not to guess the identity of a word without processing its letters. Therefore, *teaching* children to guess is not an appropriate focus for the first-grade decoding curriculum. The primary focus of the decoding curriculum is on developing knowledge of letter sounds and patterns and strategies for using them to read words.

First graders need to move from sound-by-sound decoding strategies to automatic word recognition. The only way for them to do this is to engage in extended reading practice. First graders must read and reread. Whole-class shared reading provides a context for this. In whole-class settings, teachers provide both support and opportunity for this rereading. They use different reading formats (such as choral, echo, and paired reading) to facilitate reading practice.

First graders can also develop fluency by reading and rereading books that are carefully selected for them. Any book that has been previously read in an instructional setting, or any book that contains phonics elements previously taught, is a book eligible for fluency work. Another way to build fluency for these beginning readers is to build in time for practice reading. In first grade, this practice reading is anything but silent; for all children, reading aloud to themselves to build fluency is noisy business.

For first graders, we combine vocabulary and comprehension strategies, because both can be developed effectively during a whole-class interactive read-aloud—if it is viewed as an active instructional context. Again, as with kindergartners, vocabulary and comprehension instruction for first graders is best situated within the read-aloud, because they can develop these skills and strategies far beyond their competence for reading text. In essence, we ask teachers to keep in mind that children learn to understand words and text structures orally so that they can read them later. For a complete treatment of how to plan interactive read-alouds for young children, see Beauchat, Blamey, and Philippakos, 2012. For a quick reference, and one that might be useful as a handout, we refer you to Figures 4.3 and 4.4.

Children do learn new words from listening (Elley, 1989). They can also learn much more about text and how it works from read-alouds, but only if these are interactive. Smolkin and Donovan (2002) have described the interactive read-aloud as a context for building comprehension proficiency in first grade, particularly when information texts are read aloud. Children who ask and answer questions, listen to their teacher modeling thinking skills, and make connections to other texts and to past experiences during read-alouds in which they are expected to learn new concepts are participating in a supported instructional setting.

You will see that we have highlighted the importance of writing in our first-grade diet. This is consistent with the rigor of the Common Core State Standards for Writing (2010). First graders write in school for many reasons. They write to learn to form letters easily. They write to practice segmenting oral language and representing sounds with letters. They write to practice spelling high-frequency words and spelling patterns. They write to document their experience. They write to demonstrate comprehension. They write to learn to write, and they write to learn to read. We are particularly interested in writing as a whole-class activity, because teachers can set the stage and then circulate and provide support as all students write.

Shared writing, described above in the section on kindergarten, is also part of first-grade literacy instruction. We encourage teachers to extend the writing curriculum in first grade. First graders who copy writing from the board are practicing letter formation and also learning how to copy. They are not learning how to read or spell. For that purpose, teachers can include dictation. Dictated sentences allow teachers to see how their beginning readers and writers are integrating their learning of high-frequency words (such as *the*) and phonetically regular words (such as *cat*). Writing instruction that includes a daily dictated sentence (e.g., "The cat is sad") helps first graders to use what they are learning in reading and spelling to write.

Dictation is surely not composition. First graders should generate texts to express themselves. They need support to do this. First graders can learn to compose their own texts in direct connection with their learning to understand the texts composed by others. During read-alouds, they can learn that stories have beginnings, middles, and ends. They can then use that same structure to begin to write their own stories with beginnings, middles, and ends. Writer's workshop, where children compose and share their own texts, should have its rudimentary beginnings in first grade.

Small-Group Activities

Because of its seminal importance in first-grade success, we focus our attention on developing firm decoding skills and strategies in first grade. We have written first-grade lessons, and they take 15 minutes per group (Walpole & McKenna, 2009a). An overview of the progression appears in Figure 7.10. For children with strong initial decoding performance in kindergarten, we begin with blends and digraphs. Diagnostic data, in this case from a decoding inventory, will provide you with the diagnostic information you will need to group children and determine their instructional focus. Remember that it might be one of the focus areas that we have anticipated in Figure 7.10, or it may be one of the areas highlighted for kindergarten in Figure 7.7.

First-grade small-group instruction can go a long way toward building competence and confidence in the alphabetic system. Ideally, children should master single-syllable decoding skills during the first-grade year. In order to do that, they have to master sound-by-sound decoding, even for blends, digraphs, and *r*-controlled vowels. They also have to understand that the system includes long-vowel markers, beginning with the final *e*, and then moving into vowel teams. While first graders are mastering this decoding content, they are vastly increasing their store of words recognized by sight; the act of decoding specific words and words with similar patterns can bring those words to the point of sight recognition (Share, 1995). In addition, these readers do need a continued instructional focus on high-frequency words, regardless of their spelling patterns.

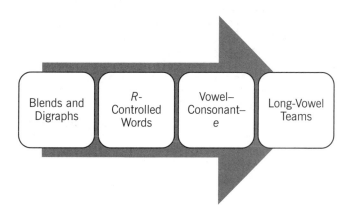

FIGURE 7.10. Small-group lessons for first grade.

In our first-grade small-group decoding lessons, there are five linked parts:

1. Phonemic awareness (segmenting and blending or isolation of medial vowel sounds).
2. Decoding (sound by sound or by pattern).
3. Spelling for sounds.
4. High-frequency word reading and spelling.
5. Decodable text reading.

We favor the use of decodable texts for beginning readers so that they can apply decoding skills just after they have been taught; they work with more natural texts during shared reading and with authentic texts in interactive read-alouds. Again, these lessons are provided in Walpole and McKenna (2009a).

INSTRUCTION FOR SECOND-GRADE READERS AND WRITERS

Second graders who master their single-syllable decoding during first grade need to consolidate and extend their learning through intensive fluency building. They also need to learn how to attack multisyllabic words. Figure 7.11 presents the second-grade Common Core State Standards (2010). You will see in Figure 7.12 that we have allocated much more fluency time for them. The second-grade year is largely a bridge between fluency and comprehension. Children reading second-grade material have large sight-word vocabularies, and they use them in texts of increasing complexity.

| **Phonics and word recognition** |
| Know and apply grade-level phonics and word-analysis skills in decoding words. |
| a. Distinguish long and short vowels when reading regularly spelled one-syllable words.
b. Know spelling–sound correspondences for additional common vowel teams.
c. Decode regularly spelled two-syllable words with long vowels.
d. Decode words with common prefixes and suffixes.
e. Identify words with inconsistent but common spelling–sound correspondences.
f. Recognize and read grade-appropriate irregularly spelled words. |
| **Fluency** |
| Read with sufficient accuracy and fluency to support comprehension. |
| a. Read on-level text with purpose and understanding.
b. Read on-level text orally with accuracy, appropriate rate, and expression on successive readings.
c. Use context to confirm or self-correct word recognition and understanding, rereading as necessary. |

FIGURE 7.11. Second-grade basic skills portion of the Common Core State Standards.

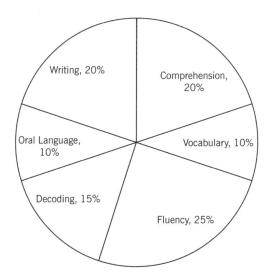

FIGURE 7.12. Instructional diet for second grade.

Whole-Class Activities

Fluency demands practice reading and rereading. During whole-class shared reading, teachers must have all children reading at once, and they have to make rereading meaningful. The trick is designing reading practice so that it is both engaged and efficient. There are many ways to do that. Peer-Assisted Learning Strategies pairs students heterogeneously so that they can engage in repeated oral reading and targeted discussions (Fuchs & Fuchs, 2005; Fuchs, Fuchs, Mathes, & Simmons, 1997).

A procedure called Reader's Theater likewise provides that practice and also focuses on oral reading performance in a way that is engaging to children. Reader's Theater uses scripts, with parts for individual readers. Children split into theater troupes and practice the parts of the scripts, switching parts at each rereading over several days, and then perform their play (without fanfare or costumes) for the rest of the class. This procedure has been used in many classrooms; Martinez, Roser, and Strecker (1999) have used it successfully to build fluency in second grade.

The texts that second graders read are different from the texts that first graders read, in that they contain new words—words that children may be able to decode, but which they do not actually know the meanings of. Vocabulary instruction has the aim of developing fully accessible, decontextualized knowledge of word meanings. In fact, knowledge of individual word meanings grows incrementally—from no knowledge to some knowledge to knowledge in context to decontextualized knowledge. Vocabulary instruction, then, is key to developing both children's vocabulary and their successful comprehension. For that instruction to be effective and efficient, it must include clear definition and context, chances for children to use the words, and discussion (Stahl, 1999).

Second graders also continue to learn concepts in science and social studies that are outside their decoding competence. These concepts are perfect targets for rich vocabulary instruction. Semantic maps, semantic feature analyses, and concept-of-definition maps all use graphic displays to indicate how concepts are related to other concepts and to prior knowledge (Stahl & Nagy, 2005). Meaningful, planned, coordinated knowledge building is essential to reading success as children get older.

Texts that second graders can read are richer contexts for comprehension than those they read in first grade; settings, plots, and characters are more fully developed, and there are more twists and surprises. One instructional procedure that we have found particularly useful to whole-group instruction in second grade is Question–Answer Relationships (QARs; Raphael, 1986; Raphael, Highfield, & Au, 2006). In QARs, teachers teach children to answer questions, and then to determine how they did it. They determine that some answers are explicit; they are "right there in the text." Other answers demand inferences within the text; these are "think-and-search" questions. Still other answers demand inferences between text information and the reader's knowledge; they are "author and you." And finally, some questions spring from text, but they are really about personal knowledge and experience; they are "on your own." QARs provide consistent strategy talk and procedures that can be used across text; this is the type of comprehension work that second-grade readers need.

Second graders can learn strategies in writing that actually develop their reading comprehension as well, and that link the curriculum in meaningful (and efficient) ways. Teaching story elements (e.g., setting, characters, events, problem, solution) directly improves reading comprehension. Clearly, story elements can be taught (and used) in both reading and writing. Therefore, writing instruction in which children are taught to use story maps to understand and plan to write stories develops comprehension skills that transfer to narrative texts written by others; this instruction will help them to meet Common Core State Standards (2010) for writing of narratives.

Small-Group Activities

Even in second grade, teacher understanding of word-recognition development is essential to addressing individual needs in decoding. In a typical heterogeneous second-grade classroom, especially prior to the institution of an evidence-based curriculum in kindergarten and first grade, decoding needs are likely to be broad. Second graders who are struggling require the small-group instruction described in the preceding sections for kindergarten and first grade. The need for assessment data for diagnosis, described in Chapter 5, will be evident here. Most normally achieving second graders will need some work with multisyllabic decoding, applying what they know about single-syllable decoding after determining syllable boundaries. Such instruction can be a very brief addition to the small-group lessons.

More common will be the need for additional work in fluency. Samuels (1979) developed the method of repeated readings for fluency building. Second graders need extensive reading practice in order to move from decoding to automaticity; they are also able to work effectively in pairs with minimal supervision. Repeated readings use short passages that pairs of children can read, albeit slowly at first. During each session, one child in each pair reads and the other tracks time, and sometimes errors. That same child rereads twice, with the other tracking the decreased time and the decreased number of errors. Then the partners switch roles. Daily progress across the three readings is documented on a chart. In a daily repeated-reading session, the teacher could pair with a different child each day, collecting assessment data. There are other models of repeated readings, but repetition is the active ingredient in all of them. For example, a stronger- and a weaker-performing reader might be paired, as in the Peer-Assisted Learning Strategies procedure we described previously. The stronger-performing reader reads a paragraph while the other listens. Then the weaker-performing reader reads the same paragraph, decoding having been supported in advance by the abler reader.

Second-grade readers need to work on integrating reading and thinking. They will do this best when they read new text that is challenging for them in a setting with support from a teacher and interaction with peers (Dowhower, 1999; Pressley et al., 1992). This small-group instruction can follow a very simple lesson structure, depicted in Figure 7.13. To learn more about it, see Walpole and McKenna (2009a).

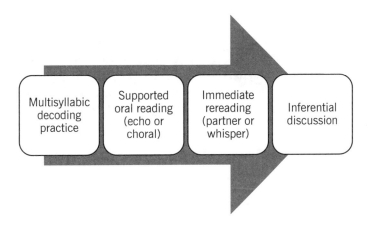

FIGURE 7.13. Small-group lesson structure for building fluency and comprehension in second grade.

INSTRUCTION FOR READERS AND WRITERS IN GRADES 3–5

Whole-Class Activities

Beginning in third grade, readers should be capitalizing on the growth in their decoding skills and their fluency to devote almost all of their cognitive attention to comprehension. At the same time, they are meeting increasingly challenging texts and tasks. Whole-class strategies can help them reinforce their learning and stretch it. While the Common Core State Standards (2010) include some attention to multisyllabic decoding for these readers, Figure 7.14 presents the Standards for fifth-grade literature, information text, and writing to highlight the high-level thinking skills that must be developed during these upper elementary years. Figure 7.15 presents our diet across these years.

Rereading is still important for upper elementary students. Because they are able to read more text in one instructional sitting, a planned cycle of rereading it before the next day's lesson will build both fluency and comprehension. Once students have attained grade-level fluency benchmarks, oral reading is unnecessary; however, if fluency is still a concern, paired oral rereadings can still be organized.

Upper elementary students see many new words in text, and they must learn how to learn new words during reading. Understanding word roots and discovering how to use them to learn new words (morphemic analysis) are important proficiencies for third-grade readers. Vocabulary instruction, then, should include instruction in sets of words related by meaning. For example, teachers can highlight the similar derivations of the words *unison*, *unicycle*, and *uniform*, and students will begin to ask themselves about other such possible relationships when they encounter new words. We have designed an upper elementary decoding curriculum that sequences these important morphemes as well as syllable types (Walpole et al., 2011).

The comprehension demands on upper elementary readers are great; the need for explanation and modeling of the thinking that happens during reading is even greater. Questioning the Author (Beck & McKeown, 2006; Beck, McKeown, Hamilton, & Kucan, 1997) is one procedure that directs attention to this during-reading thinking. Teachers ask children generic, inference-building questions during reading that direct them to make connections—both inside the text and between the text and their prior knowledge. Examples of these during-reading queries include the following:

- "What is the author trying to say here?"
- "Did the author explain this clearly?"
- "Does this make sense with what the author told us before?"
- "Why do you think the author tells us this?"

Comprehension instruction must include an emphasis on the cognitive work that readers do during reading.

Literature	Information text
Key ideas and details	
1. Quote accurately from a text when explaining what the text says explicitly and when drawing inferences from the text. 2. Determine a theme of a story, drama, or poem from details in the text, including how characters in a story or drama respond to challenges or how the speaker in a poem reflects upon a topic; summarize the text. 3. Compare and contrast two or more characters, settings, or events in a story or drama, drawing on specific details in the text (e.g., how characters interact).	1. Quote accurately from a text when explaining what the text says explicitly and when drawing inferences from the text. 2. Determine two or more main ideas of a text and explain how they are supported by key details; summarize the text. 3. Explain the relationships or interactions between two or more individuals, events, ideas, or concepts in a historical, scientific, or technical text based on specific information in the text.
Craft and structure	
4. Determine the meaning of words and phrases as they are used in a text, including figurative language such as metaphors and similes. 5. Explain how a series of chapters, scenes, or stanzas fits together to provide the overall structure of a particular story, drama, or poem. 6. Describe how a narrator's or speaker's point of view influences how events are described.	4. Determine the meaning of general academic and domain-specific words and phrases in a text relevant to a *grade 5 topic or subject area*. 5. Compare and contrast the overall structure (e.g., chronology, comparison, cause/effect, problem/solution) of events, ideas, concepts, or information in two or more texts. 6. Analyze multiple accounts of the same event or topic, noting important similarities and differences in the point of view they represent.
Integration of knowledge and ideas	
7. Analyze how visual and multimedia elements contribute to the meaning, tone, or beauty of a text (e.g., graphic novel, multimedia presentation of fiction, folktale, myth, poem). 8. (Not applicable to literature) 9. Compare and contrast stories in the same genre (e.g., mysteries and adventure stories) on their approaches to similar themes and topics.	7. Draw on information from multiple print or digital sources, demonstrating the ability to locate an answer to a question quickly or to solve a problem efficiently. 8. Explain how an author uses reasons and evidence to support particular points in a text, identifying which reasons and evidence support which point(s). 9. Integrate information from several texts on the same topic in order to write or speak about the subject knowledgeably.

(cont.)

FIGURE 7.14. Fifth-grade Common Core State Standards (2010) for literature, information text, and writing.

Range of reading and level of text complexity	
10. By the end of the year, read and comprehend literature, including stories, dramas, and poetry, at the high end of the grades 4–5 text-complexity band independently and proficiently.	10. By the end of the year, read and comprehend informational texts, including history/social studies, science, and technical texts, at the high end of the grades 4–5 text-complexity band independently and proficiently.

Writing standards

Text type and purpose

1. Write opinion pieces on topics or texts, supporting a point of view with reasons and information.
   a. Introduce a topic or text clearly, state an opinion, and create an organizational structure in which ideas are logically grouped to support the writer's purpose.
   b. Provide logically ordered reasons that are supported by facts and details.
   c. Link opinion and reasons using words, phrases, and clauses (e.g., *consequently*, *specifically*).
   d. Provide a concluding statement or section related to the opinion presented.
2. Write informative/explanatory texts to examine a topic and convey ideas and information clearly.
   a. Introduce a topic clearly and group related information in paragraphs and sections; include formatting (e.g., headings), illustrations, and multimedia when useful to aiding comprehension.
   b. Develop the topic with facts, definitions, concrete details, quotations, or other information and examples related to the topic.
   c. Link ideas within categories of information using words and phrases (e.g., *another*, *for example*, *also*, *because*).
   d. Use precise language and domain-specific vocabulary to inform about or explain the topic.
   e. Provide a concluding statement or section related to the information or explanation presented.
3. Write narratives to develop real or imagined experiences or events using effective technique, descriptive details, and clear event sequences.
   a. Orient the reader by establishing a situation and introducing a narrator and/or characters; organize an event sequence that unfolds naturally.
   b. Use dialogue and description to develop experiences and events or show the responses of characters to situations.
   c. Use a variety of transitional words and phrases to manage the sequence of events.
   d. Use concrete words and phrases and sensory details to convey experiences and events precisely.
   e. Provide a conclusion that follows from the narrated experiences or events.

Production and distribution of writing

4. Produce clear and coherent writing in which the development and organization are appropriate to task, purpose, and audience. (Grade-specific expectations for writing types are defined in standards 1–3 above.)
5. With guidance and support from peers and adults, develop and strengthen writing as needed by planning, revising, editing, rewriting, or trying a new approach.
6. With some guidance and support from adults, use technology, including the Internet, to produce and publish writing as well as to interact and collaborate with others; demonstrate sufficient command of keyboarding skills to type a minimum of two pages in a single sitting.

(cont.)

FIGURE 7.14. *(cont.)*

Research to build and present knowledge
7. Conduct short research projects that use several sources to build knowledge through investigation of different aspects of a topic.

8. Recall relevant information from experiences or gather relevant information from print and digital sources; summarize or paraphrase information in notes and finished work, and provide a list of sources.
9. Draw evidence from literary or informational texts to support analysis, reflection, and research.
   a. Apply *grade 5 reading standards* to literature (e.g., "Compare and contrast two or more characters, settings, or events in a story or a drama, drawing on specific details in the text [e.g., how characters interact]").
   b. Apply *grade 5 reading standards* to informational texts (e.g., "Explain how an author uses reasons and evidence to support particular points in a text, identifying which reasons and evidence support which point[s]").

Range of writing
10. Write routinely over extended time frames (time for research, reflection, and revision) and shorter time frames (a single sitting or a day or two) for a range of discipline-specific tasks, purposes, and audiences.

FIGURE 7.14. *(cont.)*

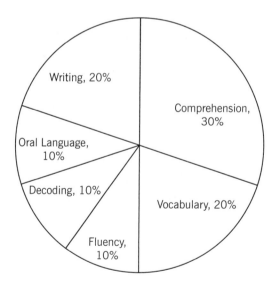

FIGURE 7.15. Instructional diet for third, fourth, and fifth grades.

Teaching children to write narrative, persuasive, and information/explanatory texts, using the common text structures that they will find when they read these texts, serves to develop strategies for both reading and writing. Third graders can write texts to compare and contrast, persuade, show a sequence or chronology, or show a problem and its resolution. If these text structures are taught with graphic organizers, these can be used both to understand text that students read and to plan text that they write.

Small-Group Activities

Children who can decode words in isolation, but struggle to read with adequate rate and prosody, need still more supported reading practice. The same cycle of multisyllabic decoding, teacher modeling, immediate rereading, and inferential discussion that we introduced for second grade applies to the upper elementary grades as well. The text will be more difficult, though, providing more opportunities to model the phrasing of complex sentences. Discussions, too, will be richer with more complex texts. In order to reach an adequate volume of text read each day, we suggest that students discuss the previous day's selection, work with multisyllabic words if necessary, then read chorally a new text section. They can reread it on their own before returning for the next day's small-group lesson.

Third graders may be able to decode, and to do so with fluency, and still be unable to really understand. One possibility is that they have inadequate knowledge of the meanings of the words in the text. Preteaching words most central to text meaning—using Stahl's (1999) frame of definition and context, children's use of the words, and discussion—is essential. This should happen before reading and after reading, especially for words central to the meaning of a narrative and definitely for core concepts in information text.

Teaching summarization is a high-utility focus for students who decode but don't necessarily understand. It has the bonus element of including both reading and writing, and it can be used with many different texts. The important characteristic of small-group work for upper elementary readers is that it includes instruction in how to summarize, rather than just a steady diet of summarization tasks. There are steps to summarization that can be taught. For example, Brown and Day (1983) suggest the following:

- Delete redundant information.
- Delete unimportant information.
- Replace lists with more general terms.
- Identify a topic sentence.
- Invent a topic sentence if none is provided.

A technique commonly taught for summarizing narratives is called Somebody-Wanted-But-So (Macon, Bewell, & Vogt, 1991). A child begins with the main character (*somebody*), states the character's goal (*wanted*), identifies the problem that prevents the character from immediately reaching that goal (*but*), and then tells how the character attempts to solve the problem (*so*). A simple summary of just a sentence or two can be produced this way for many stories.

Instruction and practice in summarization force deep processing of the text and the use of many comprehension strategies. They also result in student products that can be used to document the students' comprehension growth.

BUILDING A PROGRAM

Before we turn our attention in the next chapter to analyzing and selecting instructional materials, we want to stress that a knowledge of the instructional implications of research (which we have reviewed in Chapter 4) and an understanding of the ways that it can play out across the elementary grades (which we have described here) are essential for the literacy coach. Literacy coaches must be informed consumers themselves, and they must be creative and responsive leaders through the very difficult tasks of addressing student and teacher needs by selecting materials likely to support both. As we focus on that task in the next chapter, we caution literacy coaches to bring information from their reading so far and from their experience with children and teachers to the task ahead.

CHAPTER 8

Selecting Materials and Programs

In the first edition of this book, we offered advice about making prudent decisions when faced with the task of adopting a core program. In our experience since, we have found that few coaches enjoy the opportunity to make such choices, although they may serve on district-level selection committees. They are therefore on the receiving end of these decisions and must coach in the reality that a core program will be the mainstay of instruction. Consequently, whether one is selecting a core or helping teachers implement it, our advice remains the same—it is essential to understand how it works. This chapter offers suggestions for sizing up a core for either purpose, whether selecting or implementing. Toward that end, we believe it is important to have an idea of how core programs got to be what they are, for they are the product of many decisions through the years. And so we begin with a brief history lesson. (If you're over a hundred, feel free to skip it.)

A BRIEF HISTORY OF CORE PROGRAMS

Core programs were once referred to as basal series. The word *basal* denotes a sequence of activities that progresses from easy to difficult. The basic idea was that each child would be placed at the appropriate point on this spectrum and thereafter progress through the remainder of the sequence. For example, a new student would be preassessed using a placement test. He or she would then be placed in an appropriate reader and exposed to the corresponding instructional activities. The assumption behind a basal system was that the individual teacher had several levels available and that once an appropriate student placement was made, all easier objectives must have been accomplished and need not be repeated. In other words, a basal level had been established as a starting point for the new student.

This is the same rationale that is used in basal testing, such as intelligence measures and individually administered achievement tests. The examiner rarely starts with the easiest item, because doing so would take far too much time. This is also the idea behind a basal thermometer used to take a patient's temperature. Such a thermometer does not extend downward beyond a certain level, because it would be pointless to include temperatures below the range of living people. The manufacturer of such a thermometer simply assumes that a reasonable starting point can be set above a certain level.

The first multilevel series—clearly the forerunner of the modern basal reading series—was published by Noah Webster in 1783 and was eventually titled the *American Spelling Book* (Smith, 2002). It had three levels (beginning, intermediate, and advanced). It was used for teaching reading as well as spelling, for Webster saw spelling as a key to teaching children how to read. This series sold an amazing 24 million copies. Its moralistic tone is illustrated by the following excerpt:

> Be a good child; mind your book; love your school; and strive to learn.
>
> Tell no tales; call no ill names; you must not lie, nor swear, nor cheat, nor steal.
>
> Play not with bad boys.
>
> Play no tricks on those that sit next to you; for if you do, good boys will shun you as they would a dog they knew would bite them.

Competing series such as the *Christmas School Primer* soon appeared, and all were similar to Webster's.

During the interval from 1840 to 1880, the first reading series that contained one book for each grade appeared. This was a natural development, given the adoption in the United States of the graded school system that began in Germany. The emphasis on patriotism diminished during these years, but the moralistic flavor remained. Illustrations were greatly improved because of advances in the technology of printing.

The famous McGuffey Readers appeared between 1836 and 1844 and dominated the latter half of the 19th century. The last editions appeared between 1896 and 1907. The McGuffey Readers were the first carefully defined and graded series. The religious tone persisted, but the literary quality of the selections was generally improved. The orientation of the McGuffey Readers leaned heavily in the direction of systematic phonics instruction. However, this perspective was hotly contested even in that early era. Horace Mann, for example, opposed a decoding emphasis and once referred to letters as "skeleton-shaped, bloodless, ghostly apparitions" (cited in Adams, 1990, p. 22). During this time period, Josiah Bumstead developed a series of readers based on the whole-word, or "look–say," methodology advocated by Mann and others. Educators for the first time had choices of materials based on the pedagogy they preferred.

During the 1880s, the first supplementary materials appeared; by the turn of the 20th century, supplementary materials were becoming more prevalent as adjuncts to the individual student's reading book. Practice exercises to be done along with the reading of stories were notable in such programs as the Beacon Readers (1912–1922), produced by Ginn and Company. The 1920s brought the inclusion of specific, well-constructed teacher's manuals to accompany the children's reading books. There was also a change in the literature from predominantly fantasy-oriented fiction to nonfiction and realistic historical fiction. The expansion of supplemental materials continued during this period.

In the 1930s, a trend toward reducing the difficulty level of vocabulary and including more repetition of new words in introductory books began. In the 1940s, formal reading readiness programs became common components of reading series. More differentiation of the difficulty levels of the readers meant the inclusion of more books in a series. The artwork presented to children during this period was greatly improved and offered more varied and vivid color. The device of using story characters, like Dick and Jane, who recurred through the levels of the series was introduced during this period of time.

During the 1940s, the market-leading Scott, Foresman series (featuring Dick and Jane) emphasized a look–say (whole-word) approach. This perspective was evident in the limited phonics materials the series offered, and also in the repetition of high-frequency words. Here's a sample from the primer *The New Fun with Dick and Jane* (Gray, Artley, & Arbuthnot, 1951, pp. 6–7):

> Dick said, "Look, look.
> Look up.
> Look up, up, up."
> Jane said, "Run, run.
> Run, Dick, run.
> Run and see."

In this passage of only 20 words, *run* occurs five times, and *look* and *up* each occur four times.

Phonics continued to be back-burnered until Cold War fears led to a reexamination of the entire educational system. The *Saturday Evening Post* published critical articles with titles such as "Can Ivan Read Better Than Johnny?" (Trace, 1961). Rudolph Flesch (1955), in his best-selling book *Why Johnny Can't Read*, placed the blame squarely on too little phonics instruction. In consequence, the 1960s saw a groundswell of phonics programs and a renewed emphasis on phonics within basal series. Some series, called *linguistic readers* (merely because their authors happened to be linguists), strictly controlled vocabulary, limiting the words a child saw to those that were regular and decodable. Irregular words (such as *of, have, come,* and *said*) had to be put off until the basics of phonics were mastered. This led to some cumbersome stories. Here's an example from a 1980 *Merrill Reader,* cited in Auckerman (1987):

Nat is a cat.
Is Nat a cat?
Nat is a fat cat.

Despite evidence of the effectiveness of these materials, they tended to be boring and tedious. In addition, new theories of the reading process, introduced in the late 1960s by Kenneth Goodman and Frank Smith, challenged once again the importance of phonics. Basal publishers responded by removing vocabulary controls, so that far more difficult stories appeared in primary-level readers. Here's an excerpt from the 1981 Scott, Foresman primer (Jennings & Prince, 1981, pp. 8–9; published exactly 30 years after the excerpt from *The New Fun with Dick and Jane* quoted above):

One time there was a mother bird.
She had three little birds.
She looked after her little ones.
She found good things to eat.
She found good things to drink.
She would sing to her little birds.

Note that the vocabulary is more extensive. The repetition of words continues in this primer, but is subtler and aesthetically far more pleasing.

With the rise of the whole-language movement of the late 1980s and early 1990s, phonics was further minimized. Policy mandates in both California and Texas required adoption of reading materials consisting of unedited, authentic children's literature. Basal series were dominated by literature, and some were little more than anthologies. During the 1990s, however, it had become clear that basals and the methods they espoused were not successfully addressing the colossal reading problem faced by the United States as a nation. The basals of today employ far more decodable text, and they champion methods that have been empirically validated through scientific research. Their emphasis on phonics is strong, systematic, and sequential.

If you're interested in learning more about the history of reading materials, *American Reading Instruction,* by Nila Banton Smith (2002), provides a retrospective through the 1950s. James Hoffman (2002) tells the text story through the rest of the 20th century, and Peter Dewitz and his colleagues provide an overview of recent developments (Dewitz, Leahy, Jones, & Maslin Sullivan, 2010). Finally, the History of Literacy special-interest group of IRA maintains a website that may be of interest as well (*www.historyliteracy.org*).

PRESENT-DAY CORE PROGRAMS

Starting in the early 1990s, children were no longer placed in basal readers according to their instructional levels. Since that time, all children have been placed in the grade-level reader and the whole class reads the same selection each week. This was a major policy shift and it made the term *basal* instantly obsolete. That is why the term *core program* is now more appropriate. Figure 8.1 summarizes the key differences between the two types of programs.

But is it really a good idea to ask children who are reading considerably below average to read a grade-level selection each week? Even with high levels of teacher support, such a policy has been questioned by some teachers. Wouldn't it be better to rely on a system through which children are always matched to books based on their instructional reading level? Teaching would then occur in the sweet spot between material that is too easy and material that is frustrating. This is the conventional argument, of course, and it is quite plausible. It was the basis for assigning children to basals before the 1990s, and it is currently the basis for choosing leveled books in guided reading. But the argument has two major problems (Shanahan, 2011). One is that research has shown that children make more progress when they are pushed to engage in challenging text. This is not to say there are no limits—some text will be out of reach (and no doubt frustrating) no matter what

Before the 1990s	1990s to the present
Each child was assigned to a basal level corresponding to his or her estimated instructional level.	Each child is assigned to the grade-level book, which is used for whole-class instruction.
Differentiation occurred in all areas, because of the scope and sequence of the assigned level.	Differentiation is facilitated by means of a narrow range of leveled books, at, below, and above level.
Children read only the anthology selections for the level to which they were assigned.	Children read the grade-level anthology selection and are supported through multiple readings during the week.
Teachers relied heavily on workbooks.	Teachers rely less on workbooks.
Small groups were formed according to basal level.	Small groups are formed based (at least to some extent) on assessments.
Small groups tended to permanent.	Small groups are more flexible.

FIGURE 8.1. Core programs before and since the early 1990s.

steps are taken to make it understandable. The key is to aim higher than we have in the past, by choosing texts that are challenging but not frustrating. This is the rationale behind the use of core selections at grade level for all of the students in a classroom. The second problem with the comfort zone of the instructional level, as conventionally defined, is that the Common Core State Standards (2010) insist on more demanding texts. Coaches in Common Core states can point to the use of a core's grade-level selections as one means of ensuring that children are exposed to text of sufficient complexity for them to make real growth.

Dewitz et al. (2010) identify the year 2006 as the most recent turning point in core rationale. Prior to then, little attention was given to differentiation. Since then, teachers receive more direction about how to use the limited number of leveled books that come with each grade level. The problem, however, is that differentiation is mainly a matter of matching children with books. Other than that, there is little difference in the kind of instruction they receive. "The lessons do not noticeably differentiate tasks," these researchers concluded (p. 152). Dewitz et al. believe that the nationwide emphasis on RTI has prompted core publishers to attend more closely to differentiation. We agree, and for this reason we expect to see still more elaborate small-group guidance as well as more intervention materials in the next few editions of the major core programs. When we discuss RTI in the next chapter, we describe its relationship to the core program.

TODAY'S CORE COMPONENTS

Before we offer a system for choosing materials, we want to help you sort through the components of a typical core program. Like the parts of an automobile, some of these components are standard equipment, while others are options that can be purchased at additional cost. And, as with an automobile purchase, wise selection and combination of these components require research.

Student Anthologies

Materials for students to read are organized into a sequence of progressively difficult readers. Each reader is an anthology of selections chosen to represent a variety of genres and to be of high interest to children at a given grade level. One of the issues confronting core publishers is how many readers to include in the series. Traditionally, the following organizational pattern has been used:

Grade 1:   Three preprimers, one primer, and a first reader

Grade 2:   A 2-1 reader and a 2-2 reader (for first and second semesters)

Grade 3:   A 3-1 reader and a 3-2 reader (for first and second semesters)

Grades 4–8: A single reader per year

Teacher's Editions

A teacher's edition accompanies each student reader in the series. It provides suggestions about ways to present a selection, possible questions to ask, and activities in which to engage the students. Some programs are highly prescriptive, and the teacher's edition may provide detailed scripts of what the teacher is to say at all times. Scripting has become an issue of contention between those who argue that many teachers are ill prepared for the task of using core materials and others who argue that scripting has the effect of deprofessionalizing ("deskilling") teachers. We will address this issue later.

Practice Materials

Every core program offers student workbooks and reproducible masters that correspond to the reading selections. There is generally a wide variety of these materials, and the publisher's intent is not that all of them be used, but that they be viewed as a "smorgasbord" of possibilities. Our view is that materials may provide a kind of safety net but that in general coaches should repeat a simple mantra: *the fewer worksheets, the better.* And repeat it over and over.

Scope and Sequence

Each core is based on a system of educational objectives that are carefully sequenced from the most basic to the most sophisticated. The range of these objectives is referred to as the *scope*, whereas the order of the objectives is the *sequence*. Each commercial core offers a scope-and-sequence chart that spans the various grade levels and provides a master blueprint of the progress children should be making.

The scope and sequence of objectives is broken into several strands. These include a comprehension strand, a word-recognition strand, a study skills strand, a fluency strand, and others. A teacher at a particular grade level may be largely unfamiliar with the portions of the scope and sequence associated with other grade levels. It is up to the coach to gain an awareness of how the grade levels mesh together.

Software

Every core publisher now offers software closely aligned with the reading selections that children encounter. These programs provide a variety of experiences, often in game format, as a means of reinforcing the skills developed through the basal series. Purchasing options may involve housing the software on a local area network or allowing subscription access online, so that teachers can use it as desired. Some systems offer record-keeping and assessment features as well. Core publishers have a great deal of competition in the digital age, and it may be that online subscriptions (e.g., Reading a–z) are a cheaper option.

Resources for English Language Learners

Because of changes in the nation's demographics, core publishers are providing additional guidance to help teachers meet the challenge of English language learners. This guidance often takes the form of a separate manual containing suggestions for how to scaffold instruction.

Accessory Components

Every program offers optional components, such as wall charts, flash cards, letter cards, transparencies, big books, center activities, resources for parents, SMARTBoard and tablet apps, and other niceties that may make a teacher's life easier (if they are easy to organize and use) or harder (if they are cumbersome or superfluous to instructional goals). These components may be purchased or provided as part of the price of the student editions.

Decodable Books

Core programs typically offer decodables at kindergarten and first grade that reflect the decoding instruction in the program. These books are different from their trade book cousins, in that they are not meant to represent the full literary experience. They are constrained by the scope and sequence for word recognition of the curriculum. They are used for children to practice their decoding skills in a carefully designed context. Decodables are another area in which competition has brought down prices and provided affordable options outside the core.

Trade Books

Many series now offer sets of trade books that teachers may wish to use in going beyond the anthologized selections. *Trade books* are simply full-text pieces of children's literature just as they are sold in a bookstore. They are typically offered as classroom libraries (for students to read on their own) or read-aloud libraries (for teachers to use to support themes in a series).

Leveled Books

Leveled books were inspired by the remedial first-grade tutoring program Reading Recovery, and they represent a sequence of progressively difficult trade books. Obviously, this is exactly what a basal series was originally designed to do. However, leveled books are distinct from student readers in two important respects. First, leveled books represent many more levels. They are chosen on the basis of the text demands (readability), the illustrations, and other subjective factors. Whereas the traditional core comprises five readers at grade one, a sequence of leveled books may include as many as 10 levels. Second, leveled books are short paperbacks rather than hefty anthologies. Each lesson takes children from the beginning to the end of a single leveled book. They are easy to house in sets, and some schools have created a room for leveled books so that the teachers can share classroom sets. Leveled books are expensive, however, and they can add considerably to the cost of adoption.

A simpler (and cheaper) form of text leveling is a common middle ground in today's core programs. For each week's lesson, three sets of leveled books are included—one for students below grade level, one for students on grade level, and one for students above grade level. These books have a common theme related to the core story, and they typically repeat some common vocabulary. They are meant to be used in small groups, across the week. However, as we mentioned earlier, the instruction for each group is the same. It combines fluency, vocabulary, and comprehension.

PROS AND CONS OF A CORE PROGRAM

We are convinced that the arguments in favor of adopting a core program out-weigh those against it. The following description of what coaches and other lit-eracy leaders should expect from a core gives a fair idea of just how comprehensive such a program can be:

> Literacy leaders should look for high-quality research-based core reading programs that are integrative and balanced so that the books and materials associated with it work together to provide an instructional program that can serve all readers. The cur-riculum should align with the district's standards and contain solid core instruction. In addition, it should include instructional materials for students who need additional support and intervention from the teacher as well as those who would benefit from acceleration. Materials should include decodable and high-interest trade books acces-sible to various readers. (Dole & Nelson, 2012, p. 157)

The fact that core programs are, first and foremost, commercial products is in many ways an advantage in assuring these qualities. The competition to provide them has resulted in a healthy process of creativity through the years. On the other hand, the commercial nature of core programs has made their publishers keenly aware of market demands, and those demands have sometimes been driven by fads rather than findings.

At present, however, we feel that core programs offer a set of advantages that are hard to dispute. Tim Shanahan (2008) summarizes these advantages persua-sively. A core helps to ensure that instruction is thorough and explicit. It also lends coherence to instruction from classroom to classroom and grade to grade. A core obviously reduces (without eliminating) the demands of planning. The common set of materials and expectations provided by a core offers opportunities for profes-sional development that would not be possible if every teacher were moving to the beat of a different drummer. This argument may be strongest in inner-city schools, where the standardization a core affords is one means of offsetting inequities of access that are so commonplace. Finally, having a well-organized core in place means that not every teacher in the upper elementary grades needs to have extensive expertise in reading. Differentiated staffing at these levels can be broadened to include teachers with high levels of pedagogical content knowledge in science, math, social studies, and writing.

These are policy arguments, to be sure. But to what extent can they be substantiated with research evidence? In the previous edition of this handbook, we summarized recent studies concerning core-related issues. It makes little sense to summarize those studies now, however. One of the difficulties inherent in such investigations is that their subject is a moving target. Not only do core programs evolve and change, but they frequently do so by incorporating research findings, thus co-opting the very researchers who examine them. Consequently, research on an older version of a program should not be applied to revisions of the program (Roser, Hoffman, & Carr, 2003).

Recent investigations into core programs do offer some useful insights into current issues. One such issue is the extent to which comprehension strategy instruction is reflected in today's cores. Dewitz, Jones, and Leahy (2009) analyzed the teacher guidance for grades 3–5 in five popular programs. They reported that core developers tend to err on the side of including too extensive a range of strategies. That is, there is a tendency to include those with a limited research base, possibly (we suspect) with the goal of assuring that selection committees will see their favorites represented. They also reported that the strategies seldom follow the guidelines for explicit instruction and rarely embody a plan for gradual release of responsibility, from teacher to student. A similar analysis (Pilonieta, 2010) found that cores often err in the other direction as well, by omitting strategies with research validation. But the importance and duration of strategy instruction have themselves become targets. As we mentioned in Chapter 4, Willingham (2006–2007) has suggested that strategies are overemphasized. Likewise, McKeown, Beck, and Blake (2009), in a study of urban fifth graders, found that teaching content had a greater effect on several measures of comprehension than teaching strategies. The problem for coaches may be how to help teachers find that delicate balance between following all of the core recommendations for strategy instruction and spending enough time on vocabulary and knowledge building. That is a perfect task for a coach to consider.

We note that over time the research questions have become increasingly fine-grained. From whether or not strategies are included in a core, we have moved on to questions about which strategies and for how long. This is progress and it suggests a gradual improvement of core programs in recent years rather than the fad-driven lurches we have witnessed in the not-too-distant past. This positive trend led Foorman (2007) to conclude that "The science of reading is permeating the instructional core of primary-grade classrooms, an essential step if teachers are to have the materials needed to differentiate instruction" (p. 29).

Her conclusion suggests that coaches be mindful of the degree to which a core reflects scientific research. However, as Dewitz et al. (2010) warn:

> Determining if a core reading program is built on scientifically based reading research is an almost impossible task. Core reading programs are not subjected to rigorous experimental research with students and teachers randomly assigned to treatment and control groups. At best, the label *scientifically based reading research* means that the authors, editors, and freelance writers created instructional lessons and incorporated skills and strategies that reflected their best understanding of the reading research. (p. 175)

A far more promising route is to consider the instructional strategies embodied in the core and to make judgments on that basis. Given that there is a superabundance of suggestions, a coach who is knowledgeable about the research pedigree of particular approaches will know which to support and which to discourage.

Where does this research lead us? Unfortunately, not to the place where literacy coaches need to go—to a blueprint for making a wise, research-based choice of a core program for a particular school. There are several reasons for this:

- Research comparing the effectiveness of two or more cores does not exist.
- Researchers are likely to look at only one aspect of a program; literacy coaches must examine the entire program.
- Findings about those aspects may not apply to a subsequent edition of the same core. Core programs change over time, sometimes dramatically.
- Researchers are looking only at materials and manuals; they are not examining the match between program offerings and the local resources and needs.

The takeaway lesson is this: In order to really know what a core program has to offer, a researcher (or a literacy coach) has to engage in a carefully planned process, reading and evaluating the actual lessons with a clear and specific procedure. Some literacy coaches and administrators will admonish the research community for not providing the evidence they need to make research-based decisions. We do not. We think that the role of the research community is to develop research-based principles (such as those we have summarized in Chapter 4). It is the role of local school district personnel to learn about those principles and to look for them in the materials they choose to buy for children in their care. There is no quick or easy road to materials selection.

THOUGHTFUL SYSTEMS FOR EVALUATING MATERIALS

One thing that we (and probably you) have learned the hard way is that thoughtful use of new materials takes time. One coach with whom we work expressed frustration about this after working with us through the procedure that we introduce in

this section. "We seem to know what we need," she told us. "It's just about finding the time." In fact, thorough evaluation of materials may take months. It might
make a good summer project. It is also work that can be shared, especially with
grade-level leaders.

Such work needs a specific focus. Fortunately, a number of tools are available
to help. In the previous edition, we described the *Consumer's Guide to Analyzing
a Core Reading Program*, a detailed rubric developed at the University of Oregon.
Since then, a revision has been published (Simmons & Kame'enui, 2006), which
may be downloaded at no cost. Simmons and Kame'enui borrowed the product
rating system popularized by *Consumer Reports* to craft their own extensive
rubric to evaluate K–3 core programs in key dimensions. We believe that their
2006 revision remains useful in acquainting coaches with the many curricular
issues involved in core selection. However, the time required to apply this rubric to
a particular program, let alone to all of the commercial cores now on the market,
is daunting to say the least.

Similar tools are also available. Al Otaiba, Kosanovich-Grek, Torgesen,
Hassler, and Wahl (2005) used a rubric to evaluate the K–1 portions of six core
programs to determine the extent to which they reflected scientific research. The
Florida Center for Reading Research has developed its own *Guidelines to Review
Comprehensive Core Reading Programs* (available free at *fcrr.org*), which address
grades K–6 and include references to supplemental and intervention programs. We
especially recommend the *Guide to Program Selection*, developed by Dewitz et al.
(2010). There are actually three separate versions (one for kindergarten, one for
grades 1 and 2, and another for grades 3–6). Each is up-to-date with respect to
how present-day core programs are structured, and each may be downloaded free
at *www.reading.org/general/publications/books/bk707.aspx*.

In Figure 8.2, we suggest a general game plan for taking stock of a core reading program, whether it is being considered for adoption or is awaiting implementation.

An aspect of the core that is easily overlooked is the intervention component.
Except for the core anthology and its guidance for teachers, this is arguably the
most important component of a core program. Since 2007 all cores offer intervention materials, either directly tied to the rest of the core or as a standalone (Dewitz
et al., 2010). It is vital that the coach know whether this intervention has been (or
is likely to be) made available, and if so, how it works and for whom.

THE PROBLEM OF LAYERING

The procedures described above can really help you to make reasoned choices
about where to spend your materials money—or how to focus your coaching after
new materials have been purchased. But making such choices is not all you have
to do to ensure that you are leading a schoolwide literacy program. We have visited schools that look like museums of the history of educational materials. They

1. *Choose a rubric*. Any of the free rubrics we have identified in this chapter will help focus the examination.

2. *Form a team*. Although we recommend that a coach read the teacher's manual at every grade, others can lend additional eyes to this inspection even if they read only the manual for a single grade. Enlisting their input also serves to promote collaboration about core implementation.

3. *Establish a schedule*. You may not always be able to stick to it, but setting dates for completing tasks can be effective in making certain they are accomplished. A clear schedule, agreed upon well in advance, also contributes to the work of the team.

4. *Involve the principal*. There are many other responsibilities vying for the principal's attention, but open invitations to join team meetings will help keep the principal in the loop. So will providing periodic summaries of team findings.

5. *Form a plan to use the results*. Using a rubric to analyze the core program is bound to reveal areas of relative strength and weakness. A coach should lead the team in planning how to use this information. How will scant attention to certain skills be compensated for? By the same token, how will the problem of too many suggestions and materials be addressed? A coach must advise teachers about how to pick and choose.

FIGURE 8.2. Steps in evaluating a core program.

From *The Literacy Coach's Handbook, Second Edition*, by Sharon Walpole and Michael C. McKenna. Copyright 2013 by The Guilford Press. Permission to photocopy this figure is granted to purchasers of this book for personal use only (see copyright page for details).

have used their materials money wisely to purchase brand-new, research-based core programs. Teachers are natural hoarders! Mindful of the pendulum swings that they have experienced, many cling to their old materials and create a hybrid program that combines elements of the old with elements of the new. We caution you to be proactive in preventing this practice, which is known as *layering*. It is important to decide what the core can do and what it can't and then to consider available alternatives that might legitimately supplement core instruction. New programs and materials should not simply be layered on top of old ones.

The same is true for technology-based programs. We urge you to take a schoolwide approach; apply the descriptive rubric to all programs; be careful to avoid layering; and craft a literacy program for your school that uses commercial materials in planned, thoughtful ways. In Figure 8.3, we have provided a tool for you to use to evaluate computer-based programs. As with your core program evaluation, evaluation of a supplemental computer-based program should be conducted through a thoughtful examination of the actual lessons and a plan for how the computer-based program is an essential component of your schoolwide plan.

The use of leveled books in a reading program presents an additional challenge. Like many others, we have begun to revisit the usefulness of leveled books, especially in kindergarten and first grade. Their use must be consistent with research on how children learn to read and with the basic scope and sequence of the core program. Leveled books are not useful unless the levels of the books match the reading levels of the children, *and* unless the skills and strategies needed

A CONSUMER'S GUIDE TO EVALUATING READING SOFTWARE

This instrument is designed along the lines of *A Consumer's Guide to Analyzing a Core Reading Program, Grades K–3* by Simmons and Kame'enui (2006). This guide is intended to assist educators as they appraise software to determine how closely it is aligned with scientifically based reading research (SBRR). It is less concerned with the general design features typically appraised in all educational software. The rating symbols are similar to those adopted by Simmons and Kame'enui:

- ● Software consistently meets or exceeds the criterion.
- ◉ Software sometimes meets the criterion.
- ○ Software does not meet the criterion.
- ⊗ Software design is not relevant to this criterion.

The software is evaluated by first identifying the component(s) it addresses (phonemic awareness, phonics, etc.). The appropriate sections of this instrument are then used to appraise the software with respect to each criterion by circling or underlining the rating. Since the criteria are not necessarily of equal weight, and because some may in fact be irrelevant to a particular software design, there is no summative scoring. Rather, the ratings of all of the criteria judged must be weighed subjectively.

Phonemic Awareness

●◉○⊗ Uses oral rather than written language.

●◉○⊗ Progresses from awareness of larger phonological units (e.g., words, syllables, rhyme) to awareness of phonemes.

●◉○⊗ Includes practice with blending.

●◉○⊗ Includes practice with segmentation.

●◉○⊗ Employs a format that minimizes the effects of guessing.

●◉○⊗ Facilitates teacher monitoring of student performance.

●◉○⊗ Prescribes activities on the basis of performance.

●◉○⊗ Employs an engaging format.

(cont.)

FIGURE 8.3. An instrument for use in evaluating computer-based programs.

Phonics

●◉○⊗ Links phonics instruction to phonemic awareness.

●◉○⊗ Includes practice with letter recognition if needed.

●◉○⊗ Relies on direct approaches and minimizes the need to infer phonics content.

●◉○⊗ Progresses from alphabetic (letter-by-letter) to orthographic (spelling-pattern) decoding.

●◉○⊗ Emphasizes recognizing patterns, not learning rules.

●◉○⊗ Stresses onset-and-rime decoding.

●◉○⊗ Progresses from monosyllabic to polysyllabic words.

●◉○⊗ Maximizes time actually spent learning and reinforcing skills.

●◉○⊗ Teaches skills systematically and directly.

●◉○⊗ Employs a format that minimizes the effects of guessing.

●◉○⊗ Minimizes or eliminates jargon.

●◉○⊗ Facilitates teacher monitoring of student performance.

●◉○⊗ Prescribes activities on the basis of performance.

●◉○⊗ Employs an engaging format.

Fluency

●◉○⊗ Models appropriate phrasing and intonation (prosody).

●◉○⊗ Stresses both speed and accuracy of decoding.

●◉○⊗ Incorporates procedures for supporting reading, including repeated readings, choral reading, and echo reading.

●◉○⊗ Facilitates teacher monitoring of student performance.

●◉○⊗ Prescribes activities on the basis of performance.

●◉○⊗ Employs an engaging format.

Vocabulary

●◉○⊗ Teaches words in meaningful clusters.

●◉○⊗ Employs graphic organizers to stress interrelationships.

●◉○⊗ Selects vocabulary on the basis of utility and frequency.

●◉○⊗ Provides for multiple exposures to words.

●◉○⊗ Goes beyond simply learning definitions or synonyms.

(cont.)

●◉○⊗ Incorporates validated instructional methods (including concept sorts, feature analysis, charting, webbing, possible sentences, list–group–label, etc.).

●◉○⊗ Stresses useful word elements (prefixes, suffixes, etc.).

●◉○⊗ Combines definitions with contextual examples.

●◉○⊗ Employs a format that minimizes the effects of guessing.

●◉○⊗ Facilitates teacher monitoring of student performance.

●◉○⊗ Prescribes activities on the basis of performance.

●◉○⊗ Employs an engaging format.

Comprehension

●◉○⊗ Provides interesting and engaging texts.

●◉○⊗ Includes a variety of genres.

●◉○⊗ Requires students to reach conclusions that draw on information in more than one sentence.

●◉○⊗ Provides opportunities to transform the content of texts (e.g., into charts, summaries, graphic representations).

●◉○⊗ Teaches effective strategies (e.g., activating prior knowledge, comprehension monitoring, predicting, generating questions, summarizing).

●◉○⊗ Includes information about how, when, and why readers employ these strategies.

●◉○⊗ Avoids a specific skill mastery approach (e.g., inferring a sequence of events, noting supporting details).

●◉○⊗ Provides supported text to facilitate independent reading (e.g., online glossary, pronunciations, text simplifications, explanatory links).

●◉○⊗ Includes only hidden media effects ("hot spots") that are germane to the story.

●◉○⊗ Provides support before, during, and after reading.

●◉○⊗ Provides a listening version of texts to support weak decoders.

●◉○⊗ Recognizes prior knowledge limitations and attempts to accommodate them.

●◉○⊗ Employs graphic and semantic organizers (e.g., timelines, story maps).

●◉○⊗ Focuses on hypertext structures.

●◉○⊗ Links comprehension to writing applications.

●◉○⊗ Facilitates teacher monitoring of student performance.

●◉○⊗ Prescribes activities on the basis of performance.

to read these books are consistent with the skills and strategies taught in the core curriculum. To us, these are some broad recommendations about leveled books:

- One leveling system (letters, numbers, colors) should be used throughout the school building—in classroom libraries, in the book room, in the library—to ensure that leveled books are used in a systematic way. The leveling system should be coordinated with the core program to avoid layering.
- Leveled books for emergent readers (ideally, children in the first part of kindergarten) must be predictable, to allow them to develop their ability to track print.
- Leveled books for beginning readers (ideally, children in the second part of kindergarten and the first part of first grade) must allow them to practice their decoding. That means that these books must be matched to the developmental level of the children and to the decoding curriculum in the core program.
- Leveled books for transitional and fluent readers (ideally, children from the middle of first grade through the first part of second grade) must allow them to gain fluency through access to a great number of high-frequency and decodable words. We are convinced that many teachers are making these reader–text matches much too conservatively. Consider organizing these resources by Lexile levels to remind teachers of the new standards for text difficulty embraced in the Common Core State Standards (2010).

Organizing leveled books is a real challenge. Many literacy coaches have spent their first month on the job organizing materials full time. Although this may be tedious work, it is important work. In order for teachers to do their job well, they have to have easy access to their tools; we have visited many schools with new materials still in boxes in classrooms halfway through the school year. Literacy coaches must decide how to label and store materials so that the schoolwide program will truly be implemented schoolwide. A particular difficulty with organizing the books is the necessity of choosing between levels and topic. Why not do both? Figure 8.4 shows how cubbies can be used to organize books by level (horizontally) and by a few broad categories (vertically).

We have helped literacy coaches to establish shared book rooms, so that teachers have access to more titles to use in their needs-based fluency instruction. This is a large undertaking. However, many literacy coaches have seen the shared book room as their greatest accomplishment; because resources are pooled within the school, all teachers have more, and all children have the materials they need. In establishing a shared book room, it is important to start with a plan. First, collect existing resources from classrooms and organize them, so that you can see what you already have. Next, compare these texts to the core program; you may find that the books that you have for kindergarten and first-grade children to use for practice are inconsistent with the instruction they are getting. It may be time to

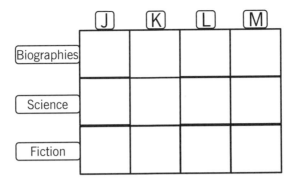

FIGURE 8.4. Example of how cubbies can be used to classify books by level and topic.

give those texts away. Finally, identify your needs and make a purchasing plan. Do you need more texts for children to practice phonics concepts? Do you need more leveled information texts? Do you need more easy chapter books for building fluency after first grade? Do you need a larger variety of high-quality literature for students at all grades who have already attained fluency?

A FINAL WORD

In our experience, selecting a core program is rarely the prerogative of one school. This decision is made by the district and is up to schools to implement the choice. There is often a mandate for implementation because of the high cost of core programs. What, then, is a coach to do? As an adoption year approaches, a coach may wish to volunteer to serve on the selection committee. This is time-consuming work, however, that might result in very little voice about the ultimate decision. A coach might also suggest that the school pilot a potential core program. Doing so may assist the district and garner free materials for the school (Dewitz et al., 2010). Such an offer should only be extended after the coach has vetted the program together with grade-level representatives.

In the end, we believe that a coach has a single overarching goal: to learn the adopted program. This means reading the teacher's edition for each grade, armed with a stack of sticky notes. We have learned much about reading development from our own close reading of core programs. Our guess is that the coach alone will have read more than one level, and it is the coach alone who will possess the long view of how the series is organized and what is expected at each grade. This knowledge is important. When a coach visits a classroom, it is essential to know what *should* be happening during core instruction. This is not to suggest the need for slavish adherence to the core, but when adaptations and departures occur it is vital to know about them. And to the coach who has studied the core, such deviations are obvious.

CHAPTER 9

Schoolwide Response to Intervention

Changes in Title I legislation led to initial design of flexible schoolwide programs for schools serving large numbers of families living in poverty. Changes in special education legislation (Individuals with Disabilities Education Improvement Act, 2004) now make flexible schoolwide intervention design possible in all schools. There are two changes. First, schools can now use a portion of their federal special education funds for prevention services. Second, they can engage in RTI plans as a part of their special education referral process.

When access to special education services is predicated only on a discrepancy between IQ and achievement, young struggling readers are denied access to intervention until they are old enough for the discrepancy to be large enough. This policy flies in the face of the evidence that early reading achievement is important and that almost all students can achieve it *if they have access to immediate and intense intervention.* In general terms, states are now allowed to reframe their special education services such that intervention comes first and testing (or eligibility) later. This idea is conceptually attractive and consistent with research. However, it is more easily embraced than enacted. It requires a new union of regular and special education. It requires new assessments of literacy on the part of all teachers. And it requires deep understanding and coordination of progressively more intense educational interventions. Our main goal here is to guide literacy coaches to anticipate specific logjams in literacy growth at each grade level, and to begin to coordinate personnel, materials, and schedules to address those logjams.

WHAT IS THE ARGUMENT FOR AGGRESSIVE EARLY INTERVENTION?

The best intervention is active, aggressive, and provided at the onset of a problem. It furnishes additional modeling, support, feedback, and practice in a particular domain. The best intervention is also intensive—usually daily, with no time wasted, provided individually or in very small groups. Moreover, the best intervention is specialized—provided by teachers with more and better training and/or with commercial materials that are more systematic. Finally, the best intervention is targeted—maximizing supported practice in a specific domain of need, rather than including all segments of the literacy diet.

Robert Slavin and his colleagues (Slavin, Madden, Karweit, Dolan, & Wasik, 1991) tell a fictitious story that makes a striking point about the value of early intervention. Imagine a town in which 30% of the children became seriously ill from drinking contaminated water. Some of them died, while others were permanently disabled. Over the years, the town spent millions on medical care, but rejected an engineer's proposal to build a water treatment plant. The plant would be too expensive, the townspeople argued. And besides, 70% of the children never became ill at all. It may seem farfetched to compare reading intervention with a life-and-death scenario like this. After all, learning to read just isn't that important. Or is it?

Early literacy failure has long-term consequences. Marie Clay (1979), the New Zealand psychologist who developed the first-grade tutoring program, Reading Recovery, has argued that the most efficient and effective time to prevent reading failure is right at the start of formal reading instruction, during first grade, when the achievement gap between normally developing and low-performing readers is smallest. She has reasoned that over time, the gap will widen, and the goal of the intervention will become more and more difficult to achieve.

Clay's (1979) charge to intervene early flies directly in the face of educational practices that are based on a developmental lag theory—the idea that children who are struggling with literacy at an early stage simply need more time to "catch up" with their peers. Children who are struggling with literacy are not simply developing more slowly; they are actually missing important knowledge and skills relative to their normally developing peers (Foorman, Francis, Shaywitz, Shaywitz, & Fletcher, 1997). Connie Juel (1988) reported that children who were struggling readers at the end of grade one had an 88% chance of struggling at the end of grade four. The first years of school, then—kindergarten and first grade—are the prime time for intervention.

The *Matthew effect*, a term coined by the sociologist Robert Merton (1968) and popularized in reading by Keith Stanovich (1986), captures the spiraling effects of reading failure. Children who struggle with reading avoid reading. This avoidance hinders the development of fluency and vocabulary that come from wide reading. At the same time, children who read easily enjoy reading. They read more.

Their fluency and vocabulary develop more and more quickly, and the difference between them and their struggling peers in terms of knowledge, skills, and strategies becomes greater and greater each year. As a result, the gap between the best and worst readers widens each year until it is unbridgeable. In the early grades, however, when the gap is narrowest, appropriate intervention stands a chance of reaching struggling readers.

In 1998, the National Research Council's report, *Preventing Reading Difficulties in Young Children* (Snow et al., 1998), described factors predicting reading failure. First, it identified child-based factors (those that could be identified through individual assessment): severe cognitive deficiencies, severe hearing and language impairments, attention problems, depressed early language development, and depressed preschool literacy skills. Individual children exhibiting one or more of these factors are *potentially* at risk. Next, the report identified family based factors (those that could be identified without any actual testing of a child): family history of reading problems, family environment with limited English-language proficiency, and low SES. Children living in environments with one or more of these factors are also *potentially* at risk. Finally, it identified community- and school-based factors (those that could be identified without specific data on families): low SES at the neighborhood level and placement in schools with a history of low achievement. Again, children living in such circumstances are *potentially* at risk.

Identification of individual-, family-, and community-based risk factors is actually an indictment of our schools' inabilities to adapt and respond to children's needs. At-risk status does not *cause* reading failure. Individual children with disabled parents learn to read. Individual children with language impairments learn to read. Individual children with no English spoken at home learn to read. Individual children from very poor families, living in very poor neighborhoods, learn to read. In a schoolwide literacy program, teachers must learn to provide especially expert instruction and to meet the needs of all children.

In fact, many children fail to learn to read because they receive poor instruction. This is one potential risk that can be removed. In a schoolwide literacy program, no individual-, family-, or community-based risk excuses the school from responsibility for preventing reading failure and/or intervening as soon as the classroom curriculum fails to address the needs of individual children. Unfortunately, when schools fail to provide the necessary instruction and intervention, individuals point to risk factors outside the school to explain it. This leads to a damaging self-fulfilling prophecy, one that can evoke a series of mantras: "These children can't learn to read because they come to school at risk for failure," "The school is powerless in light of these outside circumstances," and "The children failed to learn to read because they were initially at risk."

The total number of children who need intervention is a hotly contested issue, both within the literacy community and in the political arena. The broad message is a hopeful one: Many reading problems can be prevented altogether through consistent, research-based instruction in preschool and across the grade levels, and others can be remediated through specially targeted efforts. For a summary of this controversy, we describe the longitudinal work of Frank Vellutino and Donna Scanlon (2001), which has become a conceptual argument for RTI.

Vellutino and Scanlon's (2001) intervention studies were carefully designed. First, they tested over 1,000 kindergarten children with a variety of assessments (some of literacy achievement and others of cognitive skills) to investigate the potential underlying causes of reading problems. Next, they observed kindergarten instruction to investigate the potential relationship between the type and amount of instruction and student achievement. Next, they retested children in the middle of first grade to identify struggling readers and normally achieving readers. They provided tutoring to half of the struggling first graders. Finally, they retested children at the end of first grade, at the end of third grade, and at the end of fourth grade. This series of carefully integrated studies provides important insight into the potential effects of intervention. Here are some highlights of their findings:

- Literacy measures (letter identification and phoneme segmentation) in kindergarten were strong predictors of reading achievement at the end of first grade.
- Children who were initially weak in letter identification in kindergarten were more likely to be rated as average or strong by their first-grade teachers if they came from kindergarten classrooms where more time was spent on phonemic awareness activities.
- Children who were initially strong in letter identification in kindergarten were more likely to be rated as average or strong by their first-grade teachers if they came from kindergarten classrooms where more time was spent on shared reading activities.
- After only one semester of daily tutoring in first grade (rereading for fluency, reading new text, phonemic awareness, phonics, spelling for sounds), one-half of the tutored children scored in the average range on standardized measures of decoding and comprehension; this average range was maintained through fourth grade.
- Examining the progress of these children, the authors estimated that only 3% of children had reading impairments (standardized scores below the 30th percentile rank) and only 1.5% had severe impairments (standardized scores below the 15th percentile rank) after only one semester of tutoring.
- The ability to decode was not predictable from IQ scores. Children with both high and low IQ scores were normally achieving decoders; children with both high and low IQ scores were in the severely impaired groups.

This longitudinal work is especially important for understanding the potential for intervention. First, instruction matters. In a heterogeneous kindergarten class, both code-based and meaning-based reading instruction are important, but to different groups of children. Combining instruction with intervention, if it is intensive, targeted, and provided early, can make meaningful differences in children's literacy performance in only one semester; given instruction and early intervention, very few children will fall into the category of severely impaired.

Three of the schools where we have worked made the courageous decision to reform their K–3 reading programs based on these ideas. Theirs is a story worth telling. In 1 year, they implemented new screening and diagnostic assessments, and with the guidance of a coach they used the results to form (and reform) small groups. Children in all of the groups received 15 minutes of targeted instruction each day. For the most part, the teachers used lesson plans that we had already developed (Walpole & McKenna, 2009), saving them the time needed to plan each lesson from scratch. At the end of the year, the percentage of children who were not performing at benchmark levels fell dramatically, compared with previous years, in every one of the skills tested. In kindergarten, for example, only 3 of 217 children were still at risk overall. The results these schools brought about may seem extraordinary, but they reflect the impact of evidence-based strategies implemented systematically through the guidance and leadership of a literacy coach.

The idea that we can actually prevent most significant reading problems through our decisions and actions in school runs counter to the temptation to blame children and their families, and it also runs counter to the argument that interventions should meet struggling readers where they are and help them to feel better about reading and writing. Ann Duffy (2001) provided a definition of what she called *literacy acceleration* that we would like to co-opt for literacy coaches to characterize their interventions: "instruction that enables struggling readers to make rapid progress and read as well as or better than their peers not struggling in reading" (p. 70). Once Duffy personally conducted a summer intervention, she revisited that definition. She realized that she was able to do the difficult work of literacy acceleration because of her knowledge *and* her beliefs. As she was already an established university-based reading researcher, she had knowledge of best practices. This knowledge, though, was not what she reported as primary in her drive for literacy acceleration. Rather, it was her belief that success for children was her responsibility (not the responsibility of the students themselves or their families). She changed her own instruction to better meet the students' needs. She accepted what she called *instructional responsibility*. In a school-based program, the literacy coach must model, lead, and support a school-based culture of instructional responsibility. In our work, we have met principals, coaches, and teachers who take instructional responsibility; their efforts are tireless and their enthusiasm is infectious. But we don't have enough of these folks. We have to do a better job proving that poor literacy achievement is most likely the fault of schools and almost never of children or their families.

WHAT ARE THE SPECIFICS OF RTI?

Instructional responsibility is a hallmark of RTI. RTI requires two basic resource commitments: screening and progress-monitoring assessments *and* immediate access to successively more intensive instruction. We think that it would be easier for teachers to understand RTI if it was defined as *response to instruction*; intuitively, that is more consistent with the way schools are organized. First, we provide high-quality grade-level instruction. If that is not sufficient, we add more targeted instruction in smaller groups. If both of those together do not produce adequate achievement, we provide even more explicit instruction in an even smaller group. If we still see no improvements, we consider that the child might have a disability that is preventing success, and we move to special education evaluation and services. Essentially, we will have ruled out the more common explanation of poor reading achievement—inadequate instruction.

RTI can be applied to reading, math, and behavior. There are two schoolwide systems: problem solving and standard protocol. The problem-solving model looks more similar to a standard individualized education plan meeting. A team, including the classroom teacher and a group of specialists, meets to discuss the needs of a particular student. They consider data relevant to that student's performance, and they brainstorm strategies and systems for monitoring progress. They design the RTI model for each student, one at a time. This model seems more appropriate when the total number of students likely to need assistance is very small.

The standard protocol model may be more appropriate when the number of students to be served in interventions is larger. In that model, the school designs interventions up front. Similar to the logic of the cognitive model of reading assessment, which we presented in Chapter 5, assessments trigger interventions. For example, in a standard protocol model, if decoding assessment reveals problems, then we will provide a specific small-group decoding intervention. If, after some weeks of such small-group instruction, assessments reveal no growth, then we will stop that instruction and provide more intensive decoding instruction. Now consider another example in which data reveal intact decoding and fluency and weak comprehension, we provide intensive comprehension instruction, monitor its effects, and chart student response. Only if students receive the most intensive instruction possible and still do not improve will we think about whether a student has a disability. We will assume the standard protocol model for RTI in the rest of this chapter, because coaches who understand the standard protocol can take lessons from it to the problem-solving model.

Implementation of RTI is provided in instructional tiers, each of which must be evidence based. The first tier, *enhanced classroom instruction*, requires more attention than is usually offered in schools. Remember that the quality of this instruction will naturally be related to the number of children who need additional instruction. For us, schoolwide reading programs are grounded in initial enhancements of classroom instruction. They are, specifically:

- Design of assessment systems (see Chapter 5).
- Selection of commercial materials (see Chapter 8).
- Collaboration about exactly how each teacher at a grade level will use those materials (see below).

It makes sense for instructional leadership teams to attend to prevention-oriented classroom instruction because it will reduce the need for more costly interventions. In a time when many states are moving to new and aggressive standards, attention to the quality of Tier 1 grade-level instruction is a real opportunity to improve instruction.

The second tier, *supplemental instruction*, must be designed based on assessment data. Conceptually, students for whom data indicate that Tier 1 is insufficient must be provided with additional small-group instruction that is specifically designed to address the issues that the data have revealed. This supplemental instruction can comprise either instructional strategies (provided they are very specific) or commercial programs. There have long been small-group programs in elementary schools. What is different about tiered instruction, in our view, is the use of data to determine the focus of that instruction and to evaluate its effects. Most RTI initiatives are evaluated by plotting trend lines or slopes for each student to evaluate whether more time in the intervention is providing better results in the target skills. Progress monitoring data, then, must be very closely matched to the content of the intervention itself. If the slope of these progress monitoring trend lines is not indicating that the student is responding to the intervention, then additional interventions—more intensive ones—are warranted.

Figure 9.1 provides a visual representation of where an intervention might start. Preschool children might need an oral language intervention or a phonological awareness intervention. Kindergarten children might need a phonological awareness or an alphabet knowledge intervention; if they have extremely weak oral language, it is unlikely that such a need will be addressed without intensive oral language intervention. At first grade, these same foundational skill deficits might need to be targeted through intervention, along with other areas, such as fluency. Second graders might need any of these as well, or vocabulary and comprehension. Notice that as children get older, issues that we considered ripe for Tier 2 intervention are now in the Tier 3 category. We make this case to protect classroom teachers (who are often charged with providing Tier 2 interventions) and to protect instructional time for normally achieving children. Once children are in the upper elementary grades, they might have needs similar to kindergartners, but it is unreasonable to expect that those needs can be met in Tier 2 by classroom teachers without huge sacrifices in instructional time for the rest of the class.

Tier 3 intervention is the most intense level. It is typically provided outside of regular classroom instruction, either as a wholly alternative English language arts curriculum or during the time when other children have Tier 2 small groups and/or reading and writing practice activities. Children in these Tier 3 groups need intensely focused instruction and even more frequent progress monitoring.

Grade	Potential targets for Tier 2	Potential targets for Tier 3
Preschool	Oral language Phonological awareness	
Kindergarten	Phonological awareness Alphabet knowledge	Oral language
First grade	Phonological awareness Alphabet knowledge Decoding and spelling	Oral language
Second grade	Decoding and spelling Fluency	Oral language Alphabet knowledge Phonological awareness
Third grade	Fluency Vocabulary Comprehension Composition	Oral language Alphabet knowledge Phonological awareness Decoding and spelling Fluency Comprehension
Fourth and fifth grades	Fluency Vocabulary Comprehension Composition	Oral language Alphabet knowledge Phonological awareness Decoding and spelling Fluency Comprehension Composition

FIGURE 9.1. Tiered instruction across grade levels.

We can increase intensity for children by reducing group size, but there is little evidence that one-on-one instruction is more effective than one-on-three. We can also increase intensity by increasing intervention time, but only dramatic increases (e.g., to 2 hours per day) are associated with large effects. Finally, we can increase intensity by changing the type of intervention so that students have more time in skills practice with support and in engaged application of skills in text. Once children are in third grade, it may be best to move directly to Tier 3 interventions for students still struggling with word-level skills (Vaughn, Denton, & Fletcher, 2010). We favor the selection of very specialized commercial materials to aid teachers in addressing these intensive needs.

HOW IS RESEARCH INFORMING RTI EFFORTS?

In our experience with schools, RTI interventions are not always designed to be progressively more intensive. We think that schools may not have enough models of how an RTI framework might work. It makes sense, then, to consider the ways that researchers are designing and testing RTI. You will see, though, that research is still far from providing definitive direction. Generally, there are larger effects (and more choices) for early interventions, but there are promising practices as students get older and their needs are more complex (Wanzek & Vaughn, 2010). Design of a school-based RTI system is likely to be an important and ongoing challenge for any coach.

Preschool

We hope that many literacy coaches will consider preschools, either those now commonly housed in public school buildings or those in the community that serve future kindergartners, as an important potential intervention. Preschool teachers vary widely in their orientation to literacy and in their understanding of it. Laura Justice and Joan Kaderavek (2004) provide a reasonable conceptual orientation to RTI in preschool. Their targets are specific (phonological awareness, print concepts, alphabet knowledge, and literate language). They propose a model that is consistent with research on emergent readers and with the realities of preschool: the embedded-explicit model. They recommend explicit instruction in those four target areas and embedded experiences to develop children's positive attitudes toward literacy. This adoption of a both-and rather than an either-or orientation toward preschool intervention design is likely to resonate with teachers trained for early childhood. They recommend collection of informal data to document engagement and achievement, and collaboration between the preschool teacher and specialists (Kaderavk & Justice, 2004).

Explicit preschool tiered interventions may not need to be very lengthy. In a phonemic awareness intervention in preschool, instruction was provided for 20 minutes, twice each week, for 6 weeks. Progress monitoring data collected each week documented intervention success and also enabled enhancements. The researchers found that 71% of the children in the intervention responded adequately, and they maintained their skills over the summer to the beginning of kindergarten (Koutsoftas, Harmon, & Gray, 2009).

Kindergarten

One line of RTI research involves assessments and their interpretation. Most RTI protocols ask teachers to chart and interpret student growth. A steep slope on a growth chart will show a strong response to instruction; a flat line will indicate no response. Consequently, what we should be charting and when becomes an important question. Stephanie Al Otaiba and her colleagues investigated this question recently (Al Otaiba et al., 2011). They monitored growth for kindergarten students in schools serving large numbers of at-risk families. They also observed instruction and found that the kindergarten teachers had high-quality instructional materials and were providing effective instruction. At the end of the year, almost all children had met their kindergarten goals—a laudable outcome. Because of their entry status, though, some experienced steeper growth than others (because they had to make considerable progress to reach their goal). When researchers followed the students for an additional year, however, those steep growth curves were not extended. For students who grew the most in kindergarten literacy skills, growth had stalled in first-grade oral reading fluency. Kindergarten achievement alone, then, is not likely to be sufficient for predicting first-grade needs; we can anticipate that the same students will need additional supports when they move to more demanding tasks.

Carol Connor and her colleagues (2011) have been studying the interactions between children's assessed needs and the type and amount of instruction they receive. Basically, they have found that children with weaker alphabetic skills benefit from more time in teacher-directed code-oriented instruction; at the same time, children with stronger alphabetic skills benefit from less time in teacher-directed code instruction and more time in child-managed meaning-oriented work. These findings have informed our design of small-group Tier 2 instruction (Walpole & McKenna, 2007, 2009a). Recently, we applied this approach to kindergarten, guiding teachers to use assessment data to design a hybrid of Tier 1 and Tier 2 instruction. We think that this model, with the classroom teacher adjusting the use of the core program (Tier 1) *and* providing flexible, data-based small-group strategies (Tier 2), is an especially pragmatic approach to tiered instruction.

Carol Connor's (2011) studies of the relationship between instruction and achievement use a mathematical formula to predict the amount of time and teacher support that individual students need. In a recent study, Al Otaiba et al. (2011) applied this algorithm in kindergarten and clearly demonstrated the potential for a hybrid version of Tier 1 and Tier 2 instruction to enhance achievement. Teachers were assigned to one of two groups: RTI professional development or RTI professional development plus A2i. A2i (assessment to instruction) is the algorithm that tracks student achievement and recommends the amount of time that teachers should engage individuals in code- and meaning-based instruction. Teachers in the RTI professional development group did provide research-based Tier 1 instruction and small-group instruction. However, that small-group instruction was not differentiated. Teachers in the A2i group were able to differentiate during their reading block, and their students had higher achievement. Notably, with this combination of Tier 1 and Tier 2 instruction, only 7% of kindergarteners failed to meet benchmarks. While few literacy coaches will have access to A2i, all can guide teachers to use assessment data to adjust their whole-class work and design their small-group instruction.

First Grade

First graders have been the subject of numerous intervention studies because their end-of-year reading achievement is so important. Carolyn Denton and her colleagues have been testing a first-grade small-group intervention called responsive reading instruction (RRI). RRI includes 10 minutes of word work, 10 minutes of print concepts or fluency assessments, 10 minutes of supported reading, and 10 minutes of supported writing. First graders in RRI outperformed students in typical first-grade interventions in word reading, spelling, fluency, and reading comprehension. Most notably, this study established that the intervention could be provided in natural Tier 2 settings with no researcher supervision (Denton et al., 2010).

One persistent question is what proportion of students will actually benefit from the combination of tiered interventions. Denton, Fletcher, Anthony, and Francis (2006) asked this question. In a first-grade intervention study, they first added two small-group conditions. Students were served in groups of three and teachers followed one of two structured lesson plans for the entire year. Both contained direct phonics instruction, but they differed in the proportion of time devoted to text reading and in their choice of text (leveled vs. decodable). Students in both conditions outperformed controls and there was no difference between conditions. This structured, small-group intervention was a Tier 2 treatment, provided daily for 30 minutes for a group of three.

After the year's intervention, 22 of 298 students (7%) were still reading below average. These students were recruited for additional, Tier 3 intervention. That intervention was provided to pairs, and consisted of 8 weeks of code-based instruction followed by 8 weeks of fluency instruction. After this additional intervention, 7 of 22 students (25%) performed in the average range. The remaining 75% still had persistent reading problems. Notable for us is the fact that the Tier 2 instruction, provided across the year, addressed the needs of almost all of the students; it was of sufficient focus and intensity to do that. Tier 3, then, was reserved only for students with the most intractable reading problems. It consisted of two interventions that had not been used at Tier 2, and it further reduced the number of readers with serious reading problems.

Second Grade

By the time students enter second grade, many struggling readers have received intensive interventions in both kindergarten and first grade. Researchers working on intervention design for these students, then, are likely to call them "difficult to remediate," "slow responders," or "treatment resisters." We found Sharon Vaughn and colleagues' (2009) introduction of the alternative term, *low responders*, refreshing. It captures the fact that when we provide these intensive interventions to children, some will simply respond more slowly, reflecting their more comprehensive challenges. This research team followed students from first to second grade, increasing the intensity of intervention during second grade for low responders. The second-grade intervention lasted 50 minutes per day and included sound review, phonics and word recognition, fluency, and passage comprehension.

Low responders did outperform comparison students in word reading and comprehension, but not in fluency. It may be that fluency is a particularly difficult issue to resolve with that very small percentage of low responders, but its importance is reduced if we can demonstrate success in passage comprehension (Vaughn et al., 2009).

For most schools embracing RTI conceptually, resources for interventions will still be scarce. The designers of the comprehensive core program Success for All tested a Tier 2 computer-based program for pairs of students working with a tutor against a one-on-one tutoring program. Pairs participated in the computer program for 45 minutes four times each week. Activities included letter identification and writing, phonemic awareness, decoding, spelling, decodable text reading, fluency, comprehension questions, and graphic organizers. First graders in the paired computer tutoring outperformed students tutored one-on-one; second graders performed as well in the paired computer tutoring as in the live one-on-one treatment. Introduction of computer-based interventions in Tier 2 or in Tier 3 may allow schools to serve the needs of more struggling readers while maintaining effectiveness (Chambers et al., 2011).

Upper Elementary

As children get older, the need for interventions that target multiple areas makes Tier 2 intervention design more challenging. Carol Connor and colleagues (2011) have extended their A2i research to third grade; students with third-grade teachers who had dynamic information on their needs for teacher-directed and student-managed instruction made greater comprehension gains than teachers who did not have this information. Kristin Ritchey and colleagues argue that older struggling readers may need intervention in multisyllabic decoding, fluency, vocabulary, comprehension strategies, and motivation. Their design of a 24-lesson multicomponent intervention nested in science content for fourth graders yielded mixed results. Intervention students outperformed controls on measures of comprehension strategy use and on science knowledge, but not on word reading or fluency. It may be that older struggling readers need more intense interventions as their needs are more extensive (Ritchey, Silverman, Montanaro, Speece, & Schatschneider, 2012).

In a very different multiple-component intervention, Donna Scanlon and colleagues served fourth-grade students in special education settings with an intervention called interactive strategies approach-extended. The one-on-one approach included coordination of code and meaning-based strategies to recognize words, flexible phonics instruction, comprehension monitoring instruction, and collaborative discussion. Texts for the intervention were thematically related social studies texts at a range of difficulty levels linked to the grade-level standards. Students participated in approximately sixty 40-minute sessions. Students outperformed controls in reading accuracy and one measure of comprehension, but not in fluency (Gelzheiser, Scanlon, Vellutino, Hallgren-Flynn, & Schatschneider, 2011).

Summary

It makes sense that researchers focus more attention on preventing reading problems before they become debilitating than on remediating them with older students. Literacy coaches designing RTI approaches will have to do both. They will have to constantly support high-quality Tier 1 classroom instruction, augment it for some students with very targeted Tier 2 interventions, monitoring their effectiveness, and have Tier 3 interventions ready in the wings for those students who need them. While we don't yet have adequate research on fully formed, multiyear RTI efforts, we do have more access to research and program evaluations.

SELECTING INTERVENTION PROGRAMS AND PRACTICES

One of the biggest changes in information for literacy coaches since the first edition of this book is access to information about the evidence base for interventions. In 2002, the Institute for Education Sciences (*http://ies.ed.gov*) established the What Works Clearinghouse (*http://ies.ed.gov/ncee/wwc/*). The goal of the Clearinghouse was always to provide school-based personnel with access to credible information about the evidence that a particular intervention program or practice could be reliably associated with growth in student achievement. The Clearinghouse got off to a slow start, but as of this printing, it is a flexible and high-utility source for very important information. The Clearinghouse provides intervention reports that summarize findings about programs and practices. These reports can be essential in RTI design. They are conducted with a rigorous and transparent protocol designed to document only causal findings (those established in controlled experimental trials). Last we checked, there were 321 reports on literacy programs and practices. These can be searched by grade level, by population (general education, special education, ELL), by delivery method (individual, small group, whole class, whole school) and by type (curriculum, supplement, or practice). Summaries and full reports are easily accessible, as are customized reports that you design as you search.

The What Works Clearinghouse is a work in progress; it changes as evidence changes. Just to give you a taste, we searched literacy and practices. We found classwide peer tutoring and peer-assisted learning strategies to have potentially positive effects on reading achievement. We found interactive shared book reading and dialogic reading to have potentially positive effects on early reading and writing. Dialogic reading also had positive effects on oral language, but no effects on phonological processing. We urge you to explore the Clearinghouse and to examine the evidence both for the programs that you currently have and for the populations of children you still need to serve better.

It is important for you to understand that the level of rigor required for the What Works Clearinghouse to share evidence is very strict. There are interventions that might be effective for you that have not yet been subjected to this type of scrutiny. The Center on Instruction is another online source to consult. Scammacca, Vaughn, Roberts, Wanzek, and Torgesen (2007) provide rich descriptions of 12 intensive interventions with evidence of effectiveness. They also provide detailed information about what would be required in terms of resources to provide these interventions.

Another source of reviews is the Best Evidence Encyclopedia, developed by Robert Slavin and his colleagues (*www.bestevidence.org*). They employ slightly different criteria for deciding if studies should be included as evidence about particular programs, such as excluding studies with very small numbers of participants. We think that a good strategy is to use multiple sources and to compare and contrast the results.

Once you have investigated interventions and selected those that are likely to meet your students' needs, consider how you will monitor progress and plot student trend lines. Remember that this type of assessment must be very closely linked to the characteristics of the intervention. You are asking this question: Did the intervention as provided yield gains in the skills that were targeted? Curriculum-based measures, then, are best. We think that you need not add additional costly progress monitoring systems, but some schools choose to do this so that their progress monitoring trend lines are automated. If you would like to explore options for progress monitoring, we recommend the National Center on Response to Intervention (*www.rti4success.org*).

PLANNING AN RTI SYSTEM

We consider the contexts for intervention to include its places, times, and groupings, as well as the personnel who provide intervention as part of a schoolwide program. There is one broad theme that literacy coaches should recognize: Each of these intervention contexts has the potential to be an effective part of a schoolwide reading program, but each of these contexts is also a potentially ineffective one. Be proactive.

The traditional settings for interventions, Title I and special education, have to be part of your thinking. Remember, though, that in RTI systems *all* children can have access to *all* resources. Richard Allington and his colleagues have been sage but trenchant critics of Title I and special education as forming a "second system" of education that fragments children's learning opportunities and teachers' responsibility for that learning (e.g., Allington, 1994; Allington & McGill-Franzen, 1989; Walmsley & Allington, 1995; Johnston & Allington, 1991). The criticisms they have identified are central to the work of a literacy coach, who must ensure that these interventions are actually purposeful, integrated components of the schoolwide reading program. Here we take some of the criticisms and turn them into proactive statements for program planning:

- Special programs do not shift responsibility for educating struggling readers away from classroom teachers to specialists; special programs supplement and extend the already expert, targeted instruction provided by classroom teachers.
- Special programs need to be directly linked in philosophy to the school's program.
- Special programs need the best available materials.
- Children in special programs cannot afford to lose any time in transitions; those programs should be incorporated into the classroom whenever possible.
- Children in special programs must actually read and write more during their time in these programs than their peers who are working with the classroom teacher.

There is more to tiered intervention than meets the eye. Surely, all schools (even those not meeting the needs of their children) have intervention programs in place. For intervention, the devil is in the details. Many interventions simply do not work, especially when we define an intervention that *does* work in Ann Duffy's (2001) terms—as instruction that permits literacy acceleration. Tiered intervention systems are ways in which we take instructional responsibility for every child. This is a very tall order.

When we think about interventions that work, though, they have some important things in common. First, they all use a very structured lesson plan that directly targets a particular literacy domain. Second, they all have a specific notion of time—time during the lesson, and also days and weeks in the intervention. Third, they use specialized materials—materials that are designed to target the area of interest. Finally, interventions are interactive. During interventions, children read, write, talk about, and manipulate letters, words, and texts.

Figure 9.2 provides an illustration of the tradeoffs that you will have to make as you choose to use intervention strategies and intervention programs. If you choose intervention programs or strategies that are highly adaptive and interactive, you will need better-qualified personnel to provide them. If you choose interventions that are more scripted, you may be able to use a broader range of personnel. Either way, you will also have to plan for the professional development that your intervention providers need to deliver the instruction that you have selected.

Planning RTI is not a job for the faint of heart. Luckily, you can access a growing number of examples in schoolwide case study form. We recommend that you start on the Center on Instruction's website (*www.centeroninstruction.org*); it has a rich set of RTI resources, and all are archived there for immediate access. For example, you can read five case studies of RTI implementation, and take advantage of the frequently asked questions (and their answers!) that schools encountered.

It is unlikely that you will have to start from scratch. First, take stock of the current intervention programs. What are they? Who administers them at the district level? Engage those people in an honest discussion of the needs of students in your building and the needs revealed by data. Ask them how their programs can help. Next, move to your local personnel. Who are they? What specialized training do they have? Who do they typically serve, when, and why? How successful have they been in increasing student achievement? If your literacy program's interventions are like many of the unsuccessful ones described in the research on intervention, it is likely that they will need an overhaul. As you work with the rest of your team to build your reading program, you may want to move your existing intervention personnel into classroom-based jobs (assessing children, teaching small groups), using classroom materials. In that way, your intervention team will come to understand Tier 1 and to establish relationships with classroom teachers.

Once you have collected and summarized data on student achievement, work with grade-level teams to identify children for intervention and to describe their needs. Then locate materials that are matched directly to their needs, and set up a short-term intervention schedule. Work with the classroom teachers to be sure that the intervention schedule supplements (rather than supplants) their own instruction, in terms both of time and intensity.

At every marking period, when you have collected new data, evaluate the previous quarter's intervention decisions. Review progress monitoring trend lines. Discontinue children who have made adequate progress with the combination of intervention and expert classroom instruction. Allow children who are now lagging behind to enter into interventions.

At the end of the school year, rethink your intervention plan. Consider all of the children who were not reading on grade level. Look for patterns in their performance, and go back to your grade-level teams to consider additional interventions. RTI planning and evaluation is an ongoing component of the job of a literacy coach.

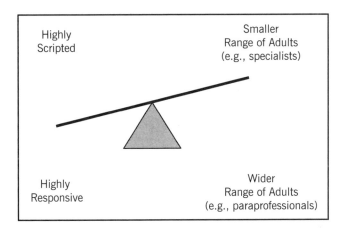

FIGURE 9.2. Matching programs and strategies with personnel.

CHAPTER 10

Providing Professional Support

Since we wrote the first edition of this text, we have been working continuously in designing, providing, and understanding professional support for teachers in schools. Looking back at our original chapter, we have a concrete reminder of how much we (and others) have learned since then. When we discussed the importance of this topic for coaches, we decided that we had to keep much of the original content and include new research findings and insights. Coaches need to know as much as possible about professional support. In fact, all of the topics in this book so far, from schoolwide curriculum and assessment design to scheduling to RTI, set the stage for the real work of coaching: providing professional support for teachers.

Professional support for all adults who work with children in a school is the key to pulling a schoolwide program together; a collaborative schoolwide culture (or at least its beginnings) is necessary for professional support to really work. We define professional support broadly to include all of the ways that literacy coaches assist teachers in understanding, implementing, and evaluating literacy development and the literacy program. Literacy coaches must make professional support count for teachers in the building so that they can make instruction count for the children they serve. In this chapter, we first review research about systems for professional support, and then suggest options for literacy coaches for specific decisions and activities that are pieces of the professional support puzzle.

PROFESSIONAL DEVELOPMENT RESEARCH

Some of the educators you know may have a fairly skeptical view of professional support; they are probably thinking of the traditional, isolated, formal workshops that are collectively referred to as professional development. They are not wrong to be skeptical. There is virtually no evidence that such sessions effect any change at all. While administrators may make loud claims that they are providing professional development for teachers that will yield increased achievement, the type and amount of professional development are not likely to change teachers' knowledge or beliefs in any perceptible way—let alone their instruction.

Professional support for teachers is a balancing act between the development of knowledge and the development of instructional skills, each addressed within a context of current knowledge and skills and within the learning environment of the school. Traditionally, professional development for inservice teachers has been targeted to address one or the other of those areas—either knowledge or skills. For example, a school or system may hire a researcher to come and give a lecture to develop knowledge in an area of concern. However, this researcher typically has no information or understanding of the curriculum or practices of the school or teachers in the audience. (We know this firsthand. We have provided such "fly-by" sessions.) The assumption behind these sessions is that knowledge building, without any reference to curriculum, will somehow transfer to altered practice. At the other end of the spectrum, a school or system may hire a representative of a publisher or a master teacher to describe or even model the use of a particular set of commercial materials or a particular teaching technique. The assumption behind these sessions is that teachers will change their practice without building knowledge or understanding of literacy and its development in schools.

Many have challenged this either–or approach to professional development. Their general message is one embracing complexity and problem solving. Shulman (1998) has proposed the use of case studies. Essentially, teachers start with samples of instruction embedded in the complex climate of the curriculum and the school, and then use them to examine and develop both knowledge and skills. Smylie (1996) has focused on problem solving. These problems come from the daily work of the teachers and the students, and solving them builds both knowledge and skills. Both suggestions are examinations of practice deeply embedded within the complex context of real instruction. Literacy coaches are probably committed to this concept, but may need some nuts-and-bolts guidance about how to proceed. Some of that guidance can come from more recent professional development research.

The literature on professional development in general is not especially large, but it is growing, and it is important to the work of coaches. A recent review available from the Institute of Education Sciences (the parent organization of the What Works Clearinghouse) summarizes existing studies (*http://ies.ed.gov/ncee/edlabs*;

Yoon, Duncan, Lee, Scarloss, & Shapley, 2007). The authors located nine studies that met the strict criteria for causal inference—the use of random assignment and a control group—in math and reading. Those studies, taken together, established that professional development *can* influence student achievement. Interestingly, the studies with positive effects had at least 14 hours of professional development delivered directly by researchers or their staff (rather than using train-the-trainer chains popular in many districts). Quality matters. And so does time. But that's not all we have learned. Teacher knowledge matters. Teacher beliefs about teaching and learning matter. And collaboration matters.

A MODEL FOR PROFESSIONAL SUPPORT

The road from professional development to achievement is indirect and winding. Joyce and Showers (1988) provided thorough analyses of the characteristics of professional development systems. What is especially striking about their work is its careful attention to context and to the development of the school as a learning community. Their analyses speak directly to the literacy coach:

- Professional development systems require new resource allocations; time, personnel, and budgetary decisions must be allocated to provide staff development within the school building and the school day.
- Virtually all teachers can learn within comprehensive systems for professional development.
- Professional development systems demand collaborative relationships between teachers and administrators.
- Professional development systems change the beliefs and practices of teachers.
- Professional development systems include cycles of theory, demonstration, practice, and feedback.

We have constructed a model for professional development that can frame the real work of coaching. We considered research on conceptual change, research on the development of self-efficacy and attitude, recent professional development intervention studies, and theoretical work in the area of professional development. We began with Desimone's (2009) conceptual framework (presented in Figure 10.1) for studying the effects of professional development on teachers and students. She argues that to develop a shared knowledge base for professional development, researchers must explore a causal chain from professional development to changes in teacher knowledge, skills, beliefs, and attitudes, to changes in instruction to changes in student achievement. All of the links in this chain are influenced by contextual factors that include individual teacher and student characteristics, leadership, curriculum, and policy.

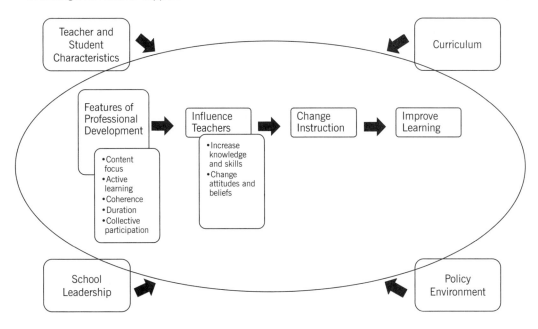

FIGURE 10.1. Desimone's (2009) framework for studying the effects of professional development.

Although Desimone's (2009) model may connote a central linear chain, we believe that the key to meaningful change lies in a more recursive process. That is why we think of professional support as a system. We assume an iterative, cyclical relationship among professional development, instructional change, improved student achievement, and changes in teacher beliefs. Out of respect for the many professionals who work in schools, we choose the title professional support rather than professional development to name our system, represented in Figure 10.2.

A truly schoolwide professional support system will have extensive contextual support from the administration, because administrators will be scheduling it, participating in it, and supporting the work of the coach. Curriculum supports will come in the form of the school's commercial and text resources and the decisions that teams have made about how to use them. We see this combination of formal professional development, classroom trials, and opportunities to reflect with a knowledgeable colleague as essential to increasing pedagogical content knowledge (PCK). PCK is a complex, situated combination of teacher knowledge and skills. It takes into account the content area, the students' knowledge, and the instructional environment. It varies from teacher to teacher (Van Driel & Berry, 2012). Individual PCK will in turn fuel additional, more expert teacher implementation, and coaches will engage teachers, in grade-level teams, in exploring changes in student achievement—further stretching individual teachers' PCK. Only when implementation and achievement are associated will teachers' beliefs (both about their own efficacy and about their students') change. Our professional support system (moving from professional development to implementation to achievement to change in

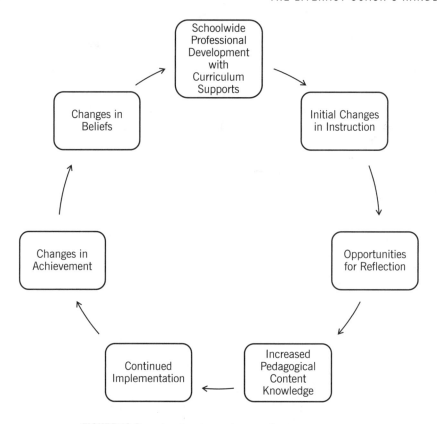

FIGURE 10.2. Schoolwide professional support system.

beliefs) is consistent with other professional development work (e.g., Mouza, 2009; Timperley & Phillips, 2003) in its incorporation of cycles of persuasion, vicarious experience, practice, and coaching (Tschannen-Moran & McMaster, 2009). It is also consistent with a basic cycle of adult learning (MacKeracher, 2004).

Schoolwide Professional Development with Curriculum Supports

A professional support system must address these facts: (1) teachers are constantly exposed to professional development that does not result in changes in their practice, and (2) their underlying beliefs play a role in this passive resistance. Guskey (1986) argued that these facts are explained by a lack of attention by professional developers to what motivates teachers to actively engage in professional development. The cognitive–affective model of conceptual change (Ebert & Crippen, 2010; Gregoire, 2003) posits that the main reasons that teachers do not change their instruction are either (1) that from the outset they do not think that the professional development applies to them personally, or (2) that even if they concede its relevance, they lack the skills or motivation to carry out the instruction. Our theory of change is based on an assumption that the professional development system must accomplish real conceptual change in order to yield sustained changes in practice, but that such conceptual change requires immediate and concrete support for implementation of specific lessons. That is why we think coaches should engage teachers in planning lessons immediately.

Initial Changes in Instruction

If teachers are to build PCK in part by seeing its effects on students, they must actually implement instruction effectively. Many teachers disengage from professional development because they lack the skills or motivation to deliver the instruction that the professional development proposes. Coaches who target implementation of very specific parts of their schoolwide literacy program are likely to see initial changes.

Opportunities for Reflection

When teachers begin to teach in new ways, individual teachers will need additional help. Coaches can provide support in the form of targeted one-on-one observation and feedback cycles to increase the effects of professional development. These cycles are similar to those first documented by Joyce and Showers (1988) and more recently provided in Teacher Quality initiatives by Sailors and Price (2010) and by Buysse, Castro, and Peisner-Feinberg (2010). In short, observation and feedback increases both the frequency and the quality of teacher implementation of new instruction.

Increased PCK

Another barrier to continued implementation of new ideas is the fact that their introduction may initially lower teacher feelings of self-efficacy. New PCK may leave teachers in the uncomfortable position of realizing that their previous knowledge was insufficient, and that the students they taught may have suffered because of it. Real feelings of guilt and low self-efficacy can be generated as teachers realize that their previous instruction may have been ineffective (Tschannen-Moran & McMaster, 2009). In schoolwide support systems, coaches identify areas that are ripe for instructional improvement, help teachers to implement new instruction, collect implementation and student achievement data, and reflect with teachers on the effects of their efforts. They first target their efficacy at providing the new instruction and then examine student achievement.

Continued Implementation

While teachers will benefit from the support of the coach, a professional support system should be structured in cycles so that teacher teams can meet to problem solve during the period of continued implementation (Buysse et al., 2010). We are influenced by (1) Bandura's (1977) theory that teachers' self-efficacy is related to their teaching effort, goals, persistence, and resilience; and (2) the theory that individual teacher learning is influenced by social interactions with peers and with teacher educators (Marrero, Woodruff, Schuster, & Riccio, 2010). The combination of (1) knowledge-building activities and lesson planning, (2) support from a coach, and (3) a structure for problem-solving meetings will allow us to leverage what Kazemi and Hubbard (2008) call the coevolution of teacher participation in professional development and their experimentation in their classrooms.

Changes in Achievement

A schoolwide professional support system includes an embedded assessment system so that teachers can see changes in their students' skills as they implement the lessons. A recent study of the effects of professional development on preschool teachers (Landry, Anthony, Swank, & Monseque-Bailey, 2009) found that the most effective professional development included a combination of theory, demonstration, and feedback about instruction, with feedback about student learning taking the form of informal curriculum-based measures. Changes in PCK and self-efficacy may require evidence that teaching efforts are yielding measurable student improvements. A structure for documenting any changes in achievement and for discussing them with peers during grade-level team meetings is the final element in our system. Without positive changes in achievement we anticipate no changes in underlying teacher belief systems. In cases where there is no growth in individual student achievement in spite of adequate implementation of the lessons, we anticipate recommendations for a more comprehensive Tier 3 intervention.

Changes in Beliefs

Although we may be able to bring about instructional change without altering teachers' beliefs, such change is likely to be transitory. If the professional development a coach is designing is to yield sustained changes in instruction, changes that remain after the professional development itself has been completed, teachers will have to change their belief structures. However, we view changes in beliefs as the natural outgrowth of the professional support system (MacKeracher, 2004) rather than as an initial outcome of the professional development (e.g., Desimone, 2009).

PROFESSIONAL SUPPORT AND COACHING

The model of professional support that we have described here derives from research on teacher learning. But what about research on coaching? Remember in Chapter 2 we reviewed that emerging research, and we proposed 10 take-home

1. Coaching does not always change instruction or achievement.
2. Use a coaching model to guide your time and activities.
3. Coaches cannot be effective unless their work is integrated with the school's climate.
4. Align your coaching goals with the goals of other leaders.
5. The needs of teachers are real and must come before the needs of coaches.
6. Be ready to learn many things on the job.
7. Be ready to differentiate for preschool teachers.
8. Be ready to build your coaching toolbox.
9. Be sure to find out whether teachers implement new approaches.
10. Use multiple assessment measures to track student achievement.

FIGURE 10.3. Take-home messages from coaching research.

messages. They are reprised in Figure 10.3. We suspect that the chapters you have read in between (Chapters 3–9) have already begun to change your understanding of these messages. Keep the messages in mind as we move from our model of professional support to the nuts and bolts of the coach's role in that model. As in all descriptions of coaching, we invite you to consider these ideas and to craft your own coaching model that draws on your strengths, improves your areas of weakness, and serves your teachers. For us, coaching requires a combination of work outside classrooms with work inside classrooms (observation, modeling). We will begin outside the classroom and move in.

PLANNING AND IMPLEMENTING SCHOOLWIDE PROFESSIONAL DEVELOPMENT

While our initial work in schoolwide professional development was informed by our own experiences working in schools, we can now reference the emerging research base for guidance. Desimone (2009) provided guidelines for professional development design, and these are listed in the left column of Figure 10.4. Actions and activities that a coach might plan to meet those guidelines are provided in the right column and described more fully. You will see that professional development outside the classroom does not involve lectures from the coach.

NUTS AND BOLTS

Coaches are in a much stronger position to help teachers build PCK than university professors because they can (and must) embed all knowledge-building time in the realities of their school. Coaches should not design any professional development without first establishing a broad description of their schoolwide literacy program. Further, we think that description should be grade-level specific. Grade-level teams

Components	Activities directed by a coach
Content focus	• Study standards, curriculum materials, and assessment data. • Read professional books related to teacher and student needs.
Active learning	• Group students for instruction. • Design lesson plans for immediate use.
Coherence	• Build professional development that addresses teacher needs directly. • Include all state and district mandates.
Duration	• Schedule regular grade-level-team professional development. • Schedule regular schoolwide professional development. • Schedule regular individual professional development.
Collective participation	• Include all adults who work with children. • Collaborate with administrators.

FIGURE 10.4. Components of high-quality initial professional development.

can be very powerful units for professional development; coaches who differentiate for teams understand that as students change, their teachers' knowledge needs change. Within each team, teachers need to begin with the nuts and bolts of the literacy program: the schedule for instruction, the data collection schedule and tools, the grouping strategy, the commercial reading materials that will be used in the program, and the plans for differentiation and intervention. Addressing these issues *is* site-based professional development.

PCK efforts must also address staff members' anxiety about making changes. It is important to build confidence. One literacy coach reported to us that her first concern in professional development was getting off to a good start. She asked herself this question before deciding on a focus for each session:

"[How] can we get [the schoolwide literacy plan] going the fastest? How can we get it started at this point in a positive sort of way?"

After attending to the basic schedule and procedures for instruction, literacy coaches can conduct knowledge-building sessions to target specific areas that teachers need to understand better. Some literacy coaches have knowledge of the school and its practices to guide them in this. Other literacy coaches do not have this advance knowledge. Using a survey to set a professional development agenda builds a collegial spirit. We recommend that coaches survey each teacher privately to identify the specific parts of the school's program for which he or she needs the most support. Then the coach can summarize these results for grade-level teams and build a professional development syllabus for the team.

Once there is basic implementation of the reading program, and a basic understanding of the needs of individuals and of the school in general, the literacy coach can truly tailor his or her professional development sessions. For example, teachers on one team needed to build understanding of how they could introduce comprehension strategies during read-alouds. Their coach started with the basics.

> "First we had to make sure that [teachers] were doing read-alouds every day, and that it became a habit, and that it was a routine in their day. Everybody expected it, and there was nobody—nobody who didn't do one. And so we got the ritual and routine down of doing the read-alouds: when they were going to do them, how often, and how much time they were going to spend."

After that, she could really focus her professional development on strategies for making the read-alouds count as instruction. She conducted informal observations, once the read-alouds were part of the instructional routine, and then she made decisions about what to target during professional development time. With routines came opportunities to build knowledge that could influence practice immediately.

USING DATA

Presenting data as part of professional development is absolutely essential. Literacy coaches build knowledge when they assist teachers in understanding the data that they have collected. In our experience, literacy coaches are expert in collecting data and expert at interpreting data for an individual child, but reluctant to look for larger trends within or across grade levels, as we discussed in Chapter 5. However, this type of professional development session has been particularly powerful in the work of many literacy coaches.

> "I think what's happening is [that] teachers are seeing the scores and listening to the children read and seeing improvements that they're making. They're finally buying into it. I think you've got to tough it out at first. Let them see that it will happen. Then they believe, and they'll do it."

Time and time again, literacy coaches report that seeing improvements in student achievement is powerful:

> "I believe the teachers are starting to express excitement about what they're seeing."

Over time, literacy coaches can direct professional development sessions so that they address both what the teachers need and what the students need; it is at this intersection that professional development is likely to be most effective. In Chapter 3 we introduced the concept of a state of the school address. This type of professional development takes the schoolwide assessment system's data and uses them to illustrate the extent to which the literacy program is having the desired effect on children. Remember that data can sometimes be disheartening; you must be prepared to engage teachers in understanding what the data mean and in problem solving around weaknesses they reveal. Data-analysis sessions with grade-level teams can follow larger state of the school presentations; teams can see the schoolwide picture first and then address their own piece of the overall puzzle. See Figure 10.5 for preparation hints. Remember to be proactive and to avoid pitting teachers against one another. Teachers must learn to see one another as sources of ideas rather than competition. These sessions are likely to reveal creative solutions from teachers who really know their children, solutions that coaches cannot think of alone.

BOOK CLUBS AND STUDY GROUPS

Professional development sessions (whether they build shared understanding of the reading program or of the building-level data) will never be quick fixes. In fact, for many literacy coaches, the second year of their work with a staff will involve revisiting ideas that were already covered. One literacy coach told us:

> "I'm looking forward to being able to go back and go over it all again, and for us to get deeper into it. You know we've skimmed the surface, and we've hit all the high points, but now I'm hoping that we can get deep, deep into it so that we're better and better and better."

Surely this type of repetition is evidence of a well-designed system rather than a failure of the first year's sessions. Another literacy coach described her first year's professional development efforts as "salesmanship." She was "selling" the new literacy program to the teachers—describing its features in detail and showing teachers how to use them. In the second year, she was able to shift her attention

---

- To save time access all data before teachers gather.
- Begin by reviewing the data sources by purpose (screening, diagnosis, progress monitoring).
- Set a task that focuses on students. Consider finding all students who have not been successful with differentiation strategies or all students who need diagnostic testing.
- Have reporting forms ready for teachers. Include a space for next steps or questions to explore.

FIGURE 10.5. Preparing to use data in grade-level team professional development sessions.

to "customer service"—tailoring her work more closely to the needs of individual teachers and children, and fine-tuning her support.

Book clubs and study groups are structures for providing professional development outside the classroom. We distinguish them from other types of knowledge-building sessions because they involve work for teachers prior to each meeting. Book clubs and study groups are important because they establish a collegial climate for teaching and learning; all participants (including the coach) are reflecting together on ideas expressed in text, and all are making connections to their prior knowledge and experience and to the building's literacy program. Practically speaking, the use of text for learning builds relationships and collegiality. A "research says" presentation conducted by a literacy coach establishes a power structure that is not conducive to building relationships. In fact, literacy coaches who "know it all" are unlikely to be effective in leading building-level change efforts (Vacca & Padak, 1990). A book club sends a different message: Literacy coaches and teachers are learners. They can work together to understand research and see how they can use it to inform their practice.

We see book clubs or study groups as cooperative learning environments. Cooperative learning is most effective when it combines group and individual accountability. Practically speaking, the management issues for book clubs or study groups are these:

- Setting a goal for the team.
- Choosing appropriate readings.
- Scheduling reading times and schedules.
- Distributing responsibilities among team members.
- Managing productive discussions.

Novice coaches will find that managing adult discussions is very different from managing student discussions!

Literacy coaches we have worked with use different strategies for identifying areas for study. At first blush, knowledge of the school and its history may provide guidance; a literacy coach may be in a position to know about specific domains in the reading program that have previously been ignored. For example, one school may really need to focus on developing knowledge and skills for teaching foundational skills. Another school may really need to focus on understanding of comprehension and its instruction, or of text complexity. Still another strategy is to sort topics by grade level. For example, the kindergarten team may engage in a book club on developing phonemic awareness. First-grade teachers may work on decoding and spelling. Second-grade teachers may target fluency. Third-grade teachers may target comprehension strategy instruction. Some topics transcend a single grade level, of course, and may lend themselves to a combined study group. However, our experience is that a group works best when it is confined to a single grade level. The teachers already have a working relationship and tend to be more candid in their discussion. It is also easier for them to tailor their talk to concerns specific to their grade level.

As a school-level reading program evolves, a literacy coach makes much more targeted decisions, and relies on data to inform these decisions. Student achievement data, for example, may indicate that the youngest learners are proficient overall in phonemic awareness and decoding, but that their language development is limited. A book club on oral language and vocabulary development may be needed. Observational data constitute another potential source of ideas. As literacy coaches observe instruction, they will learn that teachers struggle with implementation in one or more areas of the program; book clubs can be planned to develop knowledge and expertise in those areas.

After a target area is identified, literacy coaches must locate resources. Since choice is important, it may be best to identify several different texts and then to allow teachers to choose the one they are most interested in reading. Text selection is crucial. Not all published sources are equal. Literacy coaches who do not monitor text selection for book clubs run the risk of engaging teachers in long-term work with ideas inconsistent with the principles of the building-level program or with the evidence base.

A professional organization such as a school should have a professional library. Literacy coaches should spend some of the building's resources in stocking this library. Book clubs are only successful if the members read the books; in a professional support system, these books must be provided. One way to build the library is to buy sets of texts (e.g., 10 copies) so that a small group can check them out for study and then return them for use by another group. In some cases, one text may be selected and copies purchased for the entire faculty. In other cases, each grade-level team might read a different text.

Establishing a procedure for discussion up front is also important. One possibility is to move from a small-group format to a larger jigsaw format. We have learned that it is important to start with the text and then move to experience. For example, we have created discussion forms requiring that the book club members first summarize the author's argument, then compare it with their experience, and finally, formulate specific possibilities for applying the ideas in their own program and practice. If individual book clubs all engage in this procedure, the entire staff can then meet to hear about these discussions across clubs. In this sort of jigsaw discussion, small groups end their study of a particular text by preparing and presenting what they have learned to the larger group. Individual and small-group accountability are both included.

LESSON PLANNING

The work of book clubs and study groups must be connected to the real work of teaching children. One of the best ways to accomplish this is to engage grade-level teams in collaborative lesson planning. The link is natural. New ideas can be discovered and discussed, but then they should be applied specifically. We have had extensive experience with lesson planning as a part of professional development. At first, we used our book studies with teachers to create broad guidelines for lesson planning. Unfortunately, though, those guidelines were often too broad, and individual teacher lessons did not capture for us the essence of the new idea. Discussions afterward were uncomfortable because teachers had made good-faith efforts to take ideas into their classrooms, and then we were in the position of having to suggest corrections after the fact. Instead, we moved to demonstration lessons and co-planning sessions. We, as coaches, planned *for* and then *with* teachers. Lesson plans from these efforts did not contain quite the individual emotional investment. If they went well, teachers could celebrate. If they did not, we could revise and try again without damaging relationships. If you would like to read about the results of our work with demonstration lessons and lesson planning, see *How to Plan Differentiated Reading Instruction: Resources for Grades K–3* (Walpole & McKenna, 2009b) or *Differentiated Reading Instruction in Grades 4 and 5* (Walpole et al., 2011).

If you would like to get your feet wet with co-planning lessons, we recommend that you begin with read-alouds. Read-alouds are safe and likely underutilized as a venue for literacy development. Management problems are unlikely. Texts can be chosen for their theme, content, level of difficulty, or their craft and structure. They need not be chosen diagnostically. And because they are not based on any diagnostic data, read-aloud plans can be shared and used across classrooms. We suggest that you begin by sharing the guidance presented in Figures 4.3 and 4.4. As a coach, you could afterward easily provide a mentor plan, including text introduction, vocabulary instruction, questioning strategies and queries, comprehension strategy modeling, and postreading discussion questions and writing prompts. You could demonstrate using that plan, with the teachers interacting as students. Then you could discuss the plan and make improvements before the teachers took it for use in their classrooms. At the next professional development session, you could release planning responsibility to the team, with each teacher constructing one plan, trying it in the classroom, making improvement, and then sharing it with colleagues.

In our outside-the-classroom professional development sessions, we have considered nuts-and-bolts sessions, using data, book clubs and study groups, and lesson planning. To us, these professional development sessions are necessary but insufficient for a comprehensive professional support system. Rita Bean (2004a) has described coaching activities along a continuum of intensity. The least intense coaching activities include providing materials and support, developing curriculum, helping with assessments, and participating in study groups. The co-planning we have just described is moderately intense; it actually impacts teaching directly. In this category she also places formal professional development presentations, grade-level meetings, and working with assessment data. The most intense activities, however, get closer to the heart of teaching and learning, and they are absolutely essential. They include work inside classrooms: modeling and observation and feedback.

OBSERVATION AND FEEDBACK

Outside-the-classroom professional development sessions and book clubs are not enough. Literacy coaches must move inside the classroom. Classroom observations are in the "most intense" category of coaching activities for a reason. For teachers, they are intimidating and potentially embarrassing. For coaches, though, the same adjectives apply. Observations produce data for coaches, and those data are almost always actionable. For coaches, the data are not about the characteristics of individual teachers. For coaches, the data are about the quality of the professional support system that the coach is leading. Over time, observations become a mirror of the coach's efforts to effect change.

Although we stress that observation drives professional support, it also helps establish the building-level climate. Literacy coaches who do not observe find themselves making incorrect assumptions about instruction. Literacy coaches tell us that they spend too much time on outside-the-classroom activities, and then they realize that their professional development has gotten out of sync with teachers' practices:

> "I think the biggest obstacle that I've been facing is people telling me one thing that they're doing, and then they're not doing it when I go by."

Literacy coaches need to keep careful track of what teachers are actually able to take from professional development into their classrooms. If teachers are not implementing the professional development, then the professional development has not been successful and must be redesigned. Observation is the only way to know.

Teachers need to learn that observation is a normal, nonevaluative part of their professional life. This is a difficult lesson, though. Most teachers have *never* been observed except for the purpose of evaluation. Most teachers have *never* observed a colleague to learn a new teaching strategy. Some teacher unions have very limiting language about who can observe and what they can do during an observation. Coaches need to take the school's observational culture into account as they design their professional support system. They have to be clear that observers do their work for very different purposes. Figure 10.6 distinguishes among these purposes.

If a school has a climate hostile to observation, the solution is frequent observation. Frequent observations combat a climate of isolated professionalism. If teachers are reluctant to have a coach observe, they can start with peer observations. Peer observations allow teachers to learn from one another; they are in no way evaluative. One way to begin is by scheduling a standards-based walk-through

Principal	Coach	Peer
Evaluate and supervise.	Provide targeted professional support.	Learn from colleagues.

FIGURE 10.6. Observers by type and purpose.

(Roberts & Pruitt, 2008). This walk-through is conducted by all teachers when there are no students in school. It is a strategy that could be used during preplanning as soon as teachers have set up their classrooms. The coach can prepare a list of things to look for in classrooms, and then create cross-grade-level teams. Figure 10.7 provides some ideas. Note that the items are not threatening and they give teachers a chance to gather ideas from colleagues to enhance their own classroom organizational plan.

Teachers need to grow accustomed to being observed, and a standards-based walk-through can set the stage. The next step may be to move from peer observations of classrooms to peer observations of instruction. Showers and Joyce (1996) have focused careful attention on the relationship between particular aspects of a professional development session and the likelihood of transfer to actual changes in teaching behaviors. They have documented how peer coaching can be an especially important component. Peer coaching is a schoolwide system where all teachers are organized into teams that plan together and into pairs where partners observe one another. During this observation, one person is observer and the other is coach—but the definition of coach is counterintuitive. The coach is the one who is teaching; the one who is watching is being coached. Teachers support one another's growth in practice by demonstration rather than by giving any feedback.

As a climate of observation is being developed, coaches need to learn to observe. We think that the best way to start is by conducting brief and frequent classroom walk-throughs. A walk-through answers questions about the instructional schedule, management, and typical practice. Does the schedule work or does

- Instructional schedule
- Procedures for attendance and lunch count
- Systems for turning in work
- Books for read-alouds
- Books for independent reading
- Comprehension strategy posters
- Materials for writing
- Bulletin boards to display student work

FIGURE 10.7. Look-fors in a standards-based walk-through.

it need adjustment? Are teachers able to manage transitions from one activity to another? Are specialists on time and integrated into the life of classrooms? How are classrooms similar to and different from one another? Each of these questions is about the literacy program in general rather than about individual teachers.

Coaches do need to move to individual formative observations. A formative observation is designed to guide an individual teacher by providing the feedback needed to examine and improve his or her own practice. As a professional development tool, formative observation must be carefully defined and described to teachers. There are three basic categories of observational tools from which a coach can choose; they are described in Figure 10.8. In our experience, as coaches are establishing a climate for observation, checklists are the most comfortable to teachers, rubrics are less comfortable, and open-ended notes are the most uncomfortable. It may be best to start with checklists, and then move to the other tools.

We have learned that it is best to start with very targeted observations. A teacher's anxiety can be reduced if it is understood that everything else is off the table. It also lightens the coach's burden. For example, if a team has been focusing on read-alouds during professional development, the coach can observe only read-alouds. In that way, the coach is "testing" only what has been "taught." The coach and the team can actually talk about the content and format for formative observations, even creating an observation checklist. Figure 10.9 is a format for an observation of a small-group decoding lesson. You can see from the observation checklist that the coach and teachers were learning about a very specific type of instruction and that the coach's observational focus is very clear.

While fairly simple checklists can get the observational ball rolling, they are unlikely to be deep enough to guide a fully formed professional support system. Too much goes undocumented. Rubrics can be a next step. A rubric is designed to capture levels of quality, not the mere presence or absence of a component; it anticipates differences in advance. We have worked with a specific type of rubric called an innovation configuration (IC). ICs are rubrics that anticipate that, in any complex innovation, there will be varying types and amounts of implementation, some close to ideal and others quite distant (Hall & Hord, 2001; Roy & Hord, 2003). If you are working with preschool or kindergarten teachers to improve their shared storybook readings, we recommend a fully formed IC published in *The Reading*

Checklists	Rubrics	Open-ended notes
• Document presence or absence of specific items. • May be made for a specific strategy. • Typically do not capture quality.	• Apply preset categories. • May be tailored to the specifics of the school's program. • May capture quality.	• May capture both activities and time. • Demand more of the observer. • Can capture quality.

FIGURE 10.8. Observational tools for coaches.

Word Recognition and Fluency
The strategy requires that Elkonin boxes and manipulatives are used. The teacher models and students do each example following the teacher model. I noticed _____ _____ _____
The strategy requires that students have word lists. The teacher models and students chorally sound and blend. Then students practice. I noticed _____ _____ _____
The strategy requires that teachers review selected, previously taught high-frequency words and then teaches new words. I noticed _____ _____ _____

FIGURE 10.9. Sample observation checklist.

Teacher (Beauchat et al., 2009). That sample will provide a powerful model if you want to engage in the creation of an IC for your schoolwide literacy program.

The final, most intrusive observational tool is open-ended notes. The reason that we think this is the highest-stakes observation tool is that there is much less information about what the coach will be watching. Both a checklist and an IC can be provided to the teacher in advance. Not so with open-ended notes. However, we do think that open-ended notes can be a powerful tool for an experienced coach. They capture quality, allow for differentiation, and provide opportunities for real discussion of the characteristics of instruction and the needs of specific children. We tend to use open-ended notes ourselves, but remember that we have been coaching teachers for many years.

Once you have chosen your tool, individual observations should proceed in a cycle, with a preobservation meeting, a targeted observation, a reflection on what you have learned, and then feedback to the teacher. This cycle is represented in Figure 10.10.

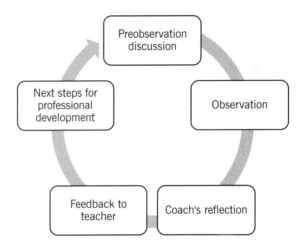

FIGURE 10.10. Observation and feedback cycle.

During the preobservation conference (which can be very brief), the nuts and bolts of the observation should be described. These should include the date and time that the observation will begin and end and what the coach will do (take notes, use a checklist, type on a laptop or tablet). The coach can ask the teacher if there is anything special to consider, and should tell the teacher exactly when and how the teacher will receive feedback. This can include a scheduled meeting or a written summary. Either way, that information must be kept confidential. One coach told us that she tells her teachers, "The only person who will find out anything about this observation is the person you tell."

During the actual observation, it is important that the coach be open to learning. When we watch, we still learn new things about teaching, reading development, the strengths and weaknesses of curriculum materials, and the real rewards and challenges of teaching. We are careful to take every observation seriously, as an invitation. We try not to think of things to change; we must spend all of our energy understanding what is actually happening.

Reflection should come after the observation—not during. A coach has to analyze and reflect on the data yielded from an observation. Two questions should be central to this thinking: "What have I learned about the state of our school-wide literacy program?" and "What have I learned about this teacher that I can use to make my professional support system more effective?" The answer to the first question is retrospective; it gives feedback to the literacy coach about the effectiveness of his or her professional development to date. The answer to the second question is prospective; it gives direction to future professional development. The answers to both questions allow literacy coaches actually to address the individual needs of their adult learners. One literacy coach shared this reflection with us:

"To some people teaching is a job, and to others it is a profession. And I think that [in some cases there's a] lack of knowledge, because my teachers come from different colleges that have different philosophies, and I think that's part of it. They just don't have that knowledge, and they're not … either they're not self-motivated to find it, or they don't even know that they don't know. And I have to realize that they're just like kids, in that they're all in different places in their knowledge. We've made a lot of assumptions here about what kids know. We've assumed that they know things that they don't, and … I have to get out of [making] that [assumption] with teachers. So it seems like I try to collect information and use that to drive the upcoming session."

The best literacy coaches we know are able to make nonjudgmental use of the information that they get from observations:

"Each teacher has a different weak- I shouldn't say weakness, but something that they need to work on. [The important things are] going in there and finding out what each teacher needs and being able to talk with them. And trying to develop a relationship with them so they won't think of me as the enemy."

The final, crucial step in the cycle of observation is sharing the information with the teacher. In our experience, teachers are very nervous about observations at first (mainly because their experience has consisted only of observations by an administrator for the purpose of evaluation). However, if feedback is quick and specific, they are grateful. Feedback can be written or oral, but it should be provided quickly, before a teacher has forgotten his or her own goals and insights for the lesson. Feedback must include positive comments, but they have to be sincere ones. Feedback must center on application and implementation of ideas previously covered in professional development. Feedback should include suggestions for improving teaching and learning, but again, these must be specific. Finally, feedback should include an offer from the literacy coach to the teacher. The session (or the written comments) should end with, "How can I help you?" (Feeney, 2007).

It may help to have a format for a feedback conference, especially if an observation has revealed real struggles. You might be surprised, but teachers often do most of the talking. Gibson (2006) suggests that coaches open by connecting to a topic that you know the teacher is concerned about or interested in. Then ask the teacher to provide observations related to that topic. The coach can clarify and respond to the teacher's observations, and invite the teacher to propose a course of action. Finally, the coach can clarify and respond to the teacher's proposal so that both coach and teacher are clear about what they have decided.

Some literacy coaches establish individual protocols for providing feedback. One literacy coach shared her system for observation and feedback:

"I took a laptop computer with me, and I have a little form that has three sections: a description of what I see, celebrations, and then considerations. I try to make the descriptions almost just like a script, as much as I can, as quickly as I can. The celebrations, that's pretty easy. I try to always make sure I give a little general one right from the onset. And then I try to get really specific things. And I don't think a day has passed yet that I've given the feedback that I haven't had a teacher approach me and say, 'I appreciate that.' If I don't write something that was a celebration, but I remembered to mention it to them later, then I think they really feel like 'She was watching when she was in there.' A lot of us have never been watched this way. You're the only one that's going to see [my observation]. That's the end of it. What happens is [that] you read it and hopefully you benefit from it, and that's all. We'll carry on, and I'll give you another [observation] next time."

Establishing a climate for observation and for collegial discussion of teaching and learning is one of the most powerful ways that a literacy coach can evaluate and improve a professional support system. Not all formative observations produce positive feedback; not all conferences with teachers are effective in changing instruction. However, a climate that embraces formative observation can set a school community on the road to continual improvement—improvement that could (if necessary) continue even without the support of the literacy coach.

MODELING

Literacy coaches often include modeling in their system for professional support. Typically, they model in two ways: First, they model instruction outside the classroom during small- and large-group sessions. This modeling is designed simply to introduce materials and techniques in the context of professional development. Because there are no students, this modeling is low risk. However, because there are no students, this modeling is also insufficient for real understanding of the use of new materials or techniques. The second type of modeling that literacy coaches do is in the classroom; they teach children while individual teachers (or sometimes groups of teachers) watch them. When a coach models during whole-class time, logistics aren't a problem. However, freeing up a teacher to observe during small-group work can be logistically difficult because the teacher has other responsibilities. One coach told us she solved this problem by taking advantage of technology. She borrowed the *teacher's* phone and created a short video of the small-group session she wished the teacher to see. The teacher could watch it later on and they could discuss what happened afterward.

Literacy coaches make very different choices about when and why they model in classrooms. Some literacy coaches model so that they can really understand the schoolwide literacy program, especially those aspects that are new; the understanding that they get from this method is very powerful.

> "I started it myself. I went into a second-grade classroom. I stayed in there 2 weeks. I did the lessons. And then I had the other teachers come and watch me. And then I modeled for them, and then after that they went out, and I started observing them. That's how [I've started] every piece that we've brought in this year."

For literacy coaches who choose to work in this way, collegial relationships with teachers are established immediately. What better way is there to start out a system for observation and feedback than to have the leader be the first one observed?

Some literacy coaches model for all teachers. First, they target a part of the day or a part of the program and introduce it outside the classroom. Next, they set up a schedule to demonstrate it in every classroom. Then they observe the teachers as they implement it.

> "Usually the morning part of my day is spent coaching. So I'm observing, I'm modeling, I'm demonstrating lessons during those blocks of time. And whatever I'm teaching in [professional development] usually parallels what I'm modeling, demonstrating, or observing, so that it is a simultaneous kind of thing. I guess some *transforming* is the right word. But I try not to evaluate anything that I haven't already taught. And I don't want to observe and I don't want to model anything that I haven't already taught before. I like it to be hand in hand."

Other literacy coaches model as needed. They initiate new goals and practices during outside-the-classroom professional development sessions, and then they observe teachers as they implement them. For teachers who are struggling, they model. At first, this may be uncomfortable; such teachers may feel singled out for poor practices. But later, it is likely that different teachers will need modeling for different aspects of the program.

> "I've had several teachers, interestingly enough, who have said, 'I would like for you to make recommendations. I want to try to implement them, and I want you to come back and see me again, and then I want you to model a lesson.'"

Over time, teachers appreciate such support and request modeling when they are struggling. At that point, literacy coaches can combine modeling, collaborating, and observing.

"I had a teacher who was at the kindergarten level, and this was her first year. She really experienced some difficulty trying to manage her groups. So I went into her classroom and I administered a center, and as the children rotated, I sat in there for about 3 hours, and I helped her to develop some better ways of having her students transition and manage her classroom. And I actually took her to visit another school so that she could observe teachers teaching kindergarten, just to go to a different environment so that she wouldn't be intimidated. I went back into her class Monday just to ask her a question, and she had already started making changes in her class, and I thought that was wonderful. She was open-minded, and she was willing to accept change."

This type of professional support for adults in a school building is actually very much like the instructional responsibility we are asking those adults to assume for children—it includes whatever it takes.

Literacy coaches are likely to be juggling many responsibilities, so we urge them to make the best possible use of their modeling time. First, they should collect artifacts that can be shared in professional development sessions: videos, student work, preparation or lesson plans, reflections. A particularly powerful artifact would be an observation (conducted by the classroom teacher) using the format that the literacy coach will then use to observe others. Literacy coaches who allow themselves to be observed have the chance to establish a very positive support system. They can actually show teachers that they are human—they make mistakes, they learn as they go, they reflect on both successes and failures.

PACING PROFESSIONAL SUPPORT

Creation of a professional support system is surely not an easy task. A literacy coach may find him- or herself in a situation in which a school building's staff must implement a totally new assessment system, a totally new schedule, and use a totally new set of commercial materials. Typically, there is little time between designing the system and the first day of school. In essence, some literacy coaches begin their professional support work in emergency mode—an ineffective mode for teaching and learning.

To create a truly comprehensive system of professional support, we urge literacy coaches to balance the time they spend providing support inside classrooms (through observations, feedback, and modeling) with time they devote to providing support outside the classroom (through knowledge-building sessions, data-based presentations, and book clubs). We urge literacy coaches to provide support both orally (through discussion) and in writing (through confidential, written feedback about teaching). We urge literacy coaches to provide support with curriculum materials (through assistance with understanding their organization and interpretation, and by locating new materials when they are needed for children). But no one can do all of those things at once. You will need to pace yourself.

ESTABLISHING COHERENCE

It may seem odd that we don't really discuss the real work of coaching until we near the end of this book. That is because no system of professional development, observations, coaching, modeling, or study groups will make a difference to teachers and children unless it directly and specifically supports a well-articulated, evidence-based, schoolwide program. A coach must make sure that everything that teachers are asked to learn and do is coherent. Everything must be clearly linked to the schoolwide design. A professional support system has three nested goals: serving individual teachers within their school, serving the school community through study of the effects of the initiative on student achievement, and serving the district community by connecting and embedding all initiatives to serve students (Joyce & Showers, 1996). A coherent system of professional support will provide powerful results.

CHAPTER 11

Leadership

We began this book with an overview of the roles, some of them quite new, that literacy coaches are creating and assuming. Taken together, these new roles constitute a radically different definition of instructional leadership. Literacy coaches are in a unique position to build the relationships that are required for teachers to enact a school's schoolwide vision—the real measure of leadership. These changes include an assessment system that informs instruction, a school-level and classroom-level instructional schedule that supports teaching and learning, a set of high-quality instructional materials and strategies, a well-integrated and flexible intervention plan, and a system of professional support that responds to the needs of all adults who work with children. To enact these changes, literacy coaches must recognize and attend to their roles as members of a leadership team. In this chapter, we share what we have learned about instructional leadership from literacy coaches and from the principals and district-level personnel who work with them.

CONCEPTUALIZING LEADERSHIP

Much has been said in the research literature about the role of the principal as instructional leader. Successful schools are in fact more likely to have principals with a deep knowledge of instruction and a commitment to time in the classrooms. Unsuccessful schools are more likely to have principals whose primary function is management of the building and personnel, and who take a bureaucratic stance toward teaching and learning (Murphy, 2004). This state of affairs is no accident. During the 1970s and 1980s, research established a clear link between a principal's subject matter expertise and pupil achievement. In the famous "Federal

Reserve Study," for example (Kean, Summers, Raivetz, & Farber, 1979), the reading achievement of a large number of Philadelphia fourth graders was examined for possible relationships with a host of factors. The principal's knowledge of reading instruction was among these significant factors. The more a principal knew about reading, the higher reading achievement tended to be, when other variables were controlled. Studies such as this led to calls for principals to lead the way for their teachers, with their personal expertise lighting the path ahead.

This notion of the principal's primary function has come to be called the *instructional leadership model*. Unfortunately, attempts to implement the model have proved somewhat disappointing. It has become clear that there is far more to raising achievement than enhancing the principal's expertise. Indeed, Hallinger, Bickman, and Davis (1996) concluded that there is no *direct* effect of a principal's expertise on reading. Rather, such expertise affects the decisions a principal makes and the school's climate.

An alternative is the *transformational model*, in which the principal facilitates a problem-solving approach. In this model, the principal acknowledges the expertise of teachers, particularly because of their proximity to and familiarity with the problems they face in their classrooms. The teachers no longer rely on the principal as the main repository of expertise. Instead, the principal draws upon and focuses the teachers' expertise in the process of addressing problems. This model may make it possible for principals to shift their focus from growth in teaching (driven by evaluative observations) to growth in learning (guided by team problem solving; DuFour, 2002). However, many principals lack the interpersonal skills needed to make such a model work. In a study of 105 California superintendents, Davis (1997) found that more than 65% listed poor interpersonal skills as a reason principals failed. Of course, this finding does not negate the transformational model, but it does suggest that not everyone can implement it.

Which of these two models is better? This is certainly a Hobson's choice, in that both models have promising attributes. Indeed, a study by Marks and Printy (2003) argues that a hybrid model works best. The most effective principals know their subject *and* can facilitate the process of teacher growth. Printy, Marks, and Bowers (2009) propose the term *integrated leadership* to capture the fact that in some schools both transformational leadership from the principal and shared instructional leadership among teachers can operate together.

Leadership in schools must be crafted at the building level, responding to the needs of adult and child learners in the school community. The Annenberg Institute for School Reform has been supporting the professional growth of instructional leaders and sharing information on the ways that these leaders are reconceptualizing their work. These "new" instructional leaders are "lead learners": They actually participate in professional development alongside teachers, and then provide follow-up sessions to direct the implementation and integration of new ideas in the building. They maintain the focus on collaborative time spent in teaching and learning (rather than on policies and procedures). They work to develop and distribute leadership responsibility within the whole school community. They create professional learning communities—where adults have regular time to meet and discuss teaching and learning, and where adults read to learn. They use data to inform their decisions, and they share that data with stakeholders both inside and outside the building. Finally, they use school-level resources (people, time, and money) creatively (King, 2002). The Annenberg leaders sound like literacy coaches. In fact, they are central office staff members, principals, and school-level professional development providers.

How do coaches enter the leadership mix? Not always easily. An interesting new line of research on the effects of teacher leaders gets to the heart of an issue that many coaches face: they resist specific parts of their role as instructional leaders. Literacy teaching and learning integrate such a broad body of knowledge and no one can know all of it; coaches cannot position themselves as the source of all instructional truth (Toll, 2005). However, coaches must be willing to position themselves as having some specialized expertise. If they do not, they tend not to deliver constructive criticism, retermed *hard feedback*, as a part of their professional support system. A reluctance to give hard feedback to individual teachers whose practice needs improvement amounts to tacit support of that practice (Mangin & Stoelinga, 2011). One of the best ways to overcome this reluctance is to think in terms of child advocacy. Children who receive poor instruction depend, without knowing it, on a coach to take action on their behalf. We find that thinking about the problem in this way makes it easier to have that courageous conversation now and then.

While coaches may not be willing to address teaching issues, many do feel personally responsible for every aspect of reading instruction in their schools. Although their conscientiousness is laudable, the result can be high levels of stress and frustration. Fostering a responsible, responsive professional community means permitting others to help shoulder the burden. Coaches should seek ways of creating leaders among the teachers they serve. This requires sharing instructional leadership, which in turn means promoting leadership in others. Doing so can result in long-lasting change. As Michael Fullan observes, "The main mark of an effective leader at the end of his or her tenure is not so much the impact on the bottom line (of profits or student achievement), but rather how many good leaders he or she leaves behind who can go even further" (2005, p. 35).

Part of the leadership work of a coach is to build teachers' sense of self-efficacy. If teachers feel their efforts have little impact on student learning, a self-fulfilling prophesy may result. Teachers need to become part of a learning community, nurtured by the coach. Such a community not only builds expertise but fosters a can-do spirit that translates into altered practice. Joyce and Showers (2002) summarize the research on school leadership this way: "Essentially, what is needed is an elevating belief system, one where the idea that schools can increase learning capability is central, rather than an accepting belief system that assumes that schools must accept the limitations of students and can do little to improve their ability" (p. 162).

ISSUES OF AUTHORITY

Although literacy coaches must accept their roles as content experts and their responsibility to help foster leadership in others, they work within a system. They are unlikely to be successful if they do not attend to leadership issues at three levels: within the district, within the building-level administration, and within the faculty. Each of these three levels has its own set of leadership challenges; we fear that some literacy coaches will find their efforts thwarted because they do not take the time (or have the personal skills) to attend to leadership issues at one or more of these levels.

Leadership within the District

Literacy coaches must attend to their position in relation to central office staff members, particularly those who have previously had responsibility for some of the coaches' work. Many of the literacy coaches we have worked with have "special" positions in their schools; in the district, some schools have won federal grants to fund the work of literacy coaches and to pay for professional development and curriculum resources, while others have not. In other cases, districts use local resources to assign coaches to some buildings but not others. This policy is likely to breed resentment and mistrust. Literacy coaches must take steps to situate their work (and even the services they provide) at their schools as a part of the shared mission of the district to improve teaching and learning.

First, it is important to have regular contact with district-level personnel. Directors of Title I, directors of special education, assistant superintendents who coordinate instruction, and even superintendents must be included in building-level planning and informed about the status of the schoolwide program. Everything that is learned in the context of the change effort—how to collect and analyze data, how to evaluate and use new curriculum materials, how to schedule the school day and year, how to integrate and conduct professional development in the school community—should be shared with the central office staff. In that way, coaches can connect their schoolwide work to other schools in the district rather than having each school operate independently.

Literacy coaches who can share this learning with humility are more likely to be successful at creating positive relationships within the district. We offer an important caveat, however. The politically astute literacy coach is ever aware of the line-and-staff organizational structure that defines supervisory relationships. Figure 11.1 illustrates the most typical structure. In this arrangement, the literacy coach reports to the building principal, who in turn reports to a central office official (often an assistant superintendent). The reason for keeping this "chain of command" in mind is that some principals may see direct contacts between the coach and the central office as jumping the chain and "going over the principal's head." The literacy coach must exercise tact by always clearing such contacts with the

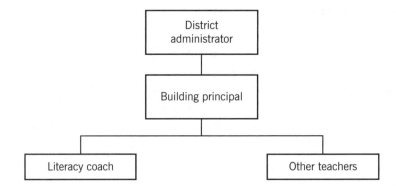

FIGURE 11.1. Typical line-and-staff organizational structure.

principal. The principal must never be caught unaware by a central office employee who has been dealing with the coach without the principal's knowledge.

Leadership within the Building-Level Administration

A coach's position is generally vested with little or no formal power. Effective coaches thrive on persuasion, tact, community building, and service. But the principal, in whom real power resides, is in a position either to further the coach's efforts, limit them through indifference, or overtly challenge them. It is up to the coach to craft a relationship in which the principal's actions are not only supportive but are *seen* as supportive by teachers. When this occurs, the coach derives power indirectly from the principal.

The ideal administrative team is collaborative. Although the principal and assistant principals in a large school building (we have worked in elementary schools with as many as 1,200 students) may by necessity have specialized roles, the "right hand" must know what the "left hand" is doing, and the focus on shared work to support teaching and learning must be maintained. One thing is certain: Literacy coaches can support change much more quickly and smoothly when they are part of an administrative team that makes decisions collaboratively and provides collegial support.

Unfortunately, the reality of many schools precludes this ideal scenario. In some schools, principals are managers who leave literacy coaches to do the instructional work alone. In such cases, the literacy coach is likely to be less effective, because the message to teachers is fragmented. The principal, who evaluates teachers' performance, does so with only incomplete knowledge of the goals of the schoolwide reading program.

What should a coach do in this situation? Even with the most reluctant principal, the literacy coach must relentlessly acknowledge that he or she works for the principal. A constant reminder of that relationship may help the principal to see his or her role as a partner over time. We have counseled many literacy coaches who struggle with this relationship to approach their principals frequently to ask two questions:

1. "How can I help you to do the work that you want to do in this building?"
2. "How will you help me to do that work more effectively?"

A principal may initially answer that the coach should know what he or she is supposed to be doing, and that it is not the principal's job to manage the coach. Over time, though, the principal may come to see that in supporting the coach, he or she is able to maintain "control" over the schoolwide program in new ways. Likewise, a coach may be a powerful leader without the formal authority of a principal once teachers see that the coach has specific expertise in areas associated with the school's mission and that they need to build their expertise with the coach's help to contribute to the mission (Dexter, Louis, & Anderson, 2009).

Leadership within the Staff

Negotiating leadership at the district level and within the administrative team is actually only a means to an end. This end is the real meat of the job—that is, leadership among teachers. There is a secret to developing a leadership position among teachers. It acknowledges and accommodates the many different personal styles and skills that literacy coaches bring to their work, and it allows them to have a common mission. The secret is not strength, wit, or knowledge of research. It is not administrative skill, research skill, teaching experience, or graduate training. The secret is service. Literacy coaches who see their mission as service to teachers, to make it easier for the teachers to provide service to children, are good leaders.

Visible, hands-on work on real issues of teaching and learning is key for literacy coaches who earn a leadership role on their staff. They do it in many ways. In effect, they do whatever it takes: they unpack boxes, copy, make lesson plans, make manipulatives, assess children, enter data, bring snacks. They do these things without being asked and without much reward, especially at first. They make themselves useful to teachers, so that they can build the relationships that allow them to be real instructional leaders.

We have worked with literacy coaches who come from inside their schools, and who struggle with issues of leadership because the teachers are reluctant to acknowledge their new role. They may suffer from the "prophets in their own country" syndrome. We have also worked with literacy coaches who come from outside their schools, and who struggle with issues of leadership because the teachers are reluctant to trust an outsider. Both sets of coaches become successful once the teachers really see them as providing a service—as responding to their individual and collective needs. And this level of buy-in gives the schoolwide program the momentum it needs.

SUPPORTING THE STRUGGLING TEACHER

The odds are high that a literacy coach will encounter some teachers whose skills are marginal. Citing both research and expert opinion, Tucker (2001) has stated bluntly that "5–15% of teachers in public classrooms perform at incompetent levels" (p. 52). Successful literacy coaches are willing to be supportive to all teachers and to differentiate this support for individual teachers in the way teachers differentiate support for individual children. The key to doing that is an absolute belief that teachers can learn, and that teachers who are struggling have the same rights as children who are struggling. They simply need more and sometimes different levels of support. Unfortunately, a struggling teacher often initially appears as a hostile teacher. To get through these dark days, a literacy coach has to look beyond the hostility and assume that the problem is simply that the teacher needs more help.

It is important to spend time listening to teachers who are struggling. A coach armed with assessment results, observational evidence, and research findings may be tempted to quickly evaluate and discount what a teacher has to say. This tendency may be reflected in interrupting the teacher or thinking about a response before the teacher finishes. The coach may be on firmer ground, to be sure, but listening actively not only conveys the impression that a teacher's thoughts are welcome; it also provides the coach with a better understanding of a teacher. "Too often," Rita Bean observes, "we listen only half-heartedly because we are busy evaluating, interpreting, or preparing our responses rather than simply trying to understand what the person is trying to communicate. Active listening is one of the key skills of an effective leader" (2004b, p. 60).

One literacy coach we know worked with a very difficult kindergarten teacher. The teacher was so resistant to the schoolwide effort that she physically turned her back during professional development sessions. She alienated the other members of her grade-level team to the point where she and they weren't speaking to each other; she thwarted the instruction and intervention schedule by having parents require that children take naps at the time designated for other things. She made every effort to insult the coach and to get other teachers to join in her rebellion.

The literacy coach was stymied, hurt, and angry. She tried to avoid this teacher, and she became physically flustered when this teacher approached her. At the January state of the school meeting, the literacy coach was sharing the grade-level assessment results. Individual teachers had copies of assessment results for their classes and were looking at the ways that their students compared with the results across classrooms. All but one of the children in need of intensive intervention came from one classroom—the difficult teacher's classroom, where children were sleeping while others received instruction and intervention. The literacy coach did not share this tidbit of information with the school, but because the reluctant teacher had her own data, she could see it for herself.

After the meeting, the teacher confronted the literacy coach. Initially, as always, she was angry and the coach was flustered. The coach steeled her resolve, though, and told the teacher that she really believed that it was not too late for the children—that they could work together immediately to rework the teacher's schedule and to change her focus. The teacher cried. The coach promised that she would teach for 1 week, to model. The coach also suggested that they meet that Friday to make a plan for that week. The teacher refused; she wanted to stay that evening and get on board the very next day.

What the coach learned was that the struggling teacher was hostile because she was afraid. This will usually be the case. When learners are afraid, they cannot learn. The literacy coach had not met the needs of this teacher, so she had become more and more afraid and hostile. This spiraling fear and hostility had caused the literacy coach herself to become afraid, so she became even less effective. We think that this is a common story. We urge literacy coaches to be effective leaders. To do so, they will have to step back from conflicts with teachers and ask themselves what they can do to support those teachers.

One thing to remember about working with teachers who are struggling is that the support for change must acknowledge and capitalize on what the teachers already know. Literacy coaches who start with teacher "deficits" rather than teacher "assets" are unlikely to be effective. This is an essential leadership quality; coaches must be able to see the strengths of their learners, and they must communicate those strengths to the learners in authentic and sincere ways.

WHAT ABOUT THE RESISTANT TEACHER?

There is a difference between "can't" and "won't." We have worked with coaches who focus almost all of their time and attention on particular teachers who simply will not participate in the schoolwide program. A few teachers will not collect data, participate in professional development sessions, open or use new materials, allow modeling, or accept observation and feedback. For many, as suggested above, this resistance will be the result of fear of change—fear that they will not be able to do what the coach is asking. Instead of admitting that fear (possibly even to themselves), these teachers may instead attempt to thwart the change by passively or actively resisting it. Given the relentless support that we are advocating, most teachers will gradually develop the confidence they need to become a part of the schoolwide effort. But not all will.

For a teacher with whom the literacy coach has exhausted all of his or her personal efforts at support to no effect, it is time to document these efforts and share them with the principal. Ultimately, it is the principal who makes administrative decisions about personnel, and who documents performance and evaluates the staff. A literacy coach cannot and should not take that evaluative work as part of his or her job; in Chapter 10 we have advocated that observation and feedback be given to teachers privately and in a nonthreatening way. Rarely, though, a literacy coach will have to admit that he or she has been unsuccessful with supporting a particular adult learner, and that it is time to ask for help from the principal.

We suggest that the literacy coach do this very formally, by writing a letter both to the teacher and to the principal that documents the general problem, the types (rather than specific details) of support the coach has provided, and the failure of that support. In this way, the literacy coach moves the locus of control into the front office; the teacher and principal will have to acknowledge that the literacy coach has failed with this teacher and decide what to do next. In some cases, the principal will be strong and supportive enough to counsel the teacher to transfer to a building where the requirements are more consistent with his or her beliefs and practices. In other cases, the literacy coach will simply have to acknowledge the failure with this particular teacher and try not to worry about it any more. This is easier said than done, but it is a reality of work in the complex environment of a school. Ultimately, it is a question of time. The coach must consider the time spent in futilely attempting to reach such a teacher, and realize that this time might be spent far more productively in working with other teachers.

MANY VOICES

Coaches Speak Out

Schoolwide change is difficult—very difficult. If you take on the role of literacy coach, you will have many difficult days. But you are likely to learn more about teaching and learning in this role than in any other you may have had. We know that this is where we have learned. Now listen to the voices of literacy coaches engaged in their first year's work. They work in many different settings: in large schools, small schools, urban schools, rural schools. Below, you will see the comments of different coaches, each answering the same two questions during different months in the same year:

1. "What is the biggest success you've had so far?"
2. "What has been the biggest obstacle for you?"

September

"The biggest success? It's really with the fluency. They taught the textbook. They put the lesson out every day. If the child wasn't learning, something's wrong with this kid, and we need to get him tested. Even just doing a little bit of fluency every day, the kids—the teachers start to see they're moving.

"The biggest obstacle? They won't come out in the open and be honest about the problems they're experiencing, and I know it's fear of change, but they try to undermine it in other ways."

"The biggest success? I think it was having our schedule organized for the beginning of the year. Our schedule is 60 minutes for whole-group phonics and read-aloud. Then we have another 60 minutes for small-group reading. Then we have another 60 minutes for writing.

"The biggest obstacle? To connect to them and make them want to change, without having to force them to change, which would make it more difficult, because when you make somebody do something, they're gonna resist and they're not gonna do as good a job as they would if they changed their mind."

October

"The biggest success? The positive enthusiasm among the teachers to want to learn. I think that's the biggest thing. And even the areas where I can see that—there are approximations at least.

"The biggest obstacle? It's a lot. It's a lot of teachers—31 teachers, total. Because of the responsibilities of ordering the classroom books and all of that, I mean, my name is called all the time. 'When are you gonna come to my room and do this?' And I want so bad to be everywhere, and that's the hardest part for me. And sometimes I drive myself crazy and work way too long and way too late and get way too tired."

"The biggest success? I think the dialogue is flowing more freely between the teachers and myself, and I feel like that's the door that I wanted to be sure was open, and that's open now.

"The biggest obstacle? There are a lot of questions coming from a lot of different directions. Different grade levels have a lot of different topics—a lot of different real, true concerns."

"The biggest success? I think I've earned some credibility with them. They see that I'm worked as hard as they are. I've done a lot of things for them.

"The biggest obstacle? The [district] policy-driven mindset that people have, whether it's really been forced upon them or whether they're creating it for themselves."

"The biggest success? I guess implementing a tutoring program [with] 144 kids, and [having] 113 tutors come in and visit those kids three times a week. I mean, that's a phenomenal thing in itself.

"The biggest obstacle? It's just an overwhelming task. It's just the sheer enormity of the school and the job."

November

"The biggest success? Really, it's the initiation of a lot of vocabulary things. I mean, I didn't think it would fly and I didn't think teachers would love it, but the kids love it and the teachers do too.

"The biggest obstacle? Coming from a middle school background, I did not understand [differentiated instruction]. And I'm not sure that I really understand it now, because I've only seen it done one way."

"The biggest success? A mother called me, and she was just really moved. You know, she said that her son was very unmotivated—that when he came home before he just hated to do his schoolwork, and he didn't want to come to school. And she said now he's excited about his schoolwork. He likes to read. She said when she walks in from work, he's already done his homework, and he's got his book in his hand waiting to read to her. She told me that we had changed her life.

"The biggest obstacle? Changing philosophies for some. People who have been in it for a long time. It's hard for me to go in and say, 'This is what you need to do,' when this person has taught for 25 years."

December

"The biggest success? The way our kindergarten got on board. They've already accomplished [with kids] now what they'd done at the end of the year last year.

"The biggest obstacle? Ugh. Time. Time is the worst thing. For me, for the teachers."

"The biggest success? My biggest success has been the reception that has been received from the teachers in administering [a developmental spelling test]. And getting that book room started and finished.

"The biggest obstacle? We need more books."

January

"The biggest success? Well, I think the shared-book room is a big success. And that the teachers have been accepting of trying to use it.

"The biggest obstacle? They're very friendly and open on one side, and then I think they go and close their door and do whatever they want to. And I cannot be in 12 rooms at any one time, so I'm going to have to do a lot more observations. I'm not spending enough time in the classrooms, and I'm not modeling enough."

"The biggest success? I've seen how difficult the change is, but ... I believe the teachers are starting to express excitement about what they're seeing.

"The biggest obstacle? The biggest obstacle has been being the new kid on the block. Not being from here, not necessarily being included."

"The biggest success? Still being alive in January. No. I think really, everything's coming together. More teachers have bought into it and at least are making the effort. [It] may not be perfect, but [they're] at least making the effort.

"The biggest obstacle? It's just hard to get to 43 classrooms and take care of those teachers' needs."

"The biggest success? I think that my biggest success is just what I have learned. I just feel that I have learned so much since we began this process.

"The biggest obstacle? Time. Just not enough time to get everything done. And I think I have enough time. I just don't think that I use it wisely."

"The biggest success? Getting them to look at the assessment data, and getting them to use it and know what it means and be able to use that to guide their instruction. Because that's something that we've never really done.

"The biggest obstacle? The mindset of the teachers toward the students below grade level. Getting them to realize that you have two groups, [and that you must] now do two different lessons. If you're gonna do the same lesson, do it whole-group. Do different things in the small groups."

February

"The biggest success? The more we learn, the better we're able to understand where our weaknesses are as a school and as a system. We've found that when teachers look at their data and they see the growth in the children, that makes it all worthwhile.

"The biggest obstacle? The job gets bigger every day. And having to prioritize what is the most important thing to do out of all the things that you have to do. I would say that's got to be the biggest thing."

"The biggest success? Winning over the teachers. I think that's the biggest success, because this is my first time doing something like this. I'm a different person because of this.

"The biggest obstacle? I think getting my data organized is an obstacle. I thought about that a lot. I wake up in the middle of the night thinking, 'What do I need to do to see this?' "

March

"The biggest success? Seeing the improvement. I love to see the growth.

"The biggest obstacle? Working with teachers who are less adaptive to change and are in denial, not wanting to step up to the plate."

"The biggest success? Working with the teachers.

"The biggest obstacle? Time. We have over 1,000 students, so sometimes I may have my day planned out, but something may come up."

"The biggest success? I guess it would be how well our kindergarten children are doing. Because those people gave me fits at first. The teachers were reluctant to step up the pace of instruction and to move to small-group instruction.

"The biggest obstacle? Setting up times for after-school study groups. We'll do that early on next year. You know, we're gonna have to protect those times."

May

"The biggest success? Actually seeing the teachers come on board has been wonderful.

"The biggest obstacle? [The] administration [is] not backing me, so [some] teachers [are] doing what they want to do. I was told to stop upsetting one teacher at one point."

"The biggest success? Our kids just seem to love to read.

"The biggest obstacle? Bringing all of the teachers over to one side. Convincing them that there is a different way, and it very well may be a better way than what they're used to doing."

"The biggest success? More people [teachers and paraprofessionals] working with children. There are two people working with children in the classroom. I think that the teachers can see where they were and the growth that their children are making.

"The biggest obstacle? Time. Meeting with them and getting them to where they need to be. I can't keep up."

Principals and Other Administrators Speak Out

Now listen to the voices of principals and district-level administrators. They are reflecting on the most important change that they've seen at each school after 1 year's schoolwide program and 1 year's collaboration with a literacy coach. They are responding in June, immediately following the year of change chronicled above. Remember that they are describing change; assume that the opposite was true at the start of the reform effort.

"I think the most important change that I've seen is, I've focused on what the research tells us about literacy instruction."

"I think in the past we've done a lot of teaching because it was expected and somebody told us this was the nice thing to do. I think this year when they teach something, they know this is what they need to be teaching and this is how they need to be teaching it. We know why we're teaching what we're teaching."

"They were assigning tasks, and I think that's one of the most profound things that I've learned through the whole process is that they didn't teach—they assigned tasks."

"Over the course of the year, I think folks have become more and more relaxed about expectations. They were real apprehensive about what kind of results they would get and were concerned that they may not have the results that they expected."

"The most important change is a more consistent, concise focus on reading and the way that we have scheduled it into our day."

"The most important change is that the children have gained a love for reading. They really have."

"I guess the most dominant effect would be the attitudes of teachers and their joy and excitement teaching reading."

"I've seen a cohesiveness among the teachers. I've seen a lot of self-confidence among the teachers and more collaborative work going on, and I think that's as a result of all of the professional development."

"The most important change is professional development, which has caused change in the classroom."

"The most important change has been the climate—the climate in terms of accepting research."

"The most important change is that I see children reading."

This last change—"I see children reading"—is the bottom line for us.

References

Adams, M. J. (1990). *Beginning to read: Thinking and learning about print.* Cambridge, MA: MIT Press.

Allington, R. L. (1994). What's special about special programs for children who find learning to read difficult? *Journal of Reading Behavior, 26,* 1–21.

Allington, R. L., & Cunningham, P. M. (2006). *Schools that work: Where all children read and write* (3rd ed.). Boston: Allyn & Bacon.

Allington, R. L., & McGill-Franzen, A. (1989). School response to reading failure: Chapter 1 and special education students in grades 2, 4, and 8. *Elementary School Journal, 89,* 529–542.

Allington, R. L., & McGill-Franzen, A. (1995). Flunking: Throwing good money after bad. In R. L. Allington & S. A. Walmsley (Eds.), *No quick fix: Rethinking literacy programs in America's elementary schools* (pp. 45–60). New York: Teachers College Press.

Almasi, J. F., Garas, K., Cho, H., Ma, W., Shanahan, L., & Augustino, A. (2004, December). *The impact of peer discussion on social, cognitive, and affective growth in literacy.* Paper presented at the 54th meeting of the National Reading Conference, San Antonio, TX.

Almasi, J. F., & Garas-York, K. (2009). Comprehension and discussion of text. In S. E. Israel & G. G. Duffy (Eds.), *Handbook of research on reading comprehension* (pp. 470–493). New York: Guilford Press.

Al Otaiba, S., Folsom, J. S., Schatschneider, C., Wanzek, J., Greulich, L., Meadows, J., et al. (2011). Predicting first-grade reading performance from kindergarten response to tier 1 instruction. *Exceptional Children, 77,* 453–470.

Al Otaiba, S., Kosanovich-Grek, M. L., Torgesen, J. K., Hassler, L., & Wahl, M. (2005). Reviewing core kindergarten and first-grade reading programs in light of No Child Left Behind: An exploratory study. *Reading and Writing Quarterly, 21,* 377–400.

Atteberry, A., & Bryk, A. S. (2011). Analyzing teacher participation in literacy coaching activities. *Elementary School Journal, 112,* 356–382.

Atwell, N. (1987). *In the middle: Writing, reading and learning with adolescents.* Portsmouth, NH: Boynton Cook/Heinemann.

Au, K. H. (2005). Negotiating the slippery slope: School change and literacy achievement. *Journal of Literacy Research, 37*, 267–288.

Auckerman, R. (1987). *The basal reading approach to reading.* New York: Wiley.

August, D., & Shanahan, T. (Eds.). (2006). *Developing literacy in second language learners.* Mahwah, NJ: Erlbaum.

Bandura, A. (1977). Self-efficacy: Toward a unifying theory of behavioral change. *Psychological Review, 84*, 191–215.

Bean, R. M. (2004a). Promoting effective literacy instruction: The challenge for literacy coaches. *The California Reader, 37*, 58–63.

Bean, R. M. (2004b). *The reading specialist: Leadership for the classroom, school, and community.* New York: Guilford Press.

Bean, R. M., Draper, J. A., Hall, V., Vandermolen, J., & Zigmond, N. (2010). Coaches and coaching in Reading First schools: A reality check. *Elementary School Journal, 111*, 87–114.

Bean, R. M., & Swan Dagen, A. (2012). *Best practices of literacy leaders.* New York: Guilford Press.

Bear, D. R., Invernizzi, M., Templeton, S., & Johnston, F. (2011). *Words their way: Word study for phonics, vocabulary, and spelling instruction* (5th ed.). Upper Saddle River, NJ: Pearson.

Bear, D. R., & Templeton, S. (1998). Explorations in developmental spelling: Foundations for learning and teaching phonics, spelling, and vocabulary. *The Reading Teacher, 52*, 222–242.

Beauchat, K., Blamey, K. L., & Philippakos, Z. A. (2012). *Effective read-alouds for early literacy: A teacher's guide for PreK–1.* New York: Guilford Press.

Beauchat, K. A., Blamey, K. L., & Walpole, S. (2009). Building preschool children's language and literacy one storybook at a time. *The Reading Teacher, 63*, 26–39.

Beauchat, K. A., Blamey, K. L., & Walpole, S. (2010). *The building blocks of preschool success.* New York: Guilford Press.

Beck, I. L., & McKeown, M. G. (2006). *Improving comprehension with questioning the author: A fresh and expanded view of a powerful approach.* New York: Scholastic.

Beck, I. L., McKeown, M. G., Hamilton, R. L., & Kucan, L. (1997). *Questioning the author: An approach for enhancing student engagement with text.* Newark, DE: International Reading Association.

Beck, I. L., McKeown, M. G., & Kucan, L. (2002). *Bringing words to life: Robust vocabulary instruction.* New York: Guilford Press.

Beck, I. L., McKeown, M. G., & Kucan, L. (2008). *Creating robust vocabulary: Frequently asked questions and extended examples.* New York: Guilford Press.

Beck, I. L., McKeown, M. G., Sandora, C., Kucan, L., & Worthy, J. (1996). Questioning the author: A yearlong classroom implementation to engage students with text. *Elementary School Journal, 96*, 385–414.

Biancarosa, G., Bryk, A. S., & Dexter, E. R. (2010). Assessing the value-added effects of literacy collaborative professional development on student learning. *Elementary School Journal, 111*, 7–34.

Biemiller, A. (2004). Teaching vocabulary in the primary grades. In J. F. Baumann & E.

J. Kame'enui (Eds.), *Vocabulary instruction: Research to practice* (pp. 28–40). New York: Guilford Press.

Biemiller, A. (2006). Vocabulary development and instruction: A prerequisite for school learning. In D. K. Dickinson & S. B. Neuman (Eds.), *Handbook of early literacy research* (Vol. 2, pp. 41–51). New York: Guilford Press.

Bjorklund, D. (1995). *Children's thinking: Developmental function and individual difference* (2nd ed.). Pacific Grove, CA: Brooks/Cole.

Blachowicz, C. Z., Buhle, R., Ogle, D., Frost, S., Correa, A., & Kinner, J. (2010). Hit the ground running: Ten ideas for preparing and supporting urban literacy coaches. *The Reading Teacher, 63*, 348–359.

Blackman, B. A., Ball, E., Black, R., & Tangel, D. (1994). Kindergarten teachers develop phonemic awareness in low-income, inner-city classrooms: Does it make a difference? *Reading and Writing: An Interdisciplinary Journal, 6*, 1–17.

Boscolo, P. (2008). Writing in primary school. In C. Bazerman (Ed.), *Handbook of research on writing* (pp. 293–309). New York: Erlbaum/Taylor & Francis.

Bowers, P. N., Kirby, J. R., & Deacon, S. H. (2010). The effects of morphological instruction on literacy skills: A systematic review of the literature. *Review of Educational Research, 80*, 144–179.

Brown, A. L., & Day, J. D. (1983). Macrorules for summarizing texts: The development of expertise. *Journal of Verbal Learning and Verbal Behavior, 22*, 1–14.

Buysse, V., Castro, D., & Peisner-Feinberg, E. (2010). Effects of a professional development program on classroom practices and outcomes for Latino dual language learners. *Early Childhood Research Quarterly, 25*, 194–206.

Caldwell, J. S., & Ford, M. P. (2002). *Where have all the bluebirds gone?: How to soar with flexible grouping.* Portsmouth, NH: Heinemann.

Carlisle, J. F., & Berebitsky, D. (2011). Literacy coaching as a component of professional development. *Reading and Writing, 24*, 773–800.

Cassady, J. C., & Smith, L. L. (2005). The impact of a structured integrated learning system on first-grade students' reading gains. *Reading and Writing Quarterly, 21*, 361–376.

Chall, J. S. (1967). *Learning to read: The great debate.* New York: McGraw-Hill.

Chall, J. S. (1996). *Learning to read: The great debate* (3rd ed.). Fort Worth, TX: Harcourt Brace College.

Chambers, B., Slavin, R. E., Madden, N. A., Abrami, P., Logan, M. K., & Gifford, R. (2011). Small-group, computer-assisted tutoring to improve reading outcomes for struggling first and second graders. *Elementary School Journal, 111*, 625–640.

Clark, A., Anderson, R. C., Kuo, L., Kim, I., Archodidou, A., & Kim, N. (2003). Collaborative reasoning: Expanding ways for children to talk and think in school. *Educational Psychology Review, 15*, 181–198.

Clay, M. M. (1979). *The early detection of reading difficulties.* Auckland, New Zealand: Heinemann.

Common Core State Standards Initiative. (2010). *Common Core State Standards for English language arts and literacy in history/social studies, science, and technical subjects.* Washington, DC: National Governors Association Center for Best Practices and the Council of Chief State School Officers.

Connor, C., Morrison, F. J., Fishman, B., Giuliani, S., Luck, M., Underwood, P. S., et al. (2011). Testing the impact of child characteristics × instruction interactions on third graders' reading comprehension by differentiating literacy instruction. *Reading Research Quarterly, 46,* 189–221.

Costa, A., & Garmston, R. (1997). *Cognitive coaching: A foundation for renaissance schools* (3rd ed.). Norwood, MA: Christopher-Gordon.

Coyne, M. D., Kame'enui, E. J., & Simmons, D. C. (2004). Improving beginning reading instruction and intervention for students with LD: Reconciling "all" with "each." *Journal of Learning Disabilities, 37,* 231–239.

Crain-Thoreson, C., & Dale, P. S. (1999). Enhancing linguistic performance: Parents and teachers as book reading partners for children with language delays. *Topics in Early Childhood Special Education, 19*(1), 28–39.

Cunningham, A. E., & Zibulsky, J. (2011). Tell me a story: Examining the benefits of shared reading. In S. B. Neuman & D. K. Dickinson (Eds.), *Handbook of early literacy research* (Vol. 3, pp. 396–411). New York: Guilford Press.

Cunningham, P. M., & Allington, R. L. (2010). *Classrooms that work: They can all read and write* (5th ed.). Boston: Pearson/Allyn & Bacon.

Cutler, L., & Graham, S. (2008). Primary grade writing instruction: A national survey. *Journal of Educational Psychology, 100,* 907–919.

Dale, P. S., Crain-Thoreson, C., Notari-Syverson, A., & Cole, K. (1996). Parent–child book reading as an intervention technique for young children with language delays. *Topics in Early Childhood Special Education, 16,* 213–235.

Danielson, C. (2002). *Enhancing student achievement: A framework for school improvement.* Alexandra, VA: Association for Supervision and Curriculum Development.

Davis, S. H. (1997). The principal's paradox: Remaining secure in a precarious position. *National Association of Secondary School Principals Bulletin 81, 592,* 73–80.

Denton, C. A., Fletcher, J. M., Anthony, J. L., & Francis, D. (2006). An evaluation of intensive intervention for students with persistent reading difficulties. *Journal of Learning Disabilities, 39,* 447–466.

Denton, C. A., Kethley, C., Nimon, K., Kurz, T. B., Mathes, P. G., Shih, M., et al. (2010). Effectiveness of a supplemental early reading intervention scaled up in multiple schools. *Exceptional Children, 76,* 394–416.

Desimone, L. M. (2009). Improving impact studies of teachers' professional development: Toward better conceptualizations and measures. *Educational Researcher, 38,* 181–199.

Dewitz, P., Jones, J., & Leahy, S. (2009). Comprehension strategy instruction in core reading programs. *Reading Research Quarterly, 44,* 102–126.

Dewitz, P., Leahy, S. B., Jones, J., & Maslin Sullivan, P. (2010). *The essential guide to selecting and using core reading programs.* Newark, DE: International Reading Association.

Dexter, S., Louis, K., & Anderson, R. E. (2009). The roles and practices of specialists in teamed institutional leadership. *Journal of School Leadership, 19,* 445–465.

Dole, J. A., & Nelson, K. L. (2012). Literacy leadership in the elementary school reading program. In R. M. Bean & A. Swan Dagen (Eds.), *Best practices of literacy leaders* (pp. 147–161). New York: Guilford Press.

Donovan, C. A., & Smolkin, L. B. (2001). Genre and other factors influencing teachers' book selections for science instruction. *Reading Research Quarterly, 38,* 412–440.

Donovan, C. A., & Smolkin, L. B. (2006). Children's understanding of genre and writing development. In C. A. MacArthur, S. Graham, & J. Fitzgerald (Eds.), *Handbook of writing research* (pp. 131–143). New York: Guilford Press.

Dowhower, S. L. (1999). Supporting a strategic stance in the classroom: A comprehension framework for helping teachers help students to be strategic. *The Reading Teacher, 52,* 672–683.

Duffy, A. M. (2001). Balance, literacy acceleration, and responsive teaching in a summer school literacy program for elementary struggling readers. *Reading Research and Instruction, 40,* 67–100.

Duffy, G. G. (2009). *Explaining reading: A resource for teaching concepts, skills, and strategies* (2nd ed.). New York: Guilford Press.

Duffy, G. G., & Hoffman, J. V. (2002). Beating the odds in literacy education: Not the "betting on" but the "bettering of" schools and teachers? In B. M. Taylor & P. D. Pearson (Eds.), *Teaching reading: Effective schools, accomplished teachers* (pp. 375–388). Mahwah, NJ: Erlbaum.

DuFour, R. (2002). The learning-centered principal. *Educational Leadership, 59*(8), 12–15.

DuFour, R., DuFour, R., & Eaker, R. (2008). *Revisiting professional learning communities at work: New insights for improving schools.* Bloomington, IN: Solution Tree.

Duke, N. K. (2000). 3.6 minutes per day: The scarcity of information texts in first grade. *Reading Research Quarterly, 35,* 202–224.

Duke, N. K. (2003). *Reading and writing informational text in the primary grades: Research-based practices.* New York: Scholastic.

Duke, N. K., & Carlisle, J. (2011). The development of comprehension. In M. L. Kamil, P. D. Pearson, E. B. Moje, & P. P. Afflerbach (Eds.), *Handbook of reading research* (Vol. 4, pp. 199–228). New York: Routledge.

Duke, N. K., Caughlan, S., Juzwik, M. M., & Martin, N. M. (2011). *Reading and writing genre with purpose in K–8 classrooms.* Portsmouth, NH: Heinemann.

Duke, N. K., Schmar-Dobler, E., & Zhang, S. (2006). Comprehension and technology. In M. C. McKenna, L. D. Labbo, R. Kieffer, & D. Reinking (Eds.), *International handbook of literacy and technology* (Vol. 2, pp. 317–326). Hillsdale, NJ: Erlbaum.

Ebert, E. K., & Crippen, K. J. (2010). Applying a cognitive-affective model of conceptual change to professional development. *Journal of Science Teacher Education, 21,* 371–388.

Elish-Piper, L., & L'Allier, S. K. (2011). Examining the relationship between literacy coaching and student reading gains in grades K–3. *Elementary School Journal, 112,* 83–106.

Elley, W. B. (1989). Vocabulary acquisition from listening to stories. *Reading Research Quarterly, 24,* 174–187.

Emig, J. (1971). *The composing processes of twelfth graders.* Urbana, IL: National Council of Teachers of English.

English, F. W. (2011). *Deciding what to teach and test: Developing, aligning, and leading the curriculum* (3rd ed.). Thousand Oaks, CA: Corwin Press.

Feeney, E. J. (2007). Quality feedback: The essential ingredient for teacher success. *The Clearinghouse, 80,* 191–197.

Fisher, D., & Frey, N. (2007). Implementing a schoolwide literacy framework: Improving achievement in an urban elementary school. *The Reading Teacher, 61,* 32–43.

Fisher, D., Frey, N., & Lapp, D. (2011). Coaching middle-level teachers to think aloud improves comprehension instruction and student reading achievement. *Teacher Educator, 46,* 231–243.

Flesch, R. F. (1955). *Why Johnny can't read—and what you can do about it.* New York: Harper.

Floyd, C. (1954). Meeting children's reading needs in the middle grades: A preliminary report. *Elementary School Journal, 55,* 99–103.

Foorman, B. R. (2007). Primary prevention in classroom reading instruction. *Teaching Exceptional Children, 39*(5), 24–30.

Foorman, B. R., & Connor, C. M. (2011). Primary grade reading. In M. L. Kamil, P. D. Pearson, E. B. Moje, & P. P. Afflerbach (Eds.), *Handbook of reading research* (Vol. 4, pp. 136–156). New York: Routledge.

Foorman, B. R., Francis, D. J., Shaywitz, S. E., Shaywitz, B. A., & Fletcher, J. M. (1997). The case for early reading intervention. In B. Blachman (Ed.), *Foundations of reading acquisition and dyslexia: Implications for early intervention* (pp. 243–264). Mahwah, NJ: Erlbaum.

Fuchs, D., & Fuchs, L. S. (2005). Peer-assisted learning strategies: Promoting word recognition, fluency, and reading comprehension in young children. *Journal of Special Education, 39,* 34–44.

Fuchs, D., Fuchs, L. S., Mathes, P. G., & Simmons, D. C. (1997). Peer-assisted learning strategies: Making classrooms more responsive to diversity. *American Educational Research Journal, 34,* 174–206.

Fullan, M. (2005). *Leadership and sustainability: System thinkers in action.* Thousand Oaks, CA: Corwin Press.

Gallucci, C., Van Lare, M., Yoon, I. H., & Boatright, B. (2010). Instructional coaching: Building theory about the role and organizational support for professional learning. *American Educational Research Journal, 47,* 919–963.

Ganske, K. (2000). *Word journeys: Assessment-guided phonics, spelling, and vocabulary instruction.* New York: Guilford Press.

Garet, M. S., Cronen, S., Eaton, M., Kurki, A., Ludwig, M., Jones, W., et al. (2008). *The impact of two professional development interventions on early reading instruction and achievement.* Washington, DC: U.S. Department of Education, National Center for Educational Evaluation and Regional Assistance.

Gelzheiser, L. M., Scanlon, D., Vellutino, F., Hallgren-Flynn, L., & Schatschneider, C. (2011). Effects of the interactive strategies approach–extended: A responsive and comprehensive intervention for intermediate-grade struggling readers. *Elementary School Journal, 112,* 280–306.

Gibson, S. A. (2006). Lesson observation and feedback: The practice of an expert reading coach. *Reading Research and Instruction, 45,* 295–318.

Gilbert, J., & Graham, S. (2010). Teaching writing to elementary students in grades 4–6: A national survey. *Elementary School Journal, 110,* 494–518.

Gillon, G. T. (2004). *Phonological awareness: From research to practice.* New York: Guilford Press.

Graham, S. (2006). Strategy instruction and the teaching of writing: A meta-analysis. In C. A. MacArthur, S. Graham, & J. Fitzgerald (Eds.), *Handbook of writing research* (pp. 187–207). New York: Guilford Press.

Graham, S., & MacArthur, C. A. (1988). Improving learning disabled students' skills at revising essays produced on a word processor: Self-instructional strategy training. *Journal of Special Education, 22,* 133–152.

Graham, S., MacArthur, C. A., & Fitzgerald, J. (Eds.). (2007). *Best practices in writing instruction.* New York: Guilford Press.

Graham, S., Morphy, P., Harris, K. R., Fink-Chorzempa, B., Saddler, B., Moran, S., et al. (2008). Teaching spelling in the primary grades: A national survey of instructional practices and adaptations. *American Educational Research Journal, 45,* 796–825.

Gray, W. S., Artley, A. S., & Arbuthnot, M. H. (1951). *The new fun with Dick and Jane.* Chicago: Scott, Foresman.

Gregoire, M. (2003). Is it a challenge or a threat? A dual-process model of teachers' cognition and appraisal processes during conceptual change. *Educational Psychology Review, 15,* 147–179.

Guskey, T. R. (1986). Staff development and the process of teacher change. *Educational Researcher, 15*(5), 5–12.

Guthrie, J. T., & McCann, A. D. (1996). Idea circles: Peer collaborations for conceptual learning. In L. B. Gambrell & J. F. Almasi (Eds.), *Lively discussions: Fostering engaged reading* (pp. 87–105). Newark, DE: International Reading Association.

Hall, G., & Hord, S. (2001). *Implementing change: Patterns, principles, and potholes.* Boston: Allyn & Bacon.

Hallinger, P., Bickman, L., & Davis, K. (1996). School context, principal leadership, and student reading achievement. *Elementary School Journal, 96,* 527–549.

Harris, K. R., & Graham, S. (1996). *Making the writing process work: Strategies for composition and self-regulation.* Cambridge, MA: Brookline.

Hart, B., & Risley, T. R. (1995). *Meaningful differences in the everyday experience of young American children.* Baltimore: Brookes.

Hidi, S., & Boscolo, P. (2006). Motivation and writing. In C. A. MacArthur, S. Graham, & J. Fitzgerald (Eds.), *Handbook of writing research* (pp. 144–157). New York: Guilford Press.

Hiebert, E. H. (2006). Becoming fluent: Repeated reading with scaffolded texts. In S. J. Samuels & A. E. Farstrup (Eds.), *What research has to say about fluency instruction* (pp. 204–226). Newark, DE: International Reading Association.

Hillocks, G., Jr. (1986). *Research on written composition.* Urbana, IL: National Council on Rehabilitation Education.

Hoffman, J. V. (2002). WORDS (On words in leveled texts for beginning readers). In D. L. Shallert, C. M. Fairbanks, J. Worthy, B. Maloch, & J. V. Hoffman (Eds.), *51st yearbook of the National Reading Conference* (pp. 59–81). Oak Creek, WI: National Reading Conference.

Hsieh, W. Y., Hemmeter, M. L., McCollum, J. A., & Ostrosky, M. M. (2009). Using coaching to increase preschool teachers' use of emergent literacy teaching strategies. *Early Childhood Research Quarterly, 24,* 229–247.

Individuals with Disabilities Education Improvement Act of 2004, Public Law No. 108-446, § 614 (b)(6)(A), § 614 (b)(2 & 3), 118 Stat. 2647 (2004).

International Reading Association. (2000). *Teaching all children to read: The roles of the reading specialist.* Newark, DE: Author. Available at *www.reading.org/resources/issues/positions_specialist.html.*

International Reading Association. (2004). *The role and qualifications of the reading coach in the United States.* Newark, DE: Author. Available at *www.reading.org/resources/issues/positions_coach.html.*

International Reading Association. (2006). *Standards for middle and high school literacy coaches.* Newark, DE: Author, in collaboration with NCTE, NCTM, NSTA, NCSS, and the Carnegie Corporation of New York. Available at *www.reading.org/General/Publications/Books/bk597.aspx.*

International Reading Association. (2010). *Standards for reading professionals–Revised 2010.* Newark, DE: Author. Available at *www.reading.org/General/Publications/Books/bk713.aspx.*

Invernizzi, M. A. (2003). Concepts, sounds, and the ABCs: A diet for the very young reader. In D. M. Barone & L. M . Morrow (Eds.), *Literacy and young children: Research-based practices* (pp. 140–156). New York: Guilford Press.

Ippolito, J. (2010). Three ways that literacy coaches balance responsive and directive relationships with teachers. *Elementary School Journal, 111,* 164–190.

Jackson, B., Larzelere, R., St. Clair, L., Corr, M., Fichter, C., & Egertson, H. (2006). The impact of HeadsUp! Reading on early childhood educators' literacy practices and preschool children's literacy skills. *Early Childhood Research Quarterly, 21,* 213–226.

Jennings, R. E., & Prince, D. E. (Eds.). (1981). *Kick up your heels.* Chicago: Scott, Foresman.

Johnson, J. F., Jr. (2002). High-performing, high-poverty, urban elementary schools. In B. M. Taylor & P. D. Pearson (Eds.), *Teaching reading: Effective schools, accomplished teachers* (pp. 89–114). Mahwah, NJ: Erlbaum.

Johnston, P., & Allington, R. (1991). Remediation. In R. Barr, M. L. Kamil, P. Mosenthal, & P. D. Pearson (Eds.), *Handbook of reading research* (Vol. 2, pp. 984–1012). White Plains, NY: Longman.

Joyce, B., & Showers, B. (1996). Staff development as a comprehensive service organization. *Journal of Staff Development, 17,* 2–6.

Joyce, B., & Showers, B. (1988). *Student achievement through staff development.* Alexandria, VA: ASCD.

Joyce, B., & Showers, B. (2002). *Student achievement through staff development* (3rd ed.). Alexandria, VA: ASCD.

Juel, C. (1988). Learning to read and write: A longitudinal study of 54 children from first through fourth grades. *Journal of Educational Psychology, 80,* 437–447.

Juel, C. (1991). Beginning reading. In R. Barr, M. L. Kamil, P. B. Mosenthal, & P. D. Pearson (Eds.), *Handbook of reading research* (Vol. 2, pp. 759–788). White Plains, NY: Longman.

Justice, L. M., & Kaderavek, J. N. (2004). Embedded-explicit emergent literacy intervention I: Background and description of approach. *Language, Speech, and Hearing Services in Schools, 35,* 201–211.

Justice, L. M., & Piasta, S. (2011). Developing children's print knowledge through adult–child storybook reading interactions: Print referencing as an instructional practice. In S. B. Neuman & D. K. Dickinson (Eds.), *Handbook of early literacy research* (Vol. 3, pp. 200–213). New York: Guilford Press.

Kaderavek, J. N., & Justice, L. M. (2004). Embedded-explicit emergent literacy intervention II: Goal selection and implementation in the early childhood classroom. *Language, Speech, and Hearing Services in Schools, 35*, 212–228.

Kazemi, E., & Hubbard, A. (2008). New directions for the design and study of professional development: Attending to the coevolution of teachers' participation across contexts. *Journal of Teacher Education, 59*, 428–441.

Kean, M., Summers, A., Raivetz, M., & Farber, I. (1979). *What works in reading?* Philadelphia: Office of Research and Evaluation and the U.S. Federal Reserve Bank.

Kear, D. J., Coffman, G. A., McKenna, M. C., & Ambrosio, A. L. (2000). Measuring attitude towards writing: A new tool for teachers. *The Reading Teacher, 54*, 10–23.

King, D. (2002). The changing shape of leadership. *Educational Leadership, 59*, 61–63.

Knight, J. (2005). A primer on instructional coaches. *Principal Leadership: High School Edition, 5*(9), 16–21.

Koutsoftas, A. D., Harmon, M., & Gray, S. (2009). The effect of tier 2 intervention for phonemic awareness in a response-to-intervention model in low-income preschool classrooms. *Language, Speech, and Hearing Services in Schools, 40*, 116–130.

Kuhn, M. R. (2008). *The hows and whys of fluency instruction.* Boston: Allyn & Bacon.

Kuhn, M. R., & Stahl, S. A. (2003). Fluency: A review of developmental and remedial practices. *Journal of Educational Psychology, 95*, 3–21.

Landry, S. H., Anthony, J., Swank, P. R., & Monseque-Bailey, P. (2009). Effectiveness of comprehensive professional development for teachers of at-risk preschoolers. *Journal of Educational Psychology, 101*, 448–465.

Landry, S. H., Swank, P. R., Smith, K. E., Assel, M. A., & Gunnewig, S. B. (2006). Enhancing early literacy skills for preschool children: Bringing a professional development model to scale. *Journal of Learning Disabilities, 39*, 306–324.

Lauer, P. A., Akiba, M., Wilkerson, S. B., Apthorp, H. S., Snow, D., & Martin-Glenn, M. L. (2006). Out-of-school-time programs: A meta-analysis of effects for at-risk students. *Review of Educational Research, 76*, 275–313.

Lockwood, J. R., McCombs, J., & Marsh, J. (2010). Linking reading coaches and student achievement: Evidence from Florida middle schools. *Educational Evaluation and Policy Analysis, 32*, 372–388.

MacArthur, C. A., Graham, S., & Harris, K. H. (2004). Insight from instructional research on revision with struggling writers. In L. Allal, L. Chanquoy, & P. Largy (Eds.), *Revision: Cognitive and instructional processes* (pp. 125–137). Dordrecht, The Netherlands: Kluwer.

MacKeracher, D. (2004). *Making sense of adult learning* (2nd ed.). Toronto, Ontario, Canada: University of Toronto Press.

Macon, J. M., Bewell, D., & Vogt, M. (1991). *Responses to literature.* Newark, DE: International Reading Association.

Mangin, M. M. (2009). Literacy coach role implementation: How district context influences reform efforts. *Educational Administration Quarterly, 45*, 759–792.

Mangin, M. M., & Stoelinga, S. (2011). Peer? Expert? *Journal of Staff Development, 32*, 48–51.

Marks, H. M., & Printy, S. M. (2003). Principal leadership and school performance: An integration of transformational and instructional leadership. *Educational Leadership Quarterly, 39,* 370–397.

Marrero, M., Woodruff, K., Schuster, G., & Riccio, J. (2010). Live, online short courses: A case study of innovative teacher professional development. *International Review of Research in Open and Distance Learning, 11,* 81–95.

Martinez, M. N., Roser, N. L., & Strecker, S. (1999). I never thought I could be a star: A reader's theater ticket to fluency. *The Reading Teacher, 52,* 326–334.

Marulis, L. M., & Neuman, S. B. (2010). The effects of vocabulary intervention on young children's word learning: A meta-analysis. *Review of Educational Research, 80,* 300–335.

Matsumura, L., Garnier, H. E., Correnti, R., Junker, B., & Bickel, D. (2010). Investigating the effectiveness of a comprehensive literacy coaching program in schools with high teacher mobility. *Elementary School Journal, 111,* 35–62.

Matsumura, L., Garnier, H. E., & Resnick, L. B. (2010). Implementing literacy coaching: The role of school social resources. *Educational Evaluation and Policy Analysis, 32,* 249–272.

Matsumura, L., Sartoris, M., Bickel, D., & Garnier, H. E. (2009). Leadership for literacy coaching: The principal's role in launching a new coaching program. *Educational Administration Quarterly, 45,* 655–693.

McCutchen, D. (2006). Cognitive factors in the development of children's writing. In C. A. MacArthur, S. Graham, & J. Fitzgerald (Eds.), *Handbook of writing research* (pp. 115–130). New York: Guilford Press.

McGee, L. M., & Schickedanz, J. A. (2007). Repeated interactive read-alouds in preschool and kindergarten. *The Reading Teacher, 60,* 742–751.

McKenna, M. C., & Robinson, R. D. (2012). *Teaching through text: Reading and writing in the content areas* (2nd ed.). Boston: Allyn & Bacon/Vango.

McKenna, M. C., & Stahl, K. A. D. (2009). *Assessment for reading instruction* (2nd ed.). New York: Guilford Press.

McKenna, M. C., & Walpole, S. (2005). How well does assessment inform our reading instruction? *The Reading Teacher, 59,* 84–86.

McKenna, M. C., & Walpole, S. (2008). *The literacy coaching challenge: Models and methods for grades K–8.* New York: Guilford Press.

McKeown, M. G., Beck, I. L., & Blake, R. G. K. (2009). Rethinking reading comprehension instruction: A comparison of instruction for strategies and content approaches. *Reading Research Quarterly, 44,* 218–253.

McMullen, M. B., Elicker, J., & Goetze, G. (2006). Using collaborative assessment to examine relationships between self-reported beliefs and the documented practices of preschool teachers. *Early Childhood Journal, 34,* 81–91.

Merton, R. K. (1968). The Matthew effect in science. *Science, 159,* 56–63.

Mesmer, E. M., & Mesmer, H. A. E. (2008). Response to intervention (RTI): What teachers of reading need to know. *The Reading Teacher, 64,* 280–290.

Metsala, J. L. (2011). Lexical reorganization and the emergence of phonological awareness. In S. B. Neuman & D. K. Dickinson (Eds.), *Handbook of early literacy research* (Vol. 3, pp. 66–82). New York: Guilford Press.

Miller, S. D. (2003). How high- and low-challenge tasks affect motivation and learning: Implications for struggling learners. *Reading and Writing Quarterly, 19,* 39–57.

Mol, S., Bus, A., & deJong, M. (2009). Interactive book reading in early education: A tool to stimulate print knowledge as well as oral language. *Review of Educational Research, 79,* 979–1007.

Moody, S. W., Schumm, J. S., Fischer, M., & Jean-Francois, B. (1999). Grouping suggestions for the classroom: What do our basal reading series tell us? *Reading Research and Instruction, 38,* 319–331.

Moore, M. T. (2012). Issues and trends in writing. In R. D. Robinson, M. C. McKenna, & K. Conradi (Eds.), *Issues and trends in literacy education* (5th ed., pp. 256–269). Boston: Pearson.

Morris, D. (1981). Concept of word: A developmental phenomenon in the beginning reading and writing process. *Language Arts, 57,* 659–668.

Morrow, L. M. (1984). Effects of retelling on young children's comprehension and sense of story structure. In J. A. Niles & L. A. Harris (Eds.), *33rd yearbook of the National Reading Conference: Changing perspectives on research in reading/language processing and instruction* (pp. 95–100). Rochester, NY: National Reading Conference.

Morrow, L. M. (2007). *Developing literacy in preschool.* New York: Guilford Press.

Morrow, L. M., & Gambrell, L. B. (Eds.). (2011). *Best practices in literacy instruction* (4th ed.). New York: Guilford Press.

Morrow, L. M., Shanahan, T., & Wixson, K. K. (Eds.). (2013a). *Teaching with the Common Core Standards for English language arts, PreK–2.* New York: Guilford Press.

Morrow, L. M., Shanahan, T., & Wixson, K. K. (Eds.). (2013b). *Teaching with the Common Core Standards for English language arts, Grades 3–5.* New York: Guilford Press.

Mosenthal, J., Lipson, M., Sortino, S., Russ, R., & Mekkelsen, J. (2002). Literacy in rural Vermont: Lessons from schools where children succeed. In B. M. Taylor & P. D. Pearson (Eds.), *Teaching reading: Effective schools, accomplished teachers* (pp. 115–140). Mahwah, NJ: Erlbaum.

Mouza, C. (2009). Does research-based professional development make a difference? A longitudinal investigation of teacher learning in technology integration. *Teachers College Record, 111,* 1195–1241.

Murphy, J. (2004). *Leadership for literacy: Research-based practice, PreK–3.* Thousand Oaks, CA: Corwin Press.

National Early Literacy Panel. (2008). *Developing early literacy.* Washington, DC: National Institute of Child Health and Development. Available at *lincs.ed.gov/publications/pdf/NELPReport09.pdf.*

National Institute of Child Health and Human Development (NICHHD). (2000). *Report of the National Reading Panel. Teaching children to read: An evidence-based assessment of the scientific research literature on reading and its implications for reading instruction* (NIH Publication No. 00-4769). Washington, DC: U.S. Government Printing Office.

Neuman, S. B. (2006). The knowledge gap: Implications for early childhood. In D. K. Dickinson & S. B. Neuman (Eds.), *Handbook of early literacy research* (Vol. 2, pp. 29–40). New York: Guilford Press.

Neuman, S. B., & Cunningham, L. (2009). The impact of professional development and coaching on early language and literacy instructional practices. *American Educational Research Journal, 46,* 532–566.

Neuman, S. B., & Dwyer, J. (2009). Missing in action: Vocabulary instruction in PreK. *The Reading Teacher, 62,* 384–392.

Neuman, S. B., & Wright, T. S. (2010). Promoting language and literacy development for early childhood educators: A mixed-methods study of coursework and coaching. *Elementary School Journal, 111,* 63–86.

No Child Left Behind Act of 2001, Pub. L. No. 107-110, 115 Stat. 1425, 20 U.S.C. § § 6310 et seq. (2001).

O'Connor, R. E. (2007). *Teaching word recognition: Effective strategies for students with learning difficulties.* New York: Guilford Press.

Pajares, F., & Valiante, G. (2006). Self-efficacy beliefs and motivation in writing development. In C. A. MacArthur, S. Graham, & J. Fitzgerald (Eds.), *Handbook of writing research* (pp. 158–170). New York: Guilford Press.

Paterson, W. A., Henry, J. J., O'Quin, K., Ceprano, M. A., & Blue, E. V. (2003). Investigating the effectiveness of an integrated learning system on early emergent readers. *Reading Research Quarterly, 38,* 172–207.

Pilonieta, P. (2010). Instruction of research-based comprehension strategies in basal reading programs. *Reading Psychology, 31,* 150–175.

Powell, D. R., Diamond, K. E., & Koehler, M. J. (2010). Use of a case-based hypermedia resource in an early literacy coaching intervention with prekindergarten teachers. *Topics in Early Childhood Special Education, 29,* 239–249.

Pressley, M., El-Dinary, P. B., Gaskins, I., Schuder, T., Bergman, J., Almasi, L., et al. (1992). Beyond direct explanation: Transactional instruction of reading comprehension strategies. *Elementary School Journal, 92,* 511–554.

Printy, S. M., Marks, H. M., & Bowers, A. J. (2009). Integrated leadership: How principals and teachers share transformational and instructional influence. *Journal of School Leadership, 19,* 504–532.

Raphael, T. E. (1986). Teaching question–answer relationships, revisited. *The Reading Teacher, 39,* 516–523.

Raphael, T. E., George, M., Weber, C. M., & Nies, A. (2009). Approaches to teaching reading comprehension. In S. E. Israel & G. G. Duffy (Eds.), *Handbook of research on reading comprehension* (pp. 449–469). New York: Guilford Press.

Raphael, T. E., Goldman, S. R., Au, K. H., Hirata, S., Weber, C. M., George, M., et al. (2006, April). *Toward second generation school reform models: A developmental model for literacy reform.* Paper presented at the meeting of the American Educational Research Association, San Francisco, CA.

Raphael, T. E., Highfield, K., & Au, K. H. (2006). *QAR Now: Question answer relationships: A powerful and practical framework that develops comprehension and higher-level thinking in all students.* New York: Scholastic.

Rasinski, T. V., Reutzel, D. R., Chard, D., & Linan-Thompson, S. (2011). Reading fluency. In M. L. Kamil, P. D. Pearson, E. B. Moje, & P. P. Afflerbach (Eds.), *Handbook of reading research* (Vol. 4, pp. 286–319). New York: Routledge.

Reading Excellence Act of 1998, PL 105-277, 112 Stat. 2681-337, 2861-393, 20 U.S.C. § 6661a *et seq.*

Reutzel, D. R. (1999). Organizing literacy instruction: Effective grouping strategies and organizational plans. In L. B. Gambrell, L. M. Morrow, S. B. Neuman, & M. Pressley (Eds.), *Best practices in literacy instruction* (pp. 271–291). New York: Guilford Press.

Ritchey, K., Silverman, R., Montanaro, E., Speece, D., & Schatschneider, C. (2012).

Effects of a tier 2 supplemental reading intervention for at-risk fourth-grade students. *Exceptional Children, 78,* 318–334.

Roberts, S. M., & Pruitt, E. Z. (2008). *Schools as professional learning communities: Collaborative activities and strategies for professional development* (2nd ed.). Thousand Oaks, CA: Corwin Press.

Roehrig, A. D., Bohn, C. M., Turner, J. E., & Pressley, M. (2008). Mentoring beginning primary teachers for exemplary teaching practices. *Teaching and Teacher Education, 24,* 684–702.

Roser, N. L., Hoffman, J. V., & Carr, N. J. (2003). See it change: A primer on the basal reader. In L. M. Morrow, L. B. Gambrell, & M. Pressley (Eds.), *Best practices in literacy instruction* (2nd ed., pp. 269–286). New York: Guilford Press.

Rowe, D. W. (2008). Development of writing abilities in childhood. In C. Bazerman (Ed.), *Handbook of research on writing* (pp. 401–419). New York: Erlbaum/Taylor & Francis.

Roy, P., & Hord, S. (2003). *Moving NSDC's staff development standards into practice: Innovation configurations, Volume I.* Oxford, OH: National Staff Development Council.

Sailors, M., & Price, L. (2010). Professional development that supports the teaching of cognitive reading strategy instruction. *Elementary School Journal, 110,* 301–322.

Samuels, S. J. (1979). The method of repeated reading. *The Reading Teacher, 32,* 403–408.

Saul, E. W., & Dieckman, D. (2005). Choosing and using information trade books. *Reading Research Quarterly, 40,* 502–513.

Scammacca, N., Vaughn, S., Roberts, G., Wanzek, J., & Torgesen, J. K. (2007). *Extensive reading interventions in grades K–3: From research to practice.* Portsmouth, NH: RMC Research Corporation, Center on Instruction.

Schickedanz, J. A., & Casbergue, R. M. (2004). *Writing in preschool: Learning to orchestrate meaning and marks.* Newark, DE: International Reading Association.

Shanahan, T. (2008, August 23). *Why use a textbook to teach reading?* Available at *shanahanonliteracy.com.*

Shanahan, T. (2011, April 10). *What is the biggest literacy teaching myth in 2011?* Available at *shanahanonliteracy.com.*

Shanahan, T., Callison, K., Carriere, C., Duke, N. K., Pearson, P. D., Schatschneider, C., et al. (2010). *Improving reading comprehension in kindergarten through 3rd grade: A practice guide* (NCEE 2010-4038). Washington, DC: National Center for Education Evaluation and Regional Assistance, Institute of Education Sciences, U.S. Department of Education. Retrieved from *whatworks.ed.gov/publications/practiceguides.*

Share, D. (1995). Phonological recoding and self-teaching: Sine qua non on reading acquisition. *Cognition, 55,* 151–218.

Showers, B., & Joyce, B. (1996, March). The evolution of peer coaching. *Educational Leadership, 53*(6), 12–16.

Shulman, L. S. (1998). Theory, practice, and the evolution of professionals. *Elementary School Journal, 98,* 511–526.

Simmons, D. C., & Kame'enui, K. J. (2006). *A consumer's guide to analyzing a core reading program, grades K–3: A critical elements analysis.* Eugene: Center on Teaching and Learning, College of Education, University of Oregon. Available at *reading.uoregon.edu/cia/curricula/con_guide.php.*

Simmons, D. C., Kuykehdall, K., King, K., Cornachione, C., & Kame'enui, E. J. (2000).

Implementation of a schoolwide reading improvement model: "No one ever told us it would be this hard!" *Learning Disabilities Research and Practice, 15*(2), 92–100.

Slavin, R. E. (1987). Ability grouping and student achievement in elementary schools: A best-evidence synthesis. *Review of Educational Research, 57*, 293–336.

Slavin, R. E., Lake, C., Chambers, B., Cheung, A., & Davis, S. (2009). Effective reading programs for the elementary grades: A best-evidence synthesis. *Review of Educational Research, 79*, 1391–1466.

Slavin, R. E., Madden, N. A., Karweit, N., Dolan, L. J., & Wasik, B. A. (1991). Research directions: Success for all: Ending reading failure from the beginning. *Language Arts, 68*, 404–409.

Slobodkina, E. (1940). *Caps for sale: A tale of a peddler, some monkeys and their monkey business.* New York: William R. Scott.

Smith, N. B. (2002). *American reading instruction* (special ed.). Newark, DE: International Reading Association.

Smolkin, L. B., & Donovan, C. A. (2002). "Oh, excellent, excellent question!" Developmental differences and comprehension acquisition. In C. C. Block & M. Pressley (Eds.), *Comprehension instruction: Research-based best practices* (pp. 140–157). New York: Guilford Press.

Smylie, M. A. (1996). From bureaucratic control to building human capital: The importance of teacher learning in education reform. *Educational Researcher, 25*, 9–11.

Snow, C. E., Burns, M. S., & Griffin, P. (1998). *Preventing reading difficulties in young children.* Washington, DC: National Academy Press.

Stahl, S. A. (1999). *Vocabulary development: From research to practice* (Vol. 2). Cambridge, MA: Brookline Books.

Stahl, S. A., Duffy-Hester, A. M., & Stahl, K. A. D. (1998). Everything you wanted to know about phonics (but were afraid to ask). *Reading Research Quarterly, 33*, 338–355.

Stahl, S. A., & Heubach, K. M. (2005). Fluency-oriented reading instruction. *Journal of Literacy Research, 37*, 25–60.

Stahl, S. A., & Nagy, W. E. (2005). *Teaching word meanings.* Mahwah, NJ: Erlbaum.

Stanovich, K. E. (1986). Matthew effects in reading: Some consequences of individual differences in the acquisition of reading. *Reading Research Quarterly, 21*, 360–406.

Stoelinga, S. R. (2008). Leading from above and below: Formal and informal teacher leadership. In M. M. Mangin & S. R. Stoelinga (Eds.), *Effective teacher leadership: Using research to inform and reform* (pp. 99–119). New York: Teachers College Press.

Sunderman, G. L., & Mickelsen, H. (2000). Implementing Title I schoolwide programs in a complex policy environment: Integrating standards and school reform in the Chicago public schools. *Journal of Negro Education, 69*, 361–374.

Supovitz, J., Sirinides, P., & May, H. (2010). How principals and peers influence teaching and learning. *Educational Administration Quarterly, 46*, 31–56.

Tardy, C. M., & Swales, J. M. (2008). Form, text organization, genre, coherence, and cohesion. In C. Bazerman (Ed.), *Handbook of research on writing* (pp. 565–581). New York: Erlbaum/Taylor & Francis.

Taylor, B. M., Pearson, P. D., Clark, K. M., & Walpole, S. (2000). Effective schools and accomplished teachers: Lessons about primary-grade reading instruction in low-income schools. *Elementary School Journal, 101*, 121–165.

Taylor, B. M., Pressley, M., & Pearson, P. D. (2002). Research-supported characteristics of teachers and schools that promote reading achievement. In B. M. Taylor & P. D. Pearson (Eds.), *Teaching reading: Effective schools, accomplished teachers* (pp. 361–374). Mahwah, NJ: Erlbaum.

Timperley, H., & Phillips, G. (2003). Changing and sustaining teachers' expectations through professional development in literacy. *Teaching and Teacher Education, 19,* 627–641.

Toll, C. A. (2005). *The literacy coach's survival guide: Essential questions and practical answers.* Newark, DE: International Reading Association.

Trace, A. S., Jr. (1961). Can Ivan read better than Johnny? *Saturday Evening Post, 234*(21), 30.

Troia, G. A. (2006). Writing instruction for students with learning disabilities. In C. A. MacArthur, S. Graham, & J. Fitzgerald (Eds.), *Handbook of writing research* (pp. 324–336). New York: Guilford Press.

Tschannen-Moran, M., & McMaster, P. (2009). Sources of self-efficacy: Four professional development formats and their relationship to self-efficacy and implementation of a new teaching strategy. *Elementary School Journal, 110,* 228–245.

Tucker, P. (2001). Helping struggling teachers. *Educational Leadership, 58*(5), 52–55.

Vacca, J. L., & Padak, N. D. (1990). Reading consultants as classroom collaborators: An emerging role. *Journal of Educational and Psychological Consultation, 1,* 99–107.

Vanderburg, M., & Stephens, D. (2010). The impact of literacy coaches: What teachers value and how teachers change. *Elementary School Journal, 111,* 141–163.

Van Driel, J., & Berry, A. (2012). Teacher professional development focusing on pedagogical content knowledge. *Educational Researcher, 41,* 26–28.

Vaughn, S., Denton, C. A., & Fletcher, J. M. (2010). Why intensive interventions are necessary for students with severe reading difficulties. *Psychology in the Schools, 47,* 432–444.

Vaughn, S., Wanzek, J., Murray, C. S., Scammacca, N., Linan-Thompson, S., & Woodruff, A. L. (2009). Response to early reading intervention: Examining higher and lower responders. *Exceptional Children, 75,* 165–183.

Vellutino, F. R., & Scanlon, D. M. (2001). Emergent literacy skills, early instruction, and individual differences as determinants of difficulties in learning to read: The case for early intervention. In S. B. Neuman & D. K. Dickinson (Eds.), *Handbook of early literacy research* (pp. 295–321). New York: Guilford Press.

Walmsley, S. A., & Allington, R. L. (1995). Redefining and reforming instructional support programs for at-risk students. In R. L. Allington & S. A. Walmsley (Eds.), *No quick fix: Rethinking literacy programs in America's elementary schools.* New York: Teachers College Press.

Walpole, S., & Blamey, K. L. (2008). Elementary literacy coaches: The reality of dual roles. *The Reading Teacher, 62,* 222–231.

Walpole, S., & McKenna, M. C. (2004). *The literacy coach's handbook: A guide to research-based practice.* New York: Guilford Press.

Walpole, S., & McKenna, M. C. (2007). *Differentiated reading instruction: Strategies for the primary grades.* New York: Guilford Press.

Walpole, S., & McKenna, M. C. (2009a). Everything you've always wanted to know about literacy coaching but were afraid to ask: A review of policy and research. In K. M.

Leander, D. W. Rowe, D. K. Dickinson, R. T. Jimenez, M. K. Hundley, & V. J. Risko (Eds.), *Fifty-ninth yearbook of the National Reading Conference* (pp. 23–33). Milwaukee, WI: National Reading Conference.

Walpole, S., & McKenna, M. C. (2009b). *How to plan differentiated reading instruction: Resources for grades K–3.* New York: Guilford Press.

Walpole, S., McKenna, M. C., & Philippakos, Z. (2011). *Differentiated reading instruction in grades 4 and 5: Strategies and resources.* New York: Guilford Press.

Walpole, S., McKenna, M. C., Uribe-Zarain, X., & Lamitina, D. (2010). The relationships between coaching and instruction in the primary grades: Evidence from high-poverty schools. *Elementary School Journal, 111,* 115–140.

Wanzek, J., & Vaughn, S. (2010). Tier 3 interventions for students with significant reading problems. *Theory into Practice, 49,* 305–314.

Wanzek, J., & Vaughn, S. (2011). Is a three-tier reading intervention model associated with reduced placement in special education? *Remedial and Special Education, 32,* 167–175.

Weaver, B. M. (2000). *Leveling books K–6: Matching readers to text.* Newark, DE: International Reading Association.

Weiser, B., & Mathes, P. (2011). Using encoding instruction to improve the reading and spelling performances of elementary students at risk for literacy difficulties: A best-evidence synthesis. *Review of Educational Research, 81,* 170–200.

Whitehurst, G. (2002, October). *Evidence-based education.* Presentation made at the Student Achievement and School Accountability Conferences. Washington, DC: U.S. Department of Education. Available at: *www2.ed.gov/nclb/methods/whatworks/eb/edlite-slide001.html.*

Whitehurst, G. J., Epstein, J. N., Angell, A. L., Payne, A. C., Crone, D. A., & Fischel, J. E. (1994). Outcomes of an emergent literacy intervention in Head Start. *Journal of Educational Psychology, 86,* 542–555.

Willingham, D. T. (2006–2007). The usefulness of brief instruction in reading comprehension strategies. *American Educator, 30*(4), 39–50.

Wohlstetter, P., & Malloy, C. L. (2001). Organizing for literacy achievement: Using school governance to improve classroom practice. *Education and Urban Society, 34,* 42–65.

Yoon, K. S., Duncan, T., Lee, S. W.-Y., Scarloss, B., & Shapley, K. (2007). *Reviewing the evidence on how teacher professional development affects student achievement* (Issues and Answers Report, REL 2007–No. 033). Washington, DC: U.S. Department of Education, Institute of Education Sciences, National Center for Education Evaluation and Regional Assistance, Regional Educational Laboratory Southwest. Retrieved from *http://ies.ed.gov/ncee/edlabs.*

Zucker, T. A., & Landry, S. H. (2010). Improving the quality of preschool read-alouds: Professional development and coaching that targets book-reading practices. In M. C. McKenna, S. Walpole, & K. Conradi (Eds.), *Promoting early reading: Research, resources, and best practices.* New York: Guilford Press.

Zutell, J. (2007). Changing perspectives on word knowledge: Spelling and vocabulary. In M. J. Fresch (Ed.), *An essential history of current reading practices* (pp. 186–206). Newark, DE: International Reading Association.

Index

An *f* following a page number indicates a figure; a *t* following a page number indicates a table.

Achievement
  coaching and, 19–20
  improving group achievement scores, 109–113, 110*f*, 114*f*
  professional support and, 194, 198
  schoolwide research and, 31–36, 35*f*
  using data as a part of professional development and, 201–202
  using multiple assessment measures to track, 29
Achievement gap, 177, 178
Administrators, 22, 228–229
AIMSweb, 98, 102. *see also* Assessments
Alphabet knowledge
  first-grade readers and writers and, 145*f*
  instructional emphasis and, 137*f*
  kindergarten readers and writers and, 141*f*, 142
  National Early Literacy Panel (NELP) and, 61
  preschool readers and writers and, 138*f*
  reading and writing skills development and, 135*f*
  schoolwide program design and, 48*f*
  tiered instruction and, 183*f*
Assessments. *see also* Reading assessment; Schoolwide assessment team (SWAT) approach; Standardized testing
  allocation of time and, 50–54, 52*f*
  assessment strategy, 99–102, 100*f*
  collecting, 37–39, 38*f*–39*f*
  communicating, 41–43, 42*f*
  core programs and, 158–159
  data from and professional development, 201–202, 202*f*
  first-grade readers and writers and, 147
  grouping configurations, 43–47, 44*f*, 45*f*, 46*f*, 47*f*
  improving group achievement scores, 109–113, 110*f*, 114*f*
  interpreting outcome scores, 102–105, 102*f*, 104*f*
  intervention and, 180
  overview, 113–114
  planning, 43
  roles of a literacy coach and, 7–10, 11–12, 105–109, 107*f*

  scheduling, 37, 38*f*–39*f*
  schoolwide program design and, 36–43, 38*f*–39*f*, 40*f*, 42*f*
  summarizing data from, 39–40, 40*f*
  tracking achievement and, 29

Bacon's law, 57–58
Basal series, 158–159, 160–161, 162–163, 162*f*. *see also* Core program
Blending individual phonemes, 60, 143, 147. *see also* Phonemic awareness

Center for the Improvement of Early Reading Achievement, 32–33
Center on Instruction, 189, 190
Checklists, 208, 208*f*, 209*f*
Classroom environment/management, 116, 117*f*, 174–175, 175*f*, 207–208. *see also* Schedules
Clustering, 44, 44*f*, 118–119. *see also* Grouping
Coaching in general. *see also* Literacy coach overview; Roles of a literacy coach
  coherence and, 215
  learning on the job, 24–25
  model for, 20–22
  modeling and, 212–214
  needs of teachers and, 23–24
  observation and feedback, 206–212, 207*f*, 208*f*, 209*f*, 210*f*
  overview, 224–229
  preschool teachers and, 24–26
  read-alouds and, 79
  research on, 17–18, 18*f*, 198–199, 199*f*
  strategies for, 29
  toolbox for, 26–27, 27*f*
Cognitive model of reading assessment, 100–102, 100*f*. *see also* Assessments
Collaboration
  coaching and, 21–22
  lesson planning and, 204–206
  modeling and, 213–214
  schedules and, 131–132, 132*f*
  schoolwide program design and, 34, 54–55

Common Core State Standards Initiative
  assessment and, 103
  core programs and, 163
  for first-grade readers and writers, 143, 144*f*, 146
  for kindergarten readers and writers, 139–140, 140*f*, 141–142
  for second-grade readers and writers, 150
  for third through fifth grade readers and writers, 152, 153*f*–155*f*
  writing and, 80, 85–86
Composition, 135*f*, 146–147, 183*f*
Comprehension
  assessment and, 101–102
  content-focused coaching (CFC) and, 20
  core programs and, 167
  evaluating computer-based programs, 173*f*
  first-grade readers and writers and, 145*f*, 146
  instructional emphasis and, 137*f*
  kindergarten readers and writers and, 141–142, 141*f*
  phonics and, 65
  preschool readers and writers and, 138*f*
  reading and writing skills development and, 135*f*
  research and, 72–79, 77*f*, 80*f*, 81*f*
  schoolwide program design and, 48*f*
  second-grade readers and writers and, 148–149, 148*f*, 149*f*
  third through fifth grade readers and writers and, 152, 155*f*
  tiered instruction and, 183*f*
Computer-based programs, 164, 170, 171*f*–173*f*
Consumer's Guide to Analyzing a Core Reading Program rubric, 169
Content, 74–75, 76, 150
Content-focused coaching (CFC), 20, 28
Core program. *see also* Curriculum
  components of, 163–166
  evaluating, 168–169, 170*f*
  history of, 158–162
  layering and, 169–175, 175*f*
  overview, 30, 158, 162–163, 162*f*, 175
  pros and cons of, 166–168
Curriculum. *see also* Core program
  alignment of, 109–111, 110*f*
  evaluating, 168–169, 170*f*
  improving group achievement scores, 109–111, 110*f*
  phonics and, 63–66
  professional support and, 195
  roles of a literacy coach and, 6, 8–9, 14*f*
  schoolwide literacy program and, 30–31
  schoolwide professional support system for, 196–197
  schoolwide program design and, 47–50, 48*f*
Curriculum map, 111. *see also* Curriculum

Data analysis, 201–202, 202*f*. *see also* Assessments
Data collection. *see* Assessments
Decoding skills
  assessment and, 101
  first-grade readers and writers and, 144–145, 145, 145*f*, 147, 148
  instructional emphasis and, 137*f*
  for kindergarten readers and writers, 141*f*

phonics and, 63, 66
  schoolwide program design and, 48*f*
  second-grade readers and writers and, 148*f*, 149*f*, 150–151
  spelling, 88
  third through fifth grade readers and writers and, 152, 155*f*, 156
  tiered instruction and, 183*f*
Developmental processes, 80–87, 82*f*, 83*f*, 84*f*, 85*f*, 135*f*, 177
Diagnosis, 11–12, 98, 147, 180. *see also* Assessments
Differentiated instruction, 119*f*, 205. *see also* Response-to-intervention (RTI); Tier 2 instruction
Direct instruction, 69–70, 74. *see also* Instruction
District-level personnel, 219–220, 220*f*, 228–229
Drawing/driting, 81
Dynamic Indicators of Basic Early Literacy Skills (DIBELS Next) battery, 97–98, 102, 106–108, 107*f*. *see also* Assessments

Early intervention, 177–180, 181–183, 183*f*. *see also* Intervention
Early Reading First, 17, 24–25
English language learners (ELL), 28, 165, 178
Enhanced classroom instruction, 181–182. *see also* Instruction; Tier 1 instruction
Evidence-based reading instruction, 58, 58*f*, 188–189. *see also* Instruction
Excel software, 106–108, 107*f*. *see also* Technology

Feedback, 206–212, 207*f*, 208*f*, 209*f*, 210*f*
First-grade readers and writers
  aggressive early intervention and, 177
  instructional emphasis and, 143–148, 144*f*, 145*f*, 147*f*
  tiered instruction and, 183*f*, 185–186
Flexibility, 44–46, 45*f*, 46*f*
Fluency
  aggressive early intervention and, 177–178
  evaluating computer-based programs, 172*f*
  first-grade readers and writers and, 144*f*, 145, 145*f*
  instructional emphasis and, 137*f*
  kindergarten readers and writers and, 140*f*
  phonics and, 65
  reading and writing skills development and, 135*f*
  research and, 66–69
  schoolwide program design and, 48*f*
  second-grade readers and writers and, 148*f*, 149, 149*f*, 151
  third through fifth grade readers and writers and, 155*f*
  tiered instruction and, 183*f*
Funding, 4–5, 6*f*, 10

Genre knowledge, 75–76, 86
Grade-level readers, 162–163, 162*f*. *see also* Leveled texts
Grade-level schedules, 116–119, 118*f*, 119*f*. *see also* Schedules
Gradual release of responsibility, 37
Grant writing, 4–5, 6*f*, 13*f*–14*f*
Grouping, 43–47, 44*f*, 45*f*, 46*f*, 47*f*, 50–54, 52*f*

Guide to Program Selection (Dewitz et al., 2010), 169

Guidelines to Review Comprehensive Core Reading Programs (Florida Center for Reading Research), 169

High-frequency word reading and spelling, 148

Implementation of new approaches, 27–28
Institute of Education Sciences (IES), 94, 193–194
Instruction. *see also* Schedules
  allocation of time, 50–54, 52*f*
  coaching and, 19–20, 26–27, 27*f*
  comprehension and, 72–79, 77*f*, 80*f*, 81*f*
  core programs and, 166–168
  emphasis of, 136–138, 136*f*, 137*f*, 138*f*
  evidence-based reading instruction, 58, 58*f*
  for first-grade readers and writers, 143–148, 144*f*, 145*f*, 147*f*
  group achievement scores, 109–113, 110*f*, 114*f*
  for kindergarten readers and writers, 139–143, 140*f*, 141*f*, 142*f*
  overview, 133–134, 157
  phonemic awareness and, 60
  phonics and, 62–66
  for preschool readers and writers, 138–139, 138*f*
  professional support and, 194–198, 195*f*, 196*f*, 200, 204–206
  schoolwide program design and, 47–50, 48*f*
  scientifically based reading instruction, 57–58
  for second-grade readers and writers, 148–151, 148*f*, 149*f*, 151*f*
  spelling and, 88–89
  stage theories in reading and spelling, 134–135, 135*f*
  for third through fifth grade readers and writers, 152–157, 153*f*–155*f*
  vocabulary and, 69–70
Instructional responsibility, 180, 181
Intensive intervention, 177–180. *see also* Intervention
Interactive read-alouds, 146. *see also* Read-alouds
Interpretation of assessment information, 102–105, 102*f*, 104*f*, 105–109, 107*f*
Intervention. *see also* Instruction; Response-to-intervention (RTI); Tier 3 instruction
  aggressive early intervention and, 177–180
  schedules and, 118, 118*f*, 131–132, 132*f*
  schoolwide program design and, 48*f*, 49
  selecting intervention programs, 188–189
  special education services and, 176
IRA'S standards and performances, 11–12, 13*f*–16*f*

Kindergarten
  aggressive early intervention and, 177
  instructional emphasis and, 139–143
  for kindergarten readers and writers, 140*f*, 141*f*, 142*f*
  tiered instruction and, 183*f*, 184–185

Leadership roles
  authority issues, 219–221, 220*f*
  overview, 216–218
  resistant teachers and, 223–224

  roles of a literacy coach and, 11–12
  struggling teachers and, 222–223
  teamwork and, 54–55
Learner role, 3–4, 5*f*, 13*f*, 24–25
Leveled texts, 162–163, 162*f*, 165–166, 170, 174–175, 175*f*
Lexiles, 104–105, 104*f*
Libraries (classroom and school), 174–175, 175*f*
Linguistic readers, 160–161. *see also* Core program
Literacy acceleration, 180
Literacy coach overview, 1–3, 2*f*, 3*f*, 4*f*. *see also* Coaching in general; Roles of a literacy coach
Literacy collaborative (LC) coaching, 20, 28
Literacy programs, 136–138, 136*f*, 137*f*, 138*f*
Literacy Research Association, 17–18
Low responders, 186–187

Matthew effect, 177–178
Modeling, 212–214
Morphology, 71, 152
Motivation, 86–87

National Center on Response to Intervention, 189
National Early Literacy Panel (NELP)
  phonemic awareness and, 61
  read-alouds and, 76–79, 80*f*, 81*f*
  vocabulary and, 70
  writing, 79–87, 82*f*, 83*f*, 84*f*, 85*f*
National Reading Conference (2009), 17–18. *see also* Literacy Research Association
National Reading Panel
  comprehension, 72–79, 77*f*, 80*f*, 81*f*
  fluency, 67–69
  phonemic awareness and, 60–62
  phonics and, 62–66
  research and, 59
  vocabulary and, 69–71
  writing, 79
National Research Council, 178
No Child Left Behind Act of 2001, 10, 17, 108–109
Nonfiction texts, 74–76

Observation, 206–212, 207*f*, 208*f*, 209*f*, 210*f*, 213–214
Open-ended notes, 208*f*, 209
Oral language
  first-grade readers and writers and, 145*f*
  instructional emphasis and, 137*f*
  kindergarten readers and writers and, 141*f*
  preschool readers and writers and, 138*f*
  reading and writing skills development and, 135*f*
  second-grade readers and writers and, 149*f*
  third through fifth grade readers and writers and, 155*f*
  tiered instruction and, 183*f*
Oral reading, 67–69, 152. *see also* Fluency
Outcome tests, 98–99, 102–105, 102*f*, 104*f*. *see also* Assessments
Out-of-school-time (OST) programs, 51

Pedagogical content knowledge (PCK), 195–196, 197, 199–201, 200*f*
Peer coaching, 207–208
PEER sequence, 139

Peer-Assisted Learning Strategies (PALS), 151
Phonemic awareness
    evaluating computer-based programs, 171*f*
    first-grade readers and writers and, 148
    kindergarten readers and writers and, 142–143
    phonics and, 65
    reading and writing skills development and, 135*f*
    research and, 59–62
    schoolwide program design and, 48*f*
    tiered instruction and, 184
Phonemic segmentation, 60, 143. *see also* Phonemic
    awareness
Phonics
    core programs and, 160–161
    evaluating computer-based programs, 172*f*
    first-grade readers and writers and, 144*f*
    kindergarten readers and writers and, 140*f*
    research and, 62–66
Phonological awareness. *see also* Phonemic
    awareness
    assessment and, 101
    first-grade readers and writers and, 144*f*, 145*f*
    instructional emphasis and, 137*f*
    kindergarten readers and writers and, 140*f*, 141*f*
    National Early Literacy Panel (NELP) and, 61
    phonemic awareness and, 60
    preschool readers and writers and, 138*f*
    schedules and, 116
    tiered instruction and, 183*f*
    vocabulary and, 70–71
Phonological Awareness Literacy Screening (PALS),
    98. *see also* Assessments
Preschool
    allocation of time and, 51
    coaching and, 24–26
    core programs and, 26
    instructional emphasis and, 138–139, 138*f*
    overview, 24–25
    spelling and writing and, 81–82
    teamwork and, 54
    tiered instruction and, 183*f*, 184
    writing, 79–80
Preventing Reading Difficulties in Young Children
    (Snow et al., 1998), 178
Principals
    coaching and, 22, 228–229
    leadership roles of coaches and, 219–221, 220*f*
    overview, 216–217
    resistance from teachers and, 223–224
Print concepts, 140*f*, 144*f*
Process writing, 82–86. *see also* Writing
Professional development. *see also* Professional support
    allocation of time and, 53–54
    book clubs and study groups, 202–204
    coaching and, 199–201, 200*f*
    coherence and, 215
    lesson planning and, 204–206
    model for, 194–198, 195*f*, 196*f*
    planning and implementing, 199
    research and, 18–19, 26, 193–194
    schedules and, 131–132, 132*f*
    teachers and, 10–11
    using data as a part of, 201–202, 202*f*
Professional learning communities (PLCs), 26,
    217–218

Professional support. *see also* Professional
    development
    coherence and, 215
    model for, 194–198, 195*f*, 196*f*
    modeling and, 212–214
    observation and feedback, 206–212, 207*f*, 208*f*,
        209*f*, 210*f*
    overview, 192
    pacing of, 214–215
    research and, 193–194, 198–199, 199*f*
    teachers and, 10–11
Profiles, 106–108, 107*f*
Progress monitoring tests. *see also* Assessments
    data from and professional development,
        201–202, 202*f*
    profiles and, 106–108, 107*f*
    reading assessment and, 98
    response-to-intervention (RTI) and, 182–183,
        184–185
Prosody, 66, 68–69. *see also* Fluency

Read-alouds
    assessment and, 101–102
    comprehension and, 74–79, 77*f*, 80*f*, 81*f*
    first-grade readers and writers and, 146, 146–147
    kindergarten readers and writers and, 141–142
    lesson planning and, 205
Reader's Theater procedure, 149
Reading, stage theory in, 134–135, 135*f*
Reading assessment. *see also* Assessments
    assessment strategy, 99–102, 100*f*
    interpreting outcome scores, 102–105, 102*f*, 104*f*
    overview, 97, 113–114
    roles of a literacy coach and, 105–109, 107*f*
    types and uses of tests and, 97–99
Reading Excellence Act, 17, 21, 28
Reading First, 17–18
Reading instruction, 57–58, 65. *see also* Instruction
Reading Recovery, 165–166, 177
Reflection, 197, 210–211
Reforms, 19, 33–35, 53
Repeated read-alouds, 78–79, 80*f*, 81*f*. *see also*
    Read-alouds
Repeated reading, 151
Research
    coaching model and, 20–22
    coaching toolbox and, 26–27, 27*f*
    comprehension, 72–79, 77*f*, 80*f*, 81*f*
    core programs and, 167–168
    evidence-based reading instruction, 58, 58*f*
    fluency, 66–69
    goals of coaching and other leaders, 22–23
    implementation of new approaches and, 27–28
    integrating the coaches work with the school's
        climate, 22
    keeping up with, 89–96, 90*f*, 91*f*, 92*f*
    learning on the job, 24–25
    National Reading Panel and, 59
    needs of teachers and, 23–24
    overview, 17–19, 18*f*, 56–57
    phonemic awareness, 59–62
    phonics, 62–66
    preschool teachers and, 24–26
    professional development, 193–194
    response-to-intervention (RTI) and, 183–188

roles of a literacy coach and, 7–10, 15*f*
schoolwide literacy program and, 31–36, 35*f*
scientifically based reading instruction, 57–58
selecting intervention programs, 188–189
spelling, 87–89
tracking achievement and, 29
variability in coaching and, 19–20
vocabulary, 69–71
writing, 79–87, 82*f*, 83*f*, 84*f*, 85*f*
Resistance to coaches, 22–23
Resources, 89–96, 90*f*, 91*f*, 92*f*
Response-to-intervention (RTI). *see also*
Intervention; Tiered instruction
core programs and, 163
overview, 179–180, 181–183, 183*f*
planning, 189–191, 191*f*
research and, 183–188
schoolwide program design and, 35–36, 35*f*, 36*f*
selecting intervention programs, 188–189
Responsive reading instruction (RRI), 186. *see also*
Response-to-intervention (RTI)
Roles of a literacy coach. *see also* Coaching in
general; Leadership roles; Professional
development
assessment and, 105–109, 107*f*
curriculum expert, 6, 14*f*
grant writer, 4–5, 6*f*, 13*f*–14*f*
improving group achievement scores, 109–113,
110*f*, 114*f*
learner, 3–4, 5*f*, 13*f*, 24–25
overview, 1–3, 2*f*, 3*f*, 4*f*, 11–12, 13*f*–16*f*
researcher, 7–10, 15*f*, 56–57
school-level planner, 5–6, 14*f*
teacher, 10–11, 15*f*–16*f*
Rubrics, 208–209, 208*f*

Schedules. *see also* Instruction
examples of, 120–131, 122*f*, 123*f*, 124*f*, 126*f*,
127*f*, 128*f*, 129*f*, 130*f*, 131*f*
improving group achievement scores, 111–112
observation and feedback and, 207–208
overview, 115, 131–132, 132*f*
professional support and, 53–54, 200
schoolwide program design and, 52–53
types of, 116–119, 117*f*, 118*f*, 119*f*
School environment, 22–23, 174–175, 175*f*, 180
School-based data collection, 7–10. *see also* Data
collection
School-level planning, 5–6, 14*f*
Schoolwide assessment team (SWAT) approach, 7,
37–39, 38*f*–39*f*. *see also* Assessments
Schoolwide leadership teams, 40
Schoolwide literacy improvement model, 33–35
Schoolwide literacy program
allocation of time, 50–54, 52*f*
commercial materials and instructional strategies
and, 47–50, 48*f*
grouping configurations and, 43–47, 44*f*, 45*f*, 46*f*,
49*f*
overview, 5–6, 30–31, 55
professional support and, 192, 200–201
research and, 31–36, 35*f*
response-to-intervention (RTI) and, 181
special education services and, 176
teamwork and, 54–55

Schoolwide planning, 36, 36*f*, 189–191
Schoolwide professional development and support,
194–198, 195*f*, 196*f*, 199. *see also* Professional
development; Professional support
Schoolwide program design, 34–35, 36–43, 38*f*–39*f*,
40*f*, 42*f*. *see also* Schoolwide literacy program
Schoolwide research, 31–36, 35*f*. *see also*
Assessments; Research
Scientifically based reading instruction, 57–58,
167–168. *see also* Instruction
Scope and sequence, core programs and, 164
Screening tests. *see also* Assessments
data from and professional development,
201–202, 202*f*
intervention and, 180
profiles and, 106–108, 107*f*
reading assessment and, 97–98
Second-grade readers and writers
instructional emphasis and, 148–151, 148*f*, 149*f*,
151*f*
tiered instruction and, 183*f*, 186–187
Segmenting individual phonemes, 60, 143. *see also*
Phonemic awareness
Self-efficacy of teachers, 197–198, 218
Shared reading, 77–78, 77*f*, 140, 145
Shared writing, 142, 146
Sight-words, 148
Small-group instruction. *see also* Instruction
for first-grade readers and writers, 147–148, 147*f*
for kindergarten readers and writers, 142–143,
142*f*
for preschool readers and writers, 139
schedules and, 116, 117*f*, 118, 118*f*
schoolwide program design and, 48*f*, 49
for second-grade readers and writers, 150–151,
151*f*
for third through fifth grade readers and writers,
156–157
Socioeconomic status (SES), 63–64, 178
Software, 164, 170, 171*f*–173*f*. *see also* Technology
Somebody-Wanted-But-So technique, 156–157
South Carolina Reading Initiative, 26–27
Special education services, 176. *see also*
Intervention; Response-to-intervention (RTI)
Spelling
first-grade readers and writers and, 148
instructional emphasis and, 137*f*
phonics and, 63
research and, 87–89
stage theory in, 134–135, 135*f*
tiered instruction and, 183*f*
writing and, 80–87, 82*f*, 83*f*, 84*f*, 85*f*
Stage theory, 134–135, 135*f*
Standardized testing, 109–113, 110*f*, 113–114, 114*f*.
see also Assessments
Standards. *see* Common Core State Standards
Initiative
Standards-Based Change Process, 75
Strategy instruction, 76, 147, 150, 156–157
Struggling readers, 177–178
Success for All program, 187
Superintendents, 219–220, 220*f*
Supplemental instruction, 30, 182. *see also*
Instruction; Tier 2 instruction
Systematic instruction, 63–66. *see also* Instruction

Teachers. *see also* Professional development;
     Professional support
  allocation of time and, 50–54, 52*f*
  assessments and, 41–43, 42*f*
  coaching and, 22–23
  content-focused coaching (CFC) and, 20
  instructional support and, 133–134
  literacy coach as, 10–11, 15*f*–16*f*
  needs of, 23–24
  observation and feedback and, 206–212, 207*f*,
     208*f*, 209*f*, 210*f*
  pedagogical content knowledge (PCK) and,
     195–196
  phonics and, 64–65
  read-alouds and, 75–76
  resistance from, 223–224
  struggling, 222–223
Technology
  core programs and, 164, 170, 171*f*–173*f*
  evaluating computer-based programs, 171*f*–173*f*
  preschool teachers and, 24–26
  profiles and, 106–108, 107*f*
  summarizing data from assessments and, 40
  vocabulary instruction and, 69–70
Third through fifth grade readers and writers,
     152–157, 153*f*–155*f*, 167, 183*f*, 187
Tier 1 instruction, 35–36, 35*f*, 181–182. *see also*
     Instruction; Response-to-intervention (RTI);
     Tiered instruction
Tier 2 instruction, 35*f*, 182. *see also* Differentiated
     instruction; Instruction; Response-to-
     intervention (RTI); Tiered instruction
Tier 3 instruction, 35*f*, 182–183. *see also*
     Instruction; Intervention; Response-to-
     intervention (RTI); Tiered instruction
Tiered instruction. *see also* Response-to-intervention
     (RTI)
  overview, 181–183, 183*f*
  planning, 189–191
  research and, 183–188
  schoolwide program design and, 35–36, 35*f*, 36*f*,
     47–50, 48*f*
  selecting intervention programs, 188–189
Time, allocation of, 50–54, 52*f*
Transactional strategy instruction, 74. *see also*
     Instruction
Transitions, 50–51

Vocabulary
  aggressive early intervention and, 177–178
  comprehension and, 65
  core programs and, 161
  evaluating computer-based programs, 172*f*–173*f*
  first-grade readers and writers and, 145*f*, 146
  instructional emphasis and, 20, 48*f*, 136–138,
     136*f*, 137*f*
  kindergarten readers and writers and, 141, 141*f*
  preschool readers and writers and, 138*f*
  reading and writing skills development and, 135*f*
  research and, 69–71
  second-grade readers and writers and, 148, 149, 149*f*
  third through fifth grade readers and writers and,
     152, 155*f*
  tiered instruction and, 183*f*

What Works Clearinghouse, 188–189, 193–194
Whole-class instruction. *see also* Instruction
  for first-grade readers and writers, 143–147, 144*f*,
     145*f*, 147*f*
  for kindergarten readers and writers, 139–142,
     140*f*, 141*f*
  for preschool readers and writers, 138–139
  schedules and, 116, 117*f*, 119*f*
  schoolwide program design and, 48, 48*f*
  for second-grade readers and writers, 149–150
  for third through fifth grade readers and writers,
     152–156, 153*f*–155*f*
Whole-language movement, 161
Wide reading, 68–69. *see also* Fluency
Word recognition
  first-grade readers and writers and, 144*f*
  kindergarten readers and writers and, 140*f*, 142
  phonics and, 66
  reading and writing skills development and, 135*f*
  second-grade readers and writers and, 148*f*, 150–151
Writing
  first-grade readers and writers and, 145*f*
  instructional emphasis and, 137*f*
  kindergarten readers and writers and, 141*f*, 142
  National Early Literacy Panel (NELP) and, 61
  preschool readers and writers and, 138*f*
  research and, 79–87, 82*f*, 83*f*, 84*f*, 85*f*
  second-grade readers and writers and, 149*f*
  third through fifth grade readers and writers and,
     155*f*